"Brad Evans' captivating history of south Wa[...] authority. It is evocative and excellent in [...] provides a cliche-free, myth-lancing account [...] by the powers that were after tearing use and r[...]less abuse. He doesn't turn away from the alchemy of poverty which 'numbed ambition' or the fates of lives corroded into disengagement, but he is tough enough to 'hold to the glimmer within the darkness'. Sometimes lyrical, never romantic he offers analytical passion, acidic candour, some love, deep melancholy, dry mirth, scorn for nostalgia about 'a past that never really existed' and an unbreakable grip on truth. Dylan Thomas wanted 'rage against the dying of the light'. Evans bids us join him in that."

NEIL KINNOCK

"*How Black Was My Valley* is more than a memoir. Its in-depth analysis captures the beauty of the South Wales Rhondda valleys, mountains and rivers; reflects the dignity of the people, whose language and rich culture has been confronted by the despair of 'poverty apartheid' inflicted on abandoned mining communities. From his reflections on the impact of personal loss and destitution, Evans writes sensitively of time, place and circumstance, unpacking the historical detail behind events that shaped the valleys and blighted their communities. Each carefully constructed sentence, every beautifully recorded or imagined moment, is placed alongside tragedy's reality, ensuring that the 'view from below', as lived by the women and men who remain in the grip of economic marginalisation, is heard."

PHIL SCRATON, AUTHOR OF *HILLSBOROUGH: THE TRUTH*

"Anybody interested in the history of working class resistance, and people's daily struggles when confronting deep poverty blighting post-industrial communities should read this devastating study."

PAUL MASON, AUTHOR OF *POSTCAPITALISM*

"Evans' beautifully crafted words and thoughts are now seared into me forever. Sit with each chapter for a while as its true devastation dawns on you. These are tales of survivance when the outcome looks preordained because of neglect and cruelty, told with a level of detail that truly immerses. Thank God these stories are now being told. The boy of the valleys has come home and roared."

LUCY EASTHOPE, AUTHOR OF *WHEN THE DUST SETTLES*

"This heartrending book summons powerful spirits from a great well of suffering. People in the valleys of South Wales remade the United Kingdom in the twentieth century, but have been far beneath the concerns of political and economic elite for decades. Brad Evans refuses to ignore these people — his people — as he tallies the steep cost of their abandonment. With striking insight, he shows how neglect has blocked the way to their future. As places in between, valleys can also be passages through. From within the darkest shadows of late Great Britain, both Evans's prose and Meza's haunting artwork allow us to glimpse a new vision of folk history from the deep: but it warns that humanity has taken the wrong path, and the light ahead may be too dim to guide us."

VINCENT BROWN, PROFESSOR OF HISTORY, HARVARD UNIVERSITY

"Brad has gone down the mines and extracted a wealth of history that had been covered in soot and given serious literary attention to a vital yet overlooked aspect of working class and south Welsh life... a passionate, political, and personal retelling of the history of a place most people aim to avoid."

RHYS THOMAS, AUTHOR OF *THE FUTURE OF WALES*

"A phenomenal, poignant memoir that pulsates with the militant passion and mordant wit of a Welsh Valleys landscape ravaged in turn by the forces of white-on-white colonialism and globalisation. Oscillating between acute socio-economic-political observation and lush, almost mystical lyricism, it is a must read for anyone interested in British social history and all fans of stunningly beautiful prose."

GARETH OWEN, HUMANITARIAN DIRECTOR, SAVE THE CHILDREN

"This is a crucial, driven, and necessary piece of work, fuelled by righteous rage and dismay at how certain social strata (living, loving, hoping human beings) are deemed dispensable once their utility has been wrung dry. The chapter on the Aberfan catastrophe illustrates the ferocity with which the establishment looks after its own; if you finish this book without a sense of furious lament, then look to the carbonisation of your soul."

NIALL GRIFFITHS, AUTHOR OF *OF TALONS AND TEETH*

HOW BLACK WAS MY VALLEY

HOW BLACK WAS MY VALLEY

POVERTY & ABANDONMENT IN A POST-INDUSTRIAL HEARTLAND

Brad Evans

Published by Repeater Books

An imprint of Watkins Media Ltd

Unit 11 Shepperton House

89-93 Shepperton Road

London

N1 3DF

United Kingdom

www.repeaterbooks.com

A Repeater Books paperback original 2024

1

Distributed in the United States by Random House, Inc., New York.

Copyright Brad Evans © 2024

Brad Evans asserts the moral right to be identified as the author of this work.

ISBN: 9781913462840

Ebook ISBN: 9781913462857

Printed and bound in the United Kingdom by TJ Books Limited

MIX

Paper from responsible sources

FSC
www.fsc.org

FSC® C013056

CONTENTS

This book is dedicated to my loving grandparents Sidney Royston Smith &
Morfydd Smith. Together you personified the heart of the valley and lived
through its enduring blackness with dignity, humour and grace. Wherever you
may be, I know your spirits will be dancing above the falling rains.

Black is the colour of the story of my life. Looking back, I now see it has worn me far more than I wore it. It is a melancholic bind holding forgotten communities together. It is the open wound — a devastating loss of innocence still cutting deep in these long-abandoned lands. Black is Home. The colour of my childhood. Deadly poor, yet still full of memories of love. Black is the tone of this tremendous fiery earth, which was once sung by choirs of promise who previously gave hallowed voice to this darkened world. Black is the suffering of my forebears and neighbours, too many lives taken too soon. Black is the cavernous depths now flooded by primordial waters. An infernal abyss, which still proved better than nothing at all. Black is the colour of an ecology of suffering, where nature has reclaimed what life never could. Black is the feeling of an atmosphere of misery, of dark forebodings and a darker comedy, laughing out of scorched forests unto the final, the last, suffocating breath. Black is the abiding memory of a permanent depression, as certain as the shadows that set over these fated lands. Black is the colour of the faces of ghosts, whose ancestral rhythms have been corroded by the dust of time. Black is a memory of pitiful sorrow. The colour of defeat dressed by those living within mountains of the mind. But black is also the story of the forgotten poets of a history. Those whose words have made the earth tremble and weep.

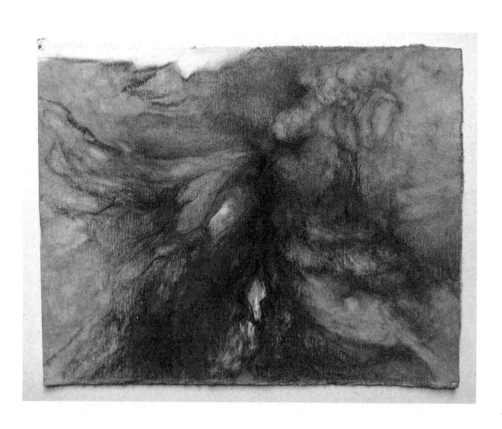

A BRIEF HISTORY OF GLOBALISATION

A familiar melancholic shadow washes over my soul as I enter back into the place I once called "home". Such a powerful and complex word. "You can take the boy out of the valleys but never the valleys out of the boy," my grandmother continually reminded when she detected I was straying too far from the ancestral fires. Only now are the depths of that simple, obvious truth fully appreciated. Poverty defines the character and shapes with fury every line that contours my worn and aged face. But my story is not unique. The people of the former mining communities of South Wales live and breathe tragedy. Even the beautiful topography conspires, holding them firmly within its landscapes of neglect. Windswept mountains strewn with familiar strips of precariously perched, grey-stoned terraced houses only add to the permanent sense of depression. Defeat here is atmospheric, as sure as the violent rains that continue to drown the hopes of a people who once lived with such dignity and pride. And I too am wracked with doubt. Maybe that book agent I summarily dismissed was right? Perhaps what the world needs is another uplifting story of people surviving in the face of adversity. Why shouldn't we see daily struggles as learning processes, which show how poverty really does have its advantages to please the resiliently minded? How I have come to loathe that word, which is so often applied to people who had their ideological gods stripped away from them, yet like wretched castaways inescapably bound to the unforgiving places, find themselves left to their own secluded misery in abandoned towns? Derelict of optimistic light, how society still finds novel concepts to justify conditions of isolation amongst the familiar post-industrial rot. But why would anybody want to read about a place, this place, which time really has forgotten? Boarded-up streets tell us nothing after all, except to cover over a gaping absence in chapters of human disposability. Yet it is impossible to write the story of globalisation without writing about these forgotten communities in the lost valleys of South Wales. For theirs is a tale of a people who went from powering the most formidable Empire the world has ever know, to one largely disappeared from memory, except to remind us from time to time of irreversible industrial decline, which for many offers no prospect of recovery.

The train is slowly leaving the market town of Pontypridd and entering into the Rhondda. This once famous valley is cut into two (the *fawr* and *fach* — literally the "big" and the "small"), much like the sense of split consciousness children in these towns have been forced to live with throughout their lives. Guilt is palpable as I now return also as an outsider who feels to have somewhat betrayed those who were "left behind", to evoke the modern parlance laboured over by the twittering classes. But maybe that feeling too is part of my own arrogance and prejudices developed over time. An old run-down carriage trudges forward by an exhausted motor of monotonous resignation as it barely clings to the precarious and corroding tracks. I wipe away the steam covering the window on the inside of the damp coach. It is still dark on this summer morning as I gaze across to the platform opposite. I recall childhood memories sat on that station, watching the last of the coal trains passing. Oblivious to their demise, I relied upon the endless number of open-topped wagons brimming with coal speeding past to practice my mathematics. Many a Saturday was spent walking with my parents amongst the bustling street markets of this once thriving town. Pontypridd used to be a much-visited place for the people of the Rhondda valleys, until the economic decline really set in and the supermarkets sucked whatever life remained from its densely crowded and often fractious independent trading streets. They appear today as empty as the dreams many have in this urban wilderness, where hopes have slowly disappeared like each of those carriages slowly vanished from the tracks of our forgotten lives. When the station was opened in 1907, it stood as the world's longest island platform dedicated to serving both the coal and steel industries. Four years after opening, however, it would be the site of an horrific crash between a passenger and freight tram, resulting in many casualties and eleven fatalities. Progress is always followed by devastation here. Now an excessive relic serving no purpose other than to ridicule those who stand in permanent wait, the lengthy platform simply reminds of a prosperity that will never return. Still, the town does have another enduring claim, which has become even more defining than the black gold that once shaped its industrial past: Tom Bloody Jones. The man in the valleys from whom everyone it seems is only two steps removed. Everyone knows someone who knows someone who knows Tom. When I was growing up, it wasn't cool to be into his music, as he tried to reinvent himself for an age that no longer wanted bare-chested crooners. I have since learned to appreciate the passion and escapism he embodied. The Elvis of the valleys, how his voice somehow speaks to those who refuse to die in these abandoned towns. Maybe there are traces of a poetic fire yet to be discovered? "Ponty" (as it is commonly called) is after all where the rapturous Welsh national anthem, "*Hen Wlad Fy Nhadau*" ("Land of My Fathers"), which sings of a land of "poets and singers" and whose old mountains are the "paradise of the bard", was first scribed.

I am the only person on the train, apart from a guard who is present at the far end of the carriage. His dark outline was observed through the distorted glass the moment I embarked. Whether he or the driver is guiding this empty vessel on its journey into nowhere is difficult to tell. A digital message board featuring a crude pixelated font warns of no alcohol consumption after the market place. Even the appearance of modern technology belongs to a bygone era that's barely fit for purpose. I suspect the authorities assume things are only going to get worse from here on in. Some 10 minutes after the train has departed, the first visible sign of the valleys past come into focus. In the distance, I can make out the imposing silhouettes of the large smoke tower and two of the pitheads winding or sheave wheels that were so iconic to the valleys' deep mining industry. Once a working pit that employed some 5,000 men producing up to one million tons of coal annually, the Rhondda Heritage Park is now just a mausoleum to its industrious past. The pit closed in 1983. Ten years later it would host the second ever National Lottery draw. The eyes of Britain briefly fell upon the valleys to anticipate which round, garishly coloured balls would be spewed out of a different rotational wheel. The show was a mitigating disaster. The weather was typically inclement as high winds were competing with the cold rain to see which could disrupt the proceedings more on that November evening. Presenters' autocue systems failed to work; though their professionalism was salvaged as they selected a few over-excited locals who provided their own animated commentary in a language which can only be described as "valleys speak". While the state-led racketeering gambit ran with the slogan "It Could Be You", a more fitting epitaph would have been "A Tax on Hope". We have to admire the ironic perversity of taking the very first travelling lottery tour to an area of the country whose people hardly needed reminding that they needed a miracle. Perhaps somebody should have told the commissioners that placing one's future in the miraculous had long since abandoned valleys folk. Once thriving Methodist churches have also been boarded up as every kind of faith was thrown into the forgotten seams of the flooded pits. In truth, for many people of the valleys, life wasn't really a lottery. They knew what awaited them. And it was often blanketed in misery.

Just over a century ago, in 1913, the South Wales coalfield was the richest in the United Kingdom. Over a quarter of a million miners were employed to cut into its seams, together extracting near a fifth of the country's coal production. This amounted to some 56 million tons of coal extorted from the ground. Coal was the element that drove globalisation. Fittingly, the coalfield was also round in shape, covering about 1000 square miles, which extended from Pontypool in the east, through Glamorgan (in which the Rhondda is situated), across to Pembrokeshire in the west. As a result of incessant demand and the job opportunities provided, population growth in the valley was rapid. Indeed, at its peak, the influx of hardened migrants even outpaced those seeking fortune by emigrating to the United States. The population of the Rhondda in 1811 was just 576, rising to 951 by 1851. By 1901 the number of people living in the area had increased to 113,735. Britain at the time was the world-leader in coal production and the valleys were its prized asset, being rich in anthracite, bituminous and steam coals. The Rhondda in particular was renowned for the high carbon quality of its coal, which was unrivalled in terms of driving the steam-powered motors of industrialisation that effectively made possible the Empire's unrivalled expansion in far-off lands. Such high carbon content, along with the valleys' more impenetrable topography, made it however altogether more dangerous to mine. Extraction proved costly, in human terms at least. Accidents were commonplace, as in 1913, which witnessed the death of 439 miners (including children) at the Universal pit in Senghenydd, near Caerphilly at the northern end of the Aber valley. Following an explosion deep underground fuelled by combustible airborne dust, many were killed as a result of "afterdamp" — a ferociously toxic mixture of carbon dioxide, carbon monoxide and nitrogen poisoning. Senghenydd was the worst mining disaster in the history of the United Kingdom.

A dense grey light starts to appear over the dawning mountainside. It gives off the aura of a sombre white hue, which promises more of the same. Even the prospect of sun appears like a random accident in these overcast towns. A copy of Richard Llewellyn's book *How Green Was My Valley* is held in my doubting hands. It would be popularized by John Ford's motion picture adaptation, which beat Orson Wells' *Citizen Kane* to the Oscar Best Picture in 1942, one of the six Oscars it won that year. The film was actually shot in the Ventura Hills in California and the only Welsh actor to feature in it was Rhys Williams, who played "Dai Bando", a local character prone to alcoholism and who took great pride in beating up the abusive school master. Overly sentimental, it's full of inaccuracies and stereotypes. Nevertheless, it does capture the transition from a rural pastureland into place brutally marked by mineral-led industrialisation, and how this extraction would disfigure the landscape and its people. And at least it put the valleys on the Hollywood map for a while, even if the glamour and whatever could be profited remained in Los Angeles. While a 1941 *New York Times* review called it a "motion picture of great poetic charm and dignity", it also duly noted how it portrayed "The story of a good people's doom, the story of how the black coal wrung so perilously from the fair earth darkens the lives of those who dig it and befouls the verdant valley in which they live". Llewellyn, however, wasn't from the valleys (or even Wales), and his claim to have known about the conditions of mining life from his grandfather were untrue. He was later revealed as being an Englishman called Vivian Lloyd, and much of his life and connection to the place was a monumental fraud. Most representations of the valleys, for better and worse, have come from authors and writers who lived outside of its terrain. The most notable being Alexander Cordell's *Rape of the Fair County* and A. J. Cronin's *The Citadel*. While the former deals with the hardship of early industrialisation, the latter, written by the Scottish doctor about his experiences in Tredegar, would be influential in laying the foundations for the National Health Service. Back to Llewellyn, despite my reservations, I am willing to grant some creative licence when dealing with the profundities of social transformation, though not in the way intended. Thoughts are starting to liberate the child within me, as my finger slowly presses into the condensation on the misty glass. I write his most poignant phrase, then as the temperature outside starts to rise, I watch the letters vanish away, knowing they will reappear again when the humidity surely returns, as it always does in parts of the world caught in between the fire and the cold. "How can there be fury felt for things that are gone to dust?"

As sure as the toxic particles have seeped deep into the wounded earth of the valleys, so the traces of its tragic past continue to mark the bodies of those who walk upon the shadows of its dark pigments. On every conceivable register, the valleys top the league tables of human suffering in the United Kingdom and indeed wider European zones. From lasting unemployment blighting generations, chronic physical health concerns and malnourishment, amongst the highest rates of depression and male suicide in the country, endemic child poverty, disturbing levels of domestic abuse, widespread alcoholism and drug addiction, the South Wales valleys are at the epicentre of the most pressing social concerns, which statisticians show are only getting worse. Desperately clinging to an appreciation of the kindness I know exists in this place, I am struggling not to be conflicted by this reality and in agreement with a BBC reporter who defined these towns as carrying an "unbearable sadness". How does a place become like this? And yet, why do I still have so many fond memories of it? Moreover, why do I continue to draw upon the lived experience of people of the valleys in response to the predictable retorts of the digital intelligentsia, who repeatedly talk of poverty and privilege without the faintest idea of what it means to live with the oppressive weight of absence year upon year, in winters of permanent discontent?

The rain continues to fall on the still deserted train as we slowly leave Tonypandy, which as I will later note is synonymous with a darker episode in the legacy of Winston Churchill. There is a reason why there are no statues to pull down of that defeater of fascism in these less-than-convinced parts. As I investigate the distance, I see the estate atop the heather-covered mountainside. Two years after I was born, my father was diagnosed with a debilitating life-long illness. He was 20 years old at the time. Due to his inability to work, the label "working class" never applied to us. Penrhys housing estate, which separated the poorest of the poor, was already infamous and a reminder that, even in destitution, things can always get worse. Our family had no option but to relocate there in 1978. Sat with our meagre possessions on the back of a relative's open truck, the move constitutes one of my earliest memories. My mother was holding me tight and trying to make an adventure of it as the precariously loaded wardrobe was colliding with the worn sofa upon which we were throned. Nothing was strapped in, though probably of little consequence as we had very little, almost nothing to show. While certainly not seeing it in those terms at the time, I now recognise the many ways poverty has its own pageantry that works to instil shame and turn misery into spectacle. Built in 1968 to much fanfare, the estate recently marked its fiftieth anniversary. In a strange twist of fate, I now live in an apartment built in exactly the same year, no doubt by architects following similar building methods inspired by post-modern dreams. Whether it was hubris or structurally induced poverty, perched some 1,170 feet above the Rhondda floor, the steep warren of grey council blocks elevated on the exposed hillside quickly became an isolated community of poverty and crime separated from the valley below. A hilltop beacon of despair, Penrhys would become a quintessential poverty trap, which for those who ended up there meant the spiral of suffering was going to get worse.

The steep one-mile road leading up to the estate was often battered by a particularly hostile weather pattern that the locals referred to as "sideways rain". While the Welsh are renowned for being lyrical with their expressions, valleys folk possess their own rather unique vocabulary that remains altogether foreign to outsiders. One such term is "tamping", which could either refer to heavy rains that are guaranteed to leave you looking like a drowned rat or a person's emotional state in which they are fuming with rage. Lyrical ecologists of a different kind, what was natural to the body was also naturally bound to weather patterns sent by unknown forces into which the continually soaked conditions of life were immersed. Whether "it's tamping down" or "I am tamping", the anger was always mixed with a healthy dose of black humour, which you learn from an early age to be essential if you are to have any chance of psychological and emotional survival. Poor people often laugh in the face of the tragic, amusing themselves at the absurdities of existence, which the middle classes have never really been able to abide. Some of the funniest people I have ever met lived in the valleys. As a young boy, I undoubtedly shed more tears of laugher than I cried. If by accident the summit at Penrhys had been reached, you would be struck by the altogether functional design of the front row housing, whose only memorable features are the brutalist sloping rooves that point to some ecological reckoning. Opposite the site is the statue of the Virgin Mary and child backdropped by the valley below. She retains a resigned look, with her head bowed in recognition of the tragedies that await her offspring. She occupies a pilgrimage site dating to the Medieval period. An earlier version would be burned down during Henry VIII's reformation and carried out by Thomas Cromwell. A key architect in the Acts of Union and the Reformation, this site was singled out for concern since its blessed waters were believed to have healing powers. While belief in such divine miracles has undoubtedly fled, the rituals of burning and the solemn demand for piety remains.

A circular roundabout with four determinable exits sits at the base of the estate. Most preferable would be to swiftly head back or across into the adjacent twinned valley in the other direction. Maybe that was the Virgin's purpose, as travellers prayed their vehicles didn't break down on top of that hill. The second and third entries were only followed if absolutely necessary or by some unceremonious fate. Connecting the east and west of the estate, they would take you onto an outer circular road, which surrounded the failed social experiment.

Delirium was part of the design, with these roads suggestive of the cyclical nature of its unending despair. We lived at 12 o'clock at the farthest point from the Virgin's glare. Penrhys is a tale of lasting suffering. It also turned Dante's nightmare vision around as the ascent was the source of one's torment. Halfway up the road to the estate stood the isolation hospital, which was opened in 1906 to contain an outbreak of smallpox. It would become a focal point years later in 1962 following the terror that spread through the valleys when another outbreak occurred, which medics suspected to have travelled from Pakistan. It was later burned by the local fire services in 1976 as the authorities hoped the bonfire on the hill would kill the unholy virus. Full of the local sinners, for whom the phrase "abandon all faith ye who enter here" had earthly meaning, the road to Penrhys was the road to Perdition. Indeed, while being closer to the heavens meant one's fate had no doubt worsened, in an eery similarity to Dante's perverse comedy, the closer one got to the inner circles of the estate, the more affliction was concentrated. Here stood maisonette flats and a local community centre, which also had several stores dispatching unhealthy food, cheap alcohol and cigarettes to ensure the poverty apartheid was as self-contained as the pox and plagues. Nobody knew if the virus was eradicated from the isolation site.

I recall the shrewd observation made by the late sociologist Zygmunt Bauman about so-called "no-go" areas. In the unlikely event of having some genuine interest or merely out of some morbid passing curiosity, it wasn't that you couldn't visit them. What defined no-go places was that their people couldn't leave even if they wished to do so. The bus stop at the bottom of Penrhys hill was avoided, frequented as it was by drunks who hurled abuse at anyone who happened to be in close enough proximity as they relieved themselves against the shelter's walls. Inebriated assaults were also directed at bus drivers, who often refused to work the route. Many drunks spent the day in the hole directly opposite the sardonically named Star Hotel. Opened in 1913, it was reputedly the oldest public house in the valleys. As the name suggested, even the celestial manages to find itself falling to the bottom here. I was around four years old and vaguely remember my mother taking me to see her parents who lived at the top of the valley near the colliery where her father had worked. Come rain or blizzard, she would walk most Sundays with my younger brother and I in a twin buggy on the 12-mile round trip. While the journey was often wet and arduous, at least there would be seasonal respite, as the estate would be largely cut off when the winter arrived. The steep incline would be covered in treacherous sheets of ice, which resulted in serious accidents for people in vehicles and most often on foot. Secluded conditions, both economically and climatically, were the norm for the unemployed in the valleys' heights.

Penrhys was initially sold as a utopian ideal. Some 954 dwellings housed around 4,000 people, who were promised the best views of the Welsh valleys. While initially seen as a prime location due to its enviable views and clean air, by the early 1970s many of the original tenants fled. It didn't take long for the social reengineers to assume control, relocating "problem families" into its cut-price dwellings. Its lauded architectural design was alienating. Unlike traditional terraced houses, the doorways faced away from neighbours, only adding to the sense of isolation. Tragically foreboding, the estate officially opened on Friday 13th September 1968. The weather was grey, windy and miserable. Residents soon discovered its revolutionary communal heating system was an abject failure. Tenants living closest to the boiler house sweltered, while those further away shivered on the expanse. Ironically, it was the soaring price of coal in the early 1970s that was absorbed into the council controlled rents which contributed to the exodus of working families. Penrhys became a void on the hillside that needed to be politically filled. A few years after opening, the estate also witnessed the brutal murder of an 11-year-old girl whose body was found in a vacant, just-completed lot. By 1976, many of the houses had been vandalised, their doors broken and windows shattered, while prone to burglaries of what meagre possessions they contained. Random violent assaults in broad daylight by other residents were commonplace. It has been suggested the name for the estate derived from the legend of the eleventh-century Welsh king Rhys-Ap-Tewdwr (a Celtic descendent of Rhodri the Great — one of the "King of the Britons") who it was said had been decapitated in 1093 by the Normans on this very site. The estate was originally named *Pen-Rhys ap Tewdwr*. Violence, it seems, was always part of the scripted design.

Over time, the estate developed a notorious reputation for violence, domestic and drug abuse, alcoholism and high rates of suicide. It even started to make national news as resident youths — unemployed agents that carried forth Cromwell's spirit — could be seen burning vacant lots. They also turned their attention to setting alight stolen cars they had been joyriding around its outer limits, until the petrol ran dry. Firefighters who arrived to douse the vandals' flames were routinely assaulted and subject to all kinds of physical and verbal abuse. The appearance of the local police only exacerbated tensions. Pelted with stones and occupational slanders, the confrontations continued until the emergency services left these twisted Cromwellian pyromaniacs to their own drug-fuelled war dances, which were at least contained and only harming those in their own community. Maybe the authorities simply knew that eventually the Virgin's tears would cascade from the sorrowful skies, thereby returning calm to this forgotten horizon of elevated destitution as sure as any comedown would dampen their disenchanted spirits for yet another day. Unemployment on the estate was put between 75 and 90%, with many claiming some form of invalidity or incapacity benefit from the State. Unemployment was permanent for most, spanning some three generations as families were born into an inescapable dereliction. Those who would be lucky enough to be relocated, or though the help of family find a way out of the patterns of its smiting winds, would nevertheless be marked out as a "Penrhyser" (like my family was) and stigmatized as being uneducated, rough, potentially violent and still liable to commit local petty crime. Moreover, even if you were accepted, the marks of prejudice always found new ways of appearing. If you lived in the valleys, similar forms of stigmatization would be experienced when you encountered those who lived beyond its natural confinements. Something that would be re-cast anew the moment you crossed the Severn Bridge. On the estate, I recall encountering the first visible signs of fascism, even if the symbolism was altogether confused. It wasn't uncommon to see the words "All coppers are bastards", "SCAB" and "Fuck the English" alongside "God Save the Queen" and the interlocking "NF" symbol of the National Front scrawled on walls using the same runny white bitumen paint, which affirmed how everything washed away. While the fate of Penrhys has changed somewhat, with its vandalized homes and its larger tenement buildings largely destroyed, personal memories and the social stigmas have still carried over into the present.

On the mountainside below Penrhys stands the derelict remains of the former Llwynypia hospital. Should you have been born in the upper Rhondda between 1935 and 1991, chances are you were born (and often died) on one of its overcrowded and underfunded wards. The hospital was originally a workhouse set up in 1903 as part of a Poor Law Union. This workhouse system was created by the 1834 Poor Law Amendment Act that abolished "outdoor relief" and demanded children be put to work to deal with the growing problem of destitute infancy. This was an endemic problem in the valleys due to the population growth associated with the vast influx of families due to the mining industry. While the harrowing plight of workhouse children was famously popularised in Charles Dickens' *Oliver Twist*, perhaps the most renowned of all children to go through its punishing system was Charles Spencer Chaplin, who would often return to themes of poverty in his silent work. Unceremoniously crowned with his iconic bowler hat, Chaplin — the quintessential Victorian Tramp — was the first global comedian, who through his art was able to break down social barriers. No one took more seriously the comic value of tragedy and was able to convey through the tears the reality of impoverishment to a global audience. For that reason alone, the people of the valleys welcomed his message with open arms. Yet, despite all the hardship the comedian faced growing up in squalor in London, he went on record to say the small valleys town of Ebbw Vale (which he stayed in while touring in his earlier years) was amongst the most depressing and surreal places he ever visited. Llwynypia hospital would become a "general" hospital in 1927 to service the entirety of the upper valley's poor.

A light drizzle falls as I survey the landscape to the westerly distance. Having travelled for a further two miles I can now see the evident signs of the valley's glaciation as the familiar round basin that dominates the horizon in the village of Ton Pentre comes into focus. While the landscape has changed significantly since I was a child, I am reassured by its familiarity. This was the town I properly called home. Having managed to escape the estate, we took up residence in Kennard Street, which was at the highest point in this village, just in front of the former Gelli Colliery that closed in 1948 following nationalisation. The fleeing industrialists at least had the courtesy to leave much of its machinery behind for us later generations to explore and turn into a makeshift playground. We were skilled improvisers, artisans of hazard turned into fun. Behind the house there was a stepped terrain of partially covered black spoil mountains leading onto a desolate expanse, which I played upon as a child. More recently, I discovered my great-grandfather took part in mountain fighting — basically boxing without the gloves, on those very same plateaus — to supplement his income from the mines with illegal payments from prize money. The adjacent mountains surrounding Ton Pentre would however be known for a more famous sporting event, when His Royal Highness the Duke of York (later King George VI) was seen whacking golf balls around the slopes in May 1924, during a paired match with the trade unionist and politician Frank Hodges (once the General Secretary of the Miners' Federation of Great Britain and then a Member of Parliament). The game took place on an amateur course established by the miners a few years earlier using very primitive equipment. Nothing quite captures the optimism and contradictions of those times than the sight of gauche miners playing golf upon terrains known for their harshness and vertical descents, which were sure to have resulted in many a loss of ball as every shot was to be played out of the rough. The match was part of a charm offensive by the Royal Family, who along with the landed aristocracy feared the growing political resentment in the valleys, who the locals rightly blamed for poor working conditions. This situation came to a head in the General Strike of 1926. It is undoubtedly romantic to imagine the creation of this golfing club in the valleys having a more radical meaning, with a group of unlikely lads reading in the local Institute library a theory about the games origins in the Scottish Highlands and considering how their Celtic compatriots learned to hit pebbles with notable accuracy to ward off wanton invaders set about putting their own plan into action!

During my teenage years, I often sat on these mountains wishing I was elsewhere. "There's nothing for you in the valleys", was repeated to the point of monotony by everyone who had the faintest glimpse of success in their eyes. But what was this nothing spoken of so freely? I am finding it hard to connect to this place. Had I not managed to successfully consign it to the past? I know its history, but it's hard to make peace with the damage I have done to myself. I feel as cold as the carriage on this early summer morn. Looking back on my childhood, the boy that appears to me now is the image of somebody I learned to murder a thousand times. They said I had to be something different if I was going to amount to anything. And surely anything is better than something, and something better than nothing at all? Or at least that was the story continually fed to us by teachers and well-meaning friends. But I now see the chill in this carriage comes from my own self-imposed affliction.

As an outsider, I am lost in a place that is still welcoming me home. My fear in staying was I would be another nobody. And my fear of returning was that nobody would care. There were many teenage years that passed when I imagined myself in this elsewhere. I travelled in my mind to places and lives better made. I believed that if you wished it enough, you could awaken in the body of another who the fortunes had looked upon more favourably. So elsewhere I became, outside of here in thought and deed, as much as in the hope of being and feeling less denied. Yet when you wish to be outside so much, the inside is punished. An inside that made me who I am, yet I struggled so hard to leave in these abandoned towns. The coldness I feel appears less in the air surrounding me, it belongs to the ice shield I have created to keep the valleys at bay. It's a constant coldness freezing over the history of my forebears, a coldness which takes a particular element to melt.

I carry on my journey, and no sooner look upon another derelict building, which locals still refer to as the EMI Factory. This dystopic monument is often populated by a contrasting set of steroid-enhanced men who can be seen walking their muscular dogs and the painfully skeletal frames of the opioid users, who are also known to sleep amongst these detritus remains. Somewhere in between these two drugged visions lays the crisis of masculinity. Twinned at birth, the steroid and heroin epidemics arrived simultaneously during the early 1980s. While gym culture had existed in the Rhondda for some time, it gained momentum as heavy lifting replaced the dignity of heavy labour. It was also fuelled by American popular culture, with Arnold Schwarzenegger's *Conan the Barbarian*, whose stiff and dulcet posture was often mimicked by the disinherited of earth whose overgrown torsos would have no doubt found it easier to get onto a wilding horse than into a modest family vehicle, and Lou Ferrigno's *Hulk*, whose anger was readapted into local serialised episodes of "roid rage". These muscle-bulging experimenters that raged against the injustice of whatever crossed paths with their medical conditioning were however less green and relied more upon home-made recoloration potions that in appearance looked more a mix of gravy browning and orange juice to induce the desired tango-kissed effect. That was until sunbed centres finally arrived, further making a mockery of any conception of "whiteness". The greyed-out faces of the heroin users, whose culture arrived from the geo-political counterpoint of Afghanistan, in contrast, were a perfect camouflage for those who blended into the grey sites of dereliction that would disguise their barely living bodies. Of course, the real tragedy is both these de-emasculated visions tended to affirm the realities of violence which are now so wrongly attributed to all types of masculinity, while ensuring that each likely succumbed to a premature and excruciating end as a result of internal organ failure. If violence is to be spoken of here, it's not simply about masculinity, but how it was replaced by vulnerability, leaving nothing to compensate, whether men of the valleys found some temporary fix in excessive and deformed growth or the slow violence of blood-draining emaciation.

Opened in the 1940s, the EMI factory set about producing valves for aircraft radar systems by local women as part of the war effort. It continued to benefit from MOD contracts until American and Japanese arms manufacturers proved more competitive. Several iterations of Fordist style production followed, none of which provided secure employment. In the 1970s, the factory became synonymous with the blank ferric oxide EMI tapes, which were cheap but terrible at recording anything at high frequency. Local kids often ransacked outside bins, hoping to recover discarded cassettes, despite the fact their twisted tape meant even the most proficient sound engineer would have given up on dreams of their salvation. What symbolism can be attached to a people asked to produce silent tapes, only for the rest of the world to add the meaningful content? Following this, workers rolled out dials for rotary phones in an operation then called Thorn EMI Dynatel that soon found itself unable to compete with the Taiwanese. Believing it was better to join the Asian Tiger economy revolution, so the shopfloor shifted its depleting energies again, this time to producing what some (notably its directors) claimed to be the very first laptop computer — the failed Wren Liberator. Weighing more than 12kg, it was hardly portable. Wren was more of a Teletext system which had little marketable value and went bust after only 1,000 sales. With the site threatened with closure, it was lastly taken over by a company specialising in the production of Christmas trimmings, notably baubles, which ran into the 1990s before it was unable to compete with Chinese imports. Unlike those who suffered from the lasting effects of the pits, at least workers wore protective masks to prevent intoxication from the dust of a more glittering kind. Today the building stands as another corroding ruin, appearing like a post-apocalyptic film that is simply awaiting the arrival of a script worthy of its attention, though unlikely to ever arrive. Like its heroin-consuming dwellers, it too is barely able to stand in the wilderness of a slow decaying bleakness, as nature takes its revenge upon the locals' memories of better times. But unlike other post-industrial wastelands such as Detroit, which at least attract photographic tourists seeking sublime images of abandoned beautification, few enter except the oversized walkers and the addicted.

A dark woodland known as Maindy forest is situated to the left of this industrial shell. Gazing upon its coverage, I recall two obscured landmarks hidden behind the density. Children of my generation grew up believing the round stone formations in one of its unkempt fields had a sacrificial purpose linked to a devil-worshiping cult. On several occasions, mischievous youths placed beheaded chickens on its central slab to further fuel the rumours. They have since become a central feature in a housing estate, featuring some of the more expensive houses in the valley. The stones were laid as part of the Eisteddfod in 1923, which was the first time this national celebration came to the Rhondda. Established in the year of the French Revolution (another moment in history with a notable penchant for decapitation), the Eisteddfod has become synonymous with

Welsh identity and culture. Not only is it an occasion when the poetic Bards of Celtic culture are commemorated, it reminds us of the importance of storytelling and oral histories. The Gorsedd stones here form a twelve-pointed circle that holds deep mystical meaning. They are also a focal point for druid ritual during the festivities. Part of the shamanic tradition, the word "druid" can be traced back to the ancient Latin "*druides*", which has been translated into "oak-seers" of wisdom. A culture that professed its sensitivity to the natural elements and saw nature itself as a sacred gift (which occasionally did lead to sacrificial happenings, thus meaning that the stories of the chickens were not as far-fetched as they seemed), the culture of the druids of Wales proved difficult to destroy precisely because of their preference for narration instead of written history. Deeper into the forest is a mountain road leading to some of the most enviable views of the valley in both directions and beyond, including across to the Breconshire Beacons range. Due to its location, it's no coincidence the hillside features the remains of a round Iron Age fort called Maindy Camp, which I ran over so many times in complete ignorance. How history can be overlooked, even by those claiming to have keen interest. I am not religious. My generation was taught to pray to gods of a more material kind. Yet there's something I can't explain each time I run through those enclosing woods. Comprised of ancient and recently planted trees, the tightly compact mass of oak, birch, alder and ash emits its own impenetrable density, pulling what's beneath the blackened earth up into the space between these natural pillars. Being looked upon by watchers in the darkness is always a prevailing feeling that takes over the sense of this place.

Here it feels like I am the ghost carried forth on a phantom train leading back through the traces of time. Close to the site of the Roman camp, another flat stone is set in the ground on the edge of a steep vertical descent. People of the valleys who venture here will know what I am referring to. The vista overlooks the magnificently carved Bwlch mountain range and across in the other direction to the valley below. This would be the place I ran to when things got too difficult, which in truth was only on a handful of occasions. We never liked to see ourselves as victims. Besides, we were all on the same shipwreck, even if revisionists have proclaimed the poor now to be on the winning team. There was a time when I sat and wondered if the world really cared if I no longer existed. At least when the sun occasionally passed behind a shadow could be set longer than was ever promised upon miniature towns in the distance. On three visits my screams raged from that stone and I listened to my anger echo down the vale, wishing it would manage to escape over the mountains as I felt no solutions on the ground. Like that shadow which nobody could see, over time I also learned to become more and more invisible. Retreating in school, company was found in the solitude of thought. I imagined what life would look like from the perspective of my death, at least dead to time in this place. After leaving, for many years I returned not wanting to be seen in these towns. Nothing was held in common, I convinced myself. Still, how the nothing returns, to sever the fibres of our most intimate selves. Admittedly, this attitude deeply pains me today, as I know there is no better than this in basic human terms. Fleeing like a troubled apparition in the night, I hollowed out my character and filled it in again like a blank canvas, which was always a deception and source of greater anguish. Lost souls are always tormented. And they are always caught in a wilderness of doubt. Still, time waits for no one upon this ghosting-carriage in which I am travelling and as the reminiscence starts to return, that deceased child is staring to awaken in the memory of my heart.

The EMI factory is situated at the edge of the village of Treorchy, which is most famous for its song. I am not referring here to Welsh legend Max Boyce, whose gold-selling album *Live at Treorchy* (produced by the EMI label) was recorded live at Treorchy Rugby Club and released in 1974, the year of my birth. The album is mainly an ode to the game with the slightly flattened ball, which remains a local and national passion, though in truth I never could understand its appeal. Formed in 1883, the sonorous tones of the Treorchy Male Voice Choir became world renowned. Theirs is a sound that once echoed as powerful as the local winds through the doors of the Nonconformist chapels and into the hearts of fellow miners from which their membership was largely recruited. More recently, however, it has become the sound of lament, often accompanying broadcasted stories of decline. Their fame also owed a great deal to the EMI label, who signed them to a record deal in the 1960s and sent them on a world tour, which brought new attention to the valleys. Their first choir won a local Eisteddfod competition in the local pub called the Red Lion (which like many of my age, I spent many a night at drinking copiously and singing terribly), performing a version of Joseph Parry's haunting "Myfanwy", which is believed to have been influenced by a fourteenth-century love story that shows the Welsh's affection for tragedy. A song that prominently featured in John Ford's adaptation of *How Green Was My Valley*, the most popular and recognisable rendition is still often attributed to the men of Treorchy. Emitting something timeless from this land of verse, their singing of this ballad is still able to cut through the loss of love with a poignant romanticism, which somehow refuses to let the melody die so long as there is a songful air to breathe.

Passing through the village's local station, my sight is bookended by the comprehensive school I attended on my left, which was built on the site of the former Tylecoch Colliery, and on the right one of the largest cemeteries in the entire South Wales valleys. Treorchy cemetery has over 70,000 graves, including most of my known deceased family. They lay in various states of happiness and misery, in the company of a few notables, including a young boy named Henry Lewis, who at 18 died in the ferocious battle at Rorke's Drift in the Anglo-Zulu War of 1879, along with a memorial to a local boxer who was en route to a fight in the USA aboard the *SS Titanic*. It is also the resting place for the male voice choir's original conductor, John Haydn Davies, and the brilliantly celebrated local footballer

Roy Paul who captained the sky-blue working-class team of Manchester to two FA cup finals in a period long before the Middle Eastern billions came flooding into the club. Another of the village's most famous sons would also have a marked impact on the beautiful game, but for all the wrong reasons. The Treorchy-born referee Clive Thomas, known as "the book" for his strict interpretation of the laws of the game, is forever associated with one of the most controversial moments in the history of the World Cup. In 1978, the Copa Mundial was hosted by Argentina, who were then under the brutal dictatorship of Jorge Rafael Videla Redondo. While not comparable to the team of the Pele years, Argentina's bitter rivals Brazil were still one of the tournament's favourites and were drawn to play the less-favoured Sweden in their opening match. With the score set at 1-1 the game entered stoppage time. The Brazilians took a corner, which was met in the air by the outstanding footballer Zico. As his head connected with the ball with only six seconds of stoppage time played, Thomas turned away and blew the final whistle, blind to the goal being scored behind him. The Rhondda man waved away the ensuing protests and marched indefatigably towards the tunnel. The Brazilians were outraged, and some even accused Thomas of foul play. Argentina would later reach the final, which they eventually won in dubious circumstances, knocking Brazil out in the process. This remains one of the most controversial televised refereeing moments in the history of the famed tournament.

Football has always been an important part of life for children in these valleys. It was the one thing that brought us together and allowed us to dream big. Of course, there were fights about who was to play Ian Rush, but there was always Mark Hughes or John Barnes in the wings should another persona be required. Children had no concern for colour or creed, unless the colour was worn by the rivals you sportingly loved to hate. What mattered was character on these pitches of life. Liverpool was our team, as brilliant as they were. When you live in misery, you hardly want to support a team that will further bring you down. But we also shared something in common with its proud and hardworking people. This unity further cemented after Hillsborough. Seeing those people fighting for breath and the state absolving itself of any complicity and guilt, we knew their story was ours, and for the very first time I found myself crying at something which didn't directly affect me. I was affected beyond all knowing. And that was the first time I really felt Thatcher was to blame. I will return to her later in this story, even if I am still reluctant to give her my words. What I do know is how the simplest things can with hindsight have the deepest of meanings, even if appreciation also only comes with the passage of time and the wisdom of age. Three ingredients were enough back then to give plentiful sustenance — a ball, a wall and daylight. We were never completely defeated so long as we had these and until the full time of the night finally descended.

Argentina then entered back into my life in 1984. I had no idea of its where or when, but I knew its colour. More than a game, Maradona was both an angel and demon incarnate as the English cried foul. How we laughed at their misfortune, even if the media told us we were all British again and the unemployed should sign up to fight for the cause. A cheap, fake Argentinian football shirt was my reward, which I like to think was defiance, but probably because it now cost the cheapest of all. I couldn't care less, for I was now Diego, and the blue shirt proved my position and streetwise credentials.

While the men of the South Wales valleys were largely recruited into the mines, the women were drawn to the factories, notably in the production of munitions and textiles. Alongside the EMI factory, the most famous facility in the entire Rhondda valley was situated at the top end of the Treorchy village in Ynyswen, historically known to locals as "Polikoffs". Whereas generations of men could find gainful employment in the deep mines, the women simply needed to turn up at this factory and found there was always an opportunity to learn to cut cloth and weave from its spherical looms. Both my mother and grandmother worked there for a time. Following a government initiative in 1937 financed by a grant administered by the newly established Nuffield Trust set up to create employment for women in "depressed areas" (it should be noted this was a time when coal production was still generating extreme wealth despite the challenges posed by oil and petroleum), the factory was set up two years later by the Russian-Jewish emigre Alfred Polikoff. He made his fortune in ladies' clothing in the East End of London during the 1920s. No sooner had the factory opened, World War II broke out, so it swiftly turned its production capacity to military clothing. A notable garment to roll from its lines would be long green army trench coats, which were said to be inspired by Russian designs to which Polikoff was accustomed. Situated on a procured site covering some 12 acres, at its peak the factory employed around 2,500 women between the ages of 14–70. Part of a wider economy of new gendered production, the impact on the valley was staggering. Prior to Polikoff's arrival, female employment was almost non-existent. Now the tables were turning, and it was the men who found themselves out of work while the women brought home the bread. There was however a notable problem with this reversal in fortunes. Women's salaries were often at the bare minimum and they were poorly unionised, hence never offering a real substitute for the miners' higher wages, while providing little of the protections the miners fought hard to secure.

Polikoff died in 1943. The operation was subsequently taken over by Great Universal (known for its mail-order and pay-monthly catalogue service) in 1948 but retained his name. It turned its production to men's and women's clothing, while also being one of the most important hubs that structured social activity throughout the local community. Workers enjoyed the use of a free bus service to and from the factory and it had its own social club a few miles down the vale. So embedded in the fabric of the Rhondda, the factory became a key social institution, helping for instance in the delivery of aid following the devastating flood that engulfed many homes during the heavy rains in 1961. Charitable replacement clothing was handed out to desperate families most affected by the disaster. It also became a principal site in administering the smallpox vaccine rollout following the local scare a year later. As the post-war consensus on achieving full employment started to crumble, and one by one the collieries started to close, so Polikoffs became the largest employer in the valleys. Through the late 1970s and 80s, however, it started to face more difficult times, and the continued threat of redundancy was ever-present as the factory was exposed to the ravages of free-market fundamentalism. The workforce would be continually cut, while wages also stagnated as workers were made acutely aware of the need to be "globally competitive". At the turn of the millennium the factory only employed some 300 skilled workers, most of which were on salaries comparable to the national minimum wage.

In 1989, the factory was taken over by high-end London fashion house Burberry (then part of Great Universal), which resulted in a decade of valleys people being uniformly dressed from head to toe in various shades of iconic brown and blue tartan. Shop-floor seconds could be bought at cheap prices since the slightest imperfections wouldn't be tolerated by those paying for aesthetic perfection. They may have been poor, but at least for a while the people of the Rhondda dressed in the highest quality fitted finery, which, marked with a Royal seal of approval, were otherwise destined for boutiques many would be too intimidated to enter, let alone be able to afford. However, despite being highly profitable, Burberry issued a statement of closure in 2006, indicating it was "refining" its global production. When translated, this meant moving its production to cheaper Chinese plants. The closure of the factory in March 2007 was the final nail in the coffin, not just for the factory, but for the history of industrial-scale production in the Rhondda valley. Like the miners who couldn't compete against the onslaught of economic and political forces beyond their control, so this last bastion of industrial heritage was whimsically discarded without any consultation. Workers cried enough to fill the celebratory champagne glasses as the company recorded record profits that year. A people who were always perversely incorporated into globalisation and the demands for maximum human capital extraction proved again to be amongst its most disposable the moment its invisible axis slightly tilted. And so, as yet another chapter in global dispossession was written, the intersections between appropriation and vulnerability played out their loaded game of rotational chance.

The end of the line has been reached. The train terminates at Treherbert station and so I'll need to make the rest of my journey on foot. On more than one occasion I would be awakened here in a drunken slumber having caught the last train home from Cardiff (where my train that brought me into the valleys began today), resulting in a maudlin run a few miles back down the empty lines, following its barely visible horizon points into the impending darkness. Guided by steeled traces of moonlight on the quiet tracks, my reddened eyes still kept watch in the hope I wouldn't encounter some less than friendly gang from a neighbouring village as I made the journey back. Valley violence was most often territorial. I make my way up to Bute Road and look upon The Bute public house, which has long enjoyed a notorious reputation. Both take their name from the Third Marquis of Bute, John Crichton Stuart, who at the time was claimed to be the richest man in the world. Stuart owned large swathes of the valleys' land, which enabled him to grant rights to various companies for mineral extraction. Engineered by the titan of industrialisation, Isambard Kingdom Brunel, the entire Taff Vale railway system that cut deep into the South Wales valleys, including the line I have been travelling for the past hour (almost to the second), owes a great deal to Stuart's business needs, financial investment and his egoistical desire to leave his mark on history. This was also driven by the naked ambition to create a network which would allow the tens of thousands of migrating workers to arrive at the seams, while the greater and more important loads of coal and profits seamlessly left in the opposite direction without any resistance. Real power has always been defined by movement, including what and who is able to decide upon the direction of travel.

Stood at the foot of the Rhigos mountain, the weaving roads marking its pass become visible. Taking this road over the top of the "Heads of the Valley" and followed around in a semi-circular motion brings the traveller to the much maligned yet historically significant town of Merthyr Tydfil. A few decades before two German intellectuals by the names of Karl Marx and Fredrich Engels theorised about worker alienation and the coming revolution, the rioters in Merthyr were the very first to birth the idea of socialism. Born from the revolutionary fires of the iron-smelting town, this idea that workers should have inalienable rights soon spread across the globe with radical, powerful and violent consequences. Such history, for those who care to remember, is woven into the memory of every hamlet here. Should I cut directly into the mountainside to my right, the neighbouring valley village of Maerdy would be entered, which was once labelled "Little Moscow" following its militancy and the financial support given to the local miners' families during the Great Strike of 1926 from Russia. Cold Siberian winds haven't always been unwelcomed in these towns. Yet how that memory so easily vanishes from record, as much as the valleys fight against the prejudicial forces of fascism. However, whilst it is tempting to idealise the radical past buried deep into the political topography of these hills, the reality is far more complex and fraught with many unresolved contradictions. The people of the valleys have been called upon, appropriated and subsequently neglected by every ideology. Whatever political stripe, the story of my forebears and contemporaries remains one of deep distrust, especially against those who promise to save them with their better ideas about what the locals truly want and tales of community enrichment.

Having walked for around 30 minutes, I arrive close to my destination at the source of the valley in Blaenrhondda.

Two generations of my family lived here, including my great-grandfather and his son, who both worked at the neighbouring Fernhill Colliery during the period leading up to the Second World War and through the equally challenging post-war years. Blaenrhondda is watched over by the most imperious of all mountains in the South Wales valleys — the strident range of Pen-Pych. Standing like a dormant volcano, majestic yet full of mysterious energy, the mountain seems to be waiting until its moment arrives and finally breaking open to reveal something tremendous from within its depths. Local mythology tells that the name for the mountain derived from a Celtic translation of "Heads of the Five Bulls". A local tribe allegedly lived on the flat top of the spur (one of only two of its kind in Europe), and their prized possession were a steed of bulls. When the Romans arrived and demanded tribute, first in the form of the land and then the taking ownership of the stock-rearing animals, the tribesmen refused. Instead of capitulating to the imperial forces, the Celtic tribesmen cut the heads off the herd and placed them on spikes on the mountaintop as a symbol of their sacrifice. The rest of the bulls' carcasses were thrown down the slopes. If their freedom and right to exist was to end, it would be on their terms, they proclaimed. The people of the valleys have a history of resistance that far predates the arrival of modernity and secular dreams of liberation. Whether the legend of the bulls is true or not is of lesser importance. If history is to mean anything, it must ignite the passion, stir the imagination and have us question what memories and hidden fires these mountains contain.

Walking along the last of the valley roads that leads directly to where the colliery was once situated, I recall a beautiful memory from the 1980s. I was ten years old. The miners' strike had begun and a procession was organised by the village's Social Club to help raise the spirits and donations. Situated at the end of the line, raising money for food parcels to give to the impoverished families in this town was essential to their survival. The local pit had already closed in 1978, but many in the community worked over the mountain at Tower Colliery in the Cynon valley at the other end of the Rhigos road. Tower's miners fought longer and more persistently than any others to stay in production and keep hold of a fading way of life. Sounds of the brass bands proudly fronted by the miners' banners which have now become a part of their living historical memory enter my thoughts. Some striking miners marched past with faces painted black, reminding the community how they looked in more dignified times. Wives marched alongside in a remarkable show of solidarity. Then in the distance appeared my grandfather, who although forcibly retired from the pits, still saw himself as one of them. He was dressed in drag, with irregular-sized balloons stuffed up his shirt for breasts, smiling through the badly-applied lipstick that covered his mouth with such gaiety. Many false preconceptions are made about the character of poor people from places like the valleys. And they often come from those who never lived or even stepped foot in such communities. Inherent prejudice is one of them, even if the anthem of there being "A Welcome in the Hillside" was romantically overplayed. Yet through the painted faces, it was clear their spirits were being crushed, much like the large boulder which supported only by rotten wood fell on my grandfather's back deep underground, cutting his working life short and making him dependent on his wits and ultimately the state. Dependency, I later discovered, is one of the most debilitating of all human conditions.

I enter into the site where the colliery once stood, and true to form the heavens open as if the elements were precipitating a deeper connection. Caught in this torrential flow of life that has me situated beneath broken clouds, I am reminded of another procession witnessed on the same street a few years later that was altogether more bizarre. Built in 1987 on the very ground I am now stood, the disastrous theme park Western World was opened, replete with its log cabins that were home to self-styled cowboys, bandits and confederate flags. It even had its own saloon bar. The opening saw a small, bemused crowd line the village road that was previously walked upon with such strident defiance by the now defeated miners, as a new band of performers and entertainers yelled out "yee-haw" while attempting to lasso bewildered locals on horseback. They were followed in line by a small convoy of Pontiac and Firebird cars. Others were dressed as Native Americans, who were invariably cast to play the part of the enemy, albeit with skin tones of a more Anglo-Saxon stock. It was an utter failure. Aside from lacking the appropriate arid climate and the authentic backdrop of cacti-strewn, deserted landscapes (they could have at least improvised), it was rather difficult to sell the idea of a colonial frontier wonderland, when such conditions resembled everyday life for a people who were now left with all the struggle but none of the prospecting. Besides, a wild west bar was hardly novel in these parts. It was open for less than a month before it ran into deep financial trouble. Maybe the organisers simply got the casting all wrong. We were after all more like the Native Americans in these mountains.

Walking through the heavy rain, I continue as far as the plateau takes me. A feeling of a terrible loss overwhelms my body. I am now caught in a psychologically disrupted landscape where past and present are forcefully colliding. Everything is concentrated and nothing appears certain anymore. Another large pit wheel stands in the open expanse, unceremoniously left without any concern and significance. Half buried in the black shale ground, it looks more like a rusty tombstone standing in memory to the gravest of injustices. The ground is covered in discarded pit waste that is loose under foot, yet like quicksand, over time it has taken firm hold of whatever it surrounds, slowly pulling everything back into its depths. Gazing upon this partially visible wheel that's corroding before my eyes, I keep asking myself, is this reality? Or am I part of some monochromatic dream in which a tragic tale finds a way to eternally return? I realise I am silently calling out like so many have silently screamed on this humble expanse. What does it mean now the wheels have finally stopped turning? My senses reawaken as I walk along the narrow tracks where the trams used to run. I look down at the clear waters in the pond that rolls into a river below. This is fed by a large waterfall, which reminds that while some things continue to have the freedom to flow, others move to a standstill. In front I see the ruins of the old building containing the waterworks pipe that connected to the reservoir at Llyn Fawr on the other side of this mountainside, which is settled in another prominent glacial circle. When deepening this reservoir in 1911 to supply more drinking water to the rapidly growing local populations, workers discovered in the waterlogged peat a significant hoard of Iron and Bronze Age objects, including two cauldrons, tools and a sword (dated to around 650 BC), which is said to be the oldest Iron Age discovery in the British Isles. It is assumed the objects belonged to the native Celtic Silures tribe, who once lived and dominated the area of South Wales and whose recognisable Hallstatt culture can be traced to Bohemia and Bavaria. They later fiercely resisted the invading army from Imperial Rome and its attempted occupation of these geographical highlands before the eventual arrival of Christianity.

Sat on the large cragged rock, I am as close as I can get to the Penpych waterfall. Looking back down the valleys, I contemplate how the mountains have returned to their green splendour. The landscape of the valleys looks as if it has been thrown back to a time before the coal was extracted from beneath this exploited earth. Still I remain unsettled. What has really been buried here? And what would happen if we uncovered what lies below? Faced with these questions, I look into the waters and see a distorted reflection. Caught in the flow of life, time itself is pulling the image I have curated of myself in conflicting directions. But I see clarity as a dark rock glistens in the water beneath my face. My generation lived a reversal of Llewellyn's transformation. *How black was my valley?* That is the proposition needing to be addressed. Having witnessed the burial of such a dark ecology, what remains of the industry are unceremonious relics that remind of an age of productivity, which can no longer be recovered. The sunken wheel only adds to a sense of tragedy as acute as anything told by ancient playwrights. A doubting wilderness of thought returns. How can I write of the past when I am both personally invested yet also someone who fled? And what of this green recovery? Surely, we don't want to be nostalgic for the black? As the winds pull my attention upward, I see, I feel, a towering deception. The mental landscapes of the mines have gone, and that for many is a rightful source for celebration and a marker that society has moved in a better direction. Dominating the vista are 76 wind turbines from the Pen-y-Cymoedd wind farm, which at the time of its erection was the largest on-shore farm of its kind in the entire United Kingdom. A prominent entrance to the site is located through the forestry road of the now-abandoned Tower Colliery. Their presence here is not unique. Constantly rotating knives mark the skyline throughout the valleys, notably towering over the village of Gilfach Goch in which Llewellyn's plot was based. As the wheel of the mining shaft has been replaced by these sleek modern blades, a new order of rotation has been inaugurated. However, no locals work at the bottom of these towers. All that was solid truly has melted into air. These imposing structures cut into the atmosphere above, while time itself is now over-present as their circular movements act as a constant reminder to forces still at work, which local people cannot do anything about as they continue to sit in conditions of widespread redundancy, depression and neglect. Failed campaigns to prevent these turbine farms from cutting across the horizon, creating noise pollution that is more searing than any natural storm while brutalising every view of its green and rugged mountainsides, is simply another chapter in the subjugation and denial of the political demands of valleys life. And so, returning to consider my earlier conflicted thoughts surrounded by contradictory memories that are marked by a colour so deep it has made an abysmal vortex of these soulful lands, I see this journey as more resonant than ever. It is not just retelling the story of the valleys. Nor is it narrating about communities as apparently broken as the ground laying before me. It is about recovering a lost jigsaw piece in the fragmented and continually evolving story of the people of the world. A people whose lives and passion still demand respect.

BLACK ECOLOGY

For centuries, everything was white as far as the sun could possibly see and the winds could tell. There were no human witnesses to this time, for the harsh conditions made the entire zone uninhabitable. All we have are fossilised relics, whose clues and signs we are still yet to properly decipher. Not everything, it seems, gets frozen in time. Much of the Northern Hemisphere was an open ice desert, reflecting the young planet back out into the wider solar system. Its crystalline hue set it apart like a diamond in the sky. Large parts of the earth were as white as the pure driven snow. But there was no romanticism to this colouration. Hostile as it was brutal. Snowstorms swirled across the surface of the concealed continental plates. Wilderness stretched tens of thousands of miles, flattening many geographical inhibitions. The ice was close to half a mile deep in places, impenetrable to any other natural force. Its expansive ambitions crushed the mightiest of settled rock formations. Temperatures had fallen to -100 Celsius. It never went into positive figures. This was a ground zero of an entirely different kind. These conditions were part of a much wider process of glacial activity which scientists have since called the Pleistocene Epoch, marked by epic changes in the earth's atmosphere, which can in part be explained by wider gravitational pulls in our wider interstellar village and our own planet's orbital tilting. Such climatic conditioning created an entirely different temporality. Slowly the ice marched and pulled, never static but moving to its own rhythms and intensities.

Beneath the ice another dynamic was taking place. Some 300 million years ago and prior to the arrival of the permafrost, the plateaus were densely covered in wetland forests. The area that is now known as Wales was overgrown and covered in tree-like structures known as lycophytes, that grew vast and died over a very quick lifespan. Their burial patterns would have a profound impact on the entire ecology of the planet. A massive build-up of peat resulted from the fallen debris that was slowly condensed on the wetland's floor. Overtime, the peat was compressed, leaving beneath the surface the hard structure of carbon deposits. Carbonisation would occur under intense heat and pressure in an oxygen-free environment. This entire process gave name to the so-called "coal forests", whose formation takes us farther back than any recorded human history. The Carboniferous period lasted about 60 million years, which appears to have resulted in the cooling of the earth's orbital parameters. This gave rise to glaciation, which it seems brought the planet perilously close to another "snowball earth" event wherein the entire surface of the globe would have been frozen. It is hypothesised that this last occurred around 700 million years ago, when extensive volcanic eruptions in a volatile range covering some 2000 miles between Alaska and Greenland (then situated closer to the equator) sent enough sulphur dioxide into the upper layers of the atmosphere to block the sun's radiation, thereby dramatically cooling the planet. This created a perfect storm made of fire and ice, which in turn took on a life of its own as the more the planet froze, the more it refracted the sun, hence literally snowballing the earth.

The ice in Wales started to melt some 15,000 years ago, though it would take another several thousand years before life properly returned. Geologists believe the process began in the Breconshire Beacons area, where the ice accumulated in dense glacial sheets before making its way southward, while cutting across as it met further geological obstacles to create the now familiar depths that we have come to call "the valleys". To the west, the melting waters turned the low-level straights between Wales and Ireland into an ocean, while the channel area below what is now Cardiff was also flooded. As the icy waters flowed away, so the marks they made into the area's once flatter plateaus were revealed. The valleys were formed as the ice cut deep into the concealed sediment and further moved the soil as the powerful drift of compression melting pushed them onward, until they eventually left the scene. A notable feature of the process here is the appearance of glaciation circles, which left distinctive rotunda carved into the mountainsides that gives the impression of either being hit by some interstellar meteorite or carved by the Gods into gigantic amphitheatres. They seem impossibly round in places, like the area north of Cwmparc ("*Cwm*" is a Welsh word that translates into "valleys" and frequently related to glacial cirques) that can be accessed from the Bwlch Road close to those aforementioned druid rocks. Some upland plateaus would remain as sites of open expanse notably exposed to the high winds. Penpych mountain in Blaenrhonnda is a wonderful example of this, which is also notable for the steep vertical descent, showing just how intent glacial activity was in this particular area. The rivers would also play their part, cutting tracks further into the top-layer of sandstone, sculpting in the process the familiar landscape that would define the region. Children of the upper Rhondda would often refer to the visible mountain ranges in these parts as the seven giants, which no doubt inspired by local tales of awakening and historical might, also historically connects to the city of Rome, which was surrounded by seven hills.

In the millennia that followed, the valleys were flourishing as nature retained its position as the defining force. Forests returned and much of the valley was covered in dense thicket. Small birds nested in the mighty oak trees, while large birds of prey could be seen surveying the land. The air was as refined as any time in history, making even the crisp breeze welcoming. Clear rivers ran through as a variety of fish swam freely up and down its babbling waters. Lynx could be seen grazing beneath the tree covering, which also provided the perfect habitat for fauna and flora to thrive. Wild horses competed in the open plateaus with red deer to see who could look the most majestic in the twilight sun as temperatures were a few degrees higher than today. When the waters did cascade due to the rains, which fell from their picturesque waterfalls into the wells of life and onward into yet to be named rivers to replenish the lands, they were absorbed into the banks and surrounding wetlands. Acres of untrampled flowers vibrantly shimmered, attracting an ecosystem of pollinating hope. Packs of white and grey wolves dominated land-bound migration patterns, periodically appearing in the woodland areas guided by the constellations. A few little homesteads were sparsely dotted across this landscape. Its habitants made use of everything, nothing went to waste and everything was recycled back into nature. Subsistence-dwelling sapiens only took what was required to maintain their existence; though from time to time they might indulge, but only on very special occasions. This was a landscape defined by atmospheric tones that marked the colour of existence. Nothing was drawn to excess, for it was known that nature required harmony as sure as the seasons would return. This at least is how the romantics might picture it, were it not for the violence and bloodshed of attempted colonisations, along with the hardships of everyday existence.

Quintessential visions of idyllic rural life later captured in Llewellyn's depictions may have been stretched somewhat, but it does still hold a certain gravity in how we picture pre-industrial valleys life. Who could not be seduced by such imaginings of serenity? As Thomas Roscoe wrote in 1836, "I had now entered into this wild and mountainous region, where nature seemed to reign in stern and unbroken silence. Not a human being besides myself appeared to be treading these solitudes, nor was there habitation to be seen." While the Welsh painter Richard Wilson was leading a new landscape movement in the north of the country, it was J. M. W. Turner who captured the rugged wilderness of the country, which in turn captivated the imagination of poets and writers alike who were drawn to its sublime beauty. Moreover, at the same time Turner was painting his *The Destruction of the Bards* (1800), Henry Gastineau and William Weston Young were turning their attention to the natural beauty of the South Wales valleys.

Clear waters on beckoning streams appear as nature intended. But all was not quite so in tune with the natural vision of the sublime purported by the philosopher who gave rise to its naming, Edmund Burke. "Untamely wild", Benjamin Heath wrote in 1803, as he confronted lands populated by people who were "thinly scattered as well as miserably poor". And less than a century later the place became largely unrecognisable to those who had earlier entered its mountain passes. While the poverty remained, the landscape would soon be devasted. This picture was captured by Thomas Alwyn Lloyd and Herbert Jackson, who lamented how "once fair valleys, with woodlands, pure streams and pastoral scenery, [were] widely despoiled". It is worth dwelling here on the significance of that word "despoil". To despoil anything, what was once visible needs to be torn asunder. While this invokes a conscious decision, it also points to something either tremendously transformative or altogether abject. But these outcomes don't necessarily need to be opposed. What is enriching and liberating for some can appear altogether dispossessing and oppressive for others. A breaking apart of the shoals by the mighty tides of progress, tied the despoiling of the land to the veritable rise of "significant people", many of which we still laud on pedestals today. Yet at the same time, these very processes further promoted the idea that there existed lesser significant landscapes populated by lesser valuable humans. A twisting gash in the moorland plateaus, the valleys' topography pointed to the violence that awaited. The violence that already lay beneath, and just needed to be set free.

Transformation was swift and brutal. Deforestation uprooted trees, so the roots of precarious humans could take their place. The earth was turned inside-out, while the lives of inhabitants were turned upside-down. As the stomachs of this ecology churned, it spewed out its own excrement and waste. The mountainside was cut, first on the surface, then as far as was possible into the bowels of this promised land. Dark soon became day, while a tidal wave of sediment killed natural streams of existence. This was history making itself visible. And it marked a new epoch inseparable from a darkness that was about to emerge. Everything began with that first assault on the rock. Now everything mattered. Time would be recorded. The past soon forgotten. In this new beginning there was an abyss, it was black, and it consumed all, and upon this terrain appeared a 12-year-old boy named John Davies. Many children in the valleys will have known John due to the iconic photo taken of him on his first day of work at the Ferndale Colliery. He appears before us with his face blackened, and yet there is such pride and optimism to his tender expression. He would become another paid prospector tasked with excavating the black gold, which was already powering the exploits of Empire and authenticating a burial of meanings in this region. I cannot possibly imagine how that young boy felt as he entered the cold steel cage on his first morning at work, having arrived in the beckoning hours, surrounded by the white eyes of battle-scarred men, feeling the bitter cold wind rise as his body descended into the darkness. So many lives were lost taking that journey and crashing at deadly speed into the chasm below. But there were always more workers, more children who in life were of less value than the pit horses. John worked underground in the carbon tunnels for most of his life. Starved of daylight, except on Sundays, like many others, the polluting atmosphere slowly killed his body by suffocating him from within. John contracted what locals referred to as "the dust" or what those in the medical profession called pneumoconiosis, which blackened his lungs and literally turned his body into ash. While thousands of miners would lose their lives as a direct result of accidents underground as collapsing shafts, underground explosions and unexpected encounters with accelerating drams often proved fatal, the torturously slow deaths of others far exceeded this number. And yet all this violence was mostly hidden away, beneath the ground or within the slow burning bodies of its victims. But still it found a way to make itself known. It always does. Anybody who grows up in the valleys knows the fatalism, and how the signs of internal scarring seep into the collective consciousness. While the ominous presence of death lingers, its cemeteries are filled with wreaths of decaying flowers left for the prematurely deceased and the permanently disinherited of this once vibrant industrial land.

Black is an ecology in the valleys of South Wales. And its seeping presence is truly mimetic. It's been raining again in the Rhondda. The heavy droplets bounce off the slate roofs, making that familiar pinging sound as they fall into the wet streets below. The tributaries at the source of the valley are already moving at a ferocious speed, building momentum as they flow and join one another. Some roll effortlessly into the rivers, while others have to make their way around the imposition of less natural structures, which change the course of their direction. But the waters always find a way to defy the barriers and follow their gravitational pull. Behind the homes built of locally quarried stone, the pits start to leak as their internal waters break. They are close to the mountainside where the tributaries continue multiplying. Some have already been redirected and put to use in the industrial process. Water would be applied in a pressurised system to separate coal from shale and to further wash the resultant coal that cleansed the financial souls of the few. Within a pulsating watery chamber, the basic principle was that the coal would float, while the shale sank. Yet even that contaminated water needs to go somewhere. And so down it goes into the valley below. What begins slowly soon becomes a cascade as the streets are full of water with no intention other than to connect with the falling volume. Those who live highest on the hills witness the merger first-hand, as the microscopic fragments of black dust mix with the waters that run past, gathering more dust along the way to darken the still. As the rain continues to fall, the unnatural tributaries now running through every village, down every hill and into every street, start to carry heavier pieces of leftover disposable rock. Some houses situated at the bottom act as a dam and stop the slurry in its tracks. Stone and carbon collide, the detritus fallout will be later witnessed when the rain subsides.

The river cutting through the centre of the valley moves at an unstoppable pace. It is as relentless as the precipitous gift from the heavens, which owes everything to the mountainous topography. A river is flowing, and it's flowing black. A blackbird can be seen flying in the distance. His silhouette barely visible through the dense grey smog billowing from the strident furnace tower below. The bird circles around its ascending mist creating its own vortex in the sky, cawing out in a language of foreboding the natives probably understand. He looks down and recognises a valley for what it has become. He has never seen that photograph of John. But the body of the earth beneath his wings resembles the same. He too is a witness to the ecological drama, which is as captivating as it is disturbing. Gaia's chest is exposed, her arteries and veins are seeping with blood that is the deepest of blacks. Even the sun seems to refract the Stygian tone, darkened by smoke and thunderous clouds that have no lining to speak of. The silver in fact has fallen to earth upon those toxic raindrops that give the carbon its seductive shine and make it glisten to rival any sub-zero crystal. The blackbird follows the river down the vale, picking up speed as it meanders and turns. The wind is at his back, like the winds of change sweeping through the valley itself. At some points, the black torrent escapes the broken banks, which simply cannot contain its tremendous power. There has always been such a thin line between the beautiful and the sublime. But how the latter became altogether more devastating once the machinery of industrialisation sped up its flows beyond all previously known measure. And so there is a devastation, and still the rains continue to fall at a punishing rate.

The higher the bird ascends, the more it sees the river's surreal black vitalism. Washed coal leaves its own oily residue, which playing children confuse for chasing rainbows. But there's no pot of gold there, at least not for them. The torrents of the River Rhondda now look like a static vein whose flows are invisible to the naked bird's eye, as it blends into the adjoining River Taff. At least, unlike Icarus, the blacked-out sun doesn't threaten his ambitions. But this is all a trick of the light. A filtering of the truth! The sun is as radiant as ever, and it's this rock which promises to be scorched. Maybe that is our deepest anxiety — fearing that black earth event? The bird recalls stories his forbears told. Of a valley covered in vibrant woodland, but soon deforested so that its wood could be used to prop up the tunnels below. The mighty tower has now replaced the mighty oak tree, giving the bird the only serious vantage point from which to rest. If only he could have read Idris Davies' *Gwalia Deserta* (*Wasteland of Wales*), at least he could connect more with the troubled souls below. Why would they bring this upon themselves? Maybe the Druids were right, and the appearance of this iridescent bird did point to the Otherworld? A world which had arrived. Davies knew the trouble the felling of the woodlands would bring. Wasted lands, wasted lives, now so easily caught in the dust that covered everything without and within. Maybe another bird of this kind returned when Jack Jones from Merthyr wrote his novel *Black Parade*, which in 1935 unapologetically noted the dark ecology at work. Polluted rivers in the valley become synonymous with suffering as "old death mowed along". No amphibians that might have emerged from the thawing ice survive here, only the infesting army of black rats perfectly attuned to this deathly terrain. Too often the birds and the rats would fight epic battles over the breaded scraps of wrath. Maybe that is how they were both marked with that complexion? Neither of which would be edible to man. What lives only brings death. Who could possibly be baptised in these waters?, Jones has us consider.

Carried by the winds, the blackbird is soaring above the Severn estuary as he follows a migration route so often denied to the wage-bound sapiens below. On his wings he carries the memory of Theophrastus the Greek scientist and successor to Aristotle, whose treatise *On Stones* provides the first ever recorded mention of the use of this black rock. He also carries around his neck the weight of the Aztec God, Xiuhtecuhtli (the Lord of Fire), whose people used the material for decorative jewellery as well as burning their sacred fires. The bird gazes across and sees a penetrating venous system openly carved in all its magnificence, drawing all its energy from source, the passionate hearts of valley life. The smoke-filled skies now seem so far away, yet their traces reveal shape-shifting phantoms whose hauntings warn of the impending decline. As he surveys the landscape with his panoramic sight, he sees how the two rivers from Rhondda's merge directly into the Taff, before coursing through a super vein on its journey down into the tidal plane at the capital city below. These ecological veins would be accompanied by the presence of others, from Neath to the Ebbw, all pushing the black blood into those waters, which were also synonymous with the selling and shipping of peoples from foreign lands. If only these waters could speak of the misery carried and witnessed, as the traces of washed over bodies collide. But even the bird finds its freedom too exhausting to bear. Becoming too disoriented having flown far from the proverbial nest. There is only so far a bird can fly with polluted lungs. And so, it gazes finally upon the now radiant sun, before plummeting to earth in a vision as close as you could get to some ethereal re-enactment of Gustave Doré's depiction of Lucifer's fall. The valley is full of fallen angels, none which believed in any salvation beyond.

In the subterranean depths, the picture is repeated. Nature is often mimicked when tyrants preside. And there's nothing tyrants enjoy more than cutting deeper and deeper into the flesh of the earth. The network of carved tunnels is also a nervous system. A highway for trams and other traffic in the dark seams of the earth, they reached for miles under the surface, carved out by miners whose humour was as dry as the dust that filled their mouths and found its way into the bottom of their hearts. And their infernal colour is as black as the setting melancholic sun. Some of the tunnels are filling with water, the rest have become still with damp, which is a danger to every lifeform walking around its cavernous depths. These flows too also bring tragedy, sometimes rushing at pace, drowning the workers like they did at the harrowing and heroized Tynewydd Colliery disaster in 1877. The water moves, which in turn moves everything else. It also seeps out into the towns, polluting the wells from which the poor children drink. A billion years of non-linear history, now concentrated, but only for the wretched to witness en masse. Deep underground waters add more complexity to the patterns marked by the tributaries above. Weaving their own discernible threads, together they create a tapestry of lines that would be formidable to behold if only we could see each and every level upon which they reside. Some appear as permanent as any main artery, following the strenuous energies of man. Many however only spring when the conditions are just right, which is rather frequent in these wetland parts. But falling rains are not separate to this visual drama. Pushed by the winds, they descend in continuous formation, like a volley of arrows that leave fleeting marks across the secluded horizon. So many bodies, layered with openings through which the shadows flow. Only to be drowned by the ambitions of those who would dam these reservoirs of wealth, making the living and the damned appear one and the same. There will be a time when much of this will also be forgotten. Yet so many of those arteries buried below have become permanently flooded, filled with icy cold waters that will also collapse with time. While the grassed over mountains and their embankments of sorrow promise more of the same. How many of those waters and hills continue to be haunted by those gasping for breath?

Flowing black waters threatening to consume life belongs to the worst of our nightmares. Yet it was a sight the miners knew all too intimately. The water content of their bodies was dyed as much as the dust coursing through their veins. Before the arrival of the pithead showers, which many still looked upon with suspicion and superstition, the ritual cleansing of the body of its black coated skin was an integral part of the family routine. While the miners drowned their sorrows or "dampened the dust" still dirty and wet in the local pubs, doting wives prepared the scalding water to be poured into the tin baths. Husbands, sons and lodgers would later submerge themselves in the boiled cauldron, which was necessary to ward off the subterranean cold's lasting impressions. Water was often reused as the cost of reheating it was beyond all means and measures. Casting aside the dark remnants of another day, later the children would bathe in the now blackened ocean that was situated beside the coal fires where the "black-pats" or cockroaches also resided. Bathing in stained waters was also a rite of passage, which for the boys provided a vision of a world to come, and the girls of what was dutifully expected. How many of those children watched their fathers coughing black blood as the heat pulled the unsettled fragments of soot from their lungs, unaware of the mass still residing within? And how many were completely blind to the toil of the mothers, who would be outside in the cold beating the dirt from the clothes, only to repeat it most other days? The deeper the miners worked, the harder it was for them to breathe the air. Lack of oxygen meant lights often went out and the matches were incapable of firing. Lungs would be compressed and the waters filling the tunnels a permanent feature. Still, they dug away in the dark, wielding their mandrils and piling the torn away rocks high behind them, like a surrounding mausoleum that was part of the prophetic reckoning. And the further down miners worked, the more they increased their chances of contracting the dust. By some estimates up to 85% of all miners in the United Kingdom who contracted pneumoconiosis worked in the mines of the South Wales valleys. A toxic mixture of coal-type, pit-depth and polluting atmosphere all conspired to wage their own war upon the bodies of men. But even these conditions were an improvement on the early days of coal prospecting, in which children were afforded no protections or distinction. What historian who studied this past could not be affected by the testimonies of William Isaac, who stood before the 1841 commission on child labour with his face burned and eyes enflamed, or tender words of the little six-year-old Mary Davies, whose lamp went out and was later found sleeping in the dark against a rock, recounting how she thought the rats who were camouflaged by the pitch black ate her food. Still, for the boys, from cradle to pit was the expectation, as the future was dominated by the hereditary shadows of the pithead and the impending loss of light.

, A black Klondike was born in the valleys of South Wales, as it was in Appalachia and elsewhere where the mining took hold. Many might have even found a home in those mountainous regions of Kentucky, born of their own continental drifts, volcanic explosions and platinic collisions, finding sympathy with one another as they looked into the burning embers. Poverty invokes a geography of its own, cragged, worn and marked by its unique measures of depth. It is also shaped by the fates of hostile ecologies, geologies of hardship, which too often translates into the character of community life. Villages around the world have been rooted into where the black could be found. It was the foundational stone of where many people would permanently reside. Territories then were discovered by the appearance of a colour, more natural than any which bleeds from flags adorning the map. If there was a flag to be flown in places like the Rhondda, it would be made of the smouldering black clouds that billowed out across the horizon from a thousand towering poles. Smoke pennants of allegiance raised to announce an age marked by the sovereignty of the stone, under which marching men fought. The fiery red would come later as the bellowing earth inevitably caught alight in the changing winds. A colour worn as much as the tragedy cloaking these towns — overdyed with the hint of a tragic procession whose congregations lived so close to death. A colour of mourning drawn from the intractable earth; but non-conforming all the same.

Yet everything would be guided by the light in this wilderness; at least that's what the lyrics to John Hughes' "Cwm Rhondda" had us believe, as a nation would soon find solace singing of its bread from heaven. Without the light, the miners would have surely perished as too much time in the abyss would fully consume their minds through its own depression sickness. Candles were lifelines. And the only other vibrant sign of colour — the timid canary — were caged as messengers of impending disaster that emerged from shadows in the densely compacted air. How could so much be wagered on the importance of the naked flame? Then again, how could it be any other way? The flame wasn't just about survival, it lived and breathed the ambitions of these men, and the meagre hopes that were dug out in the cavernous depths beneath their homes. The flame guided through the impenetrable darkness; yet its poetry and mission always carried the darkness along, for it was the black setting that gave the flame its most meaningful purpose and clarion calling. So deeper and deeper the flame was carried, opening onto caves of extraction, and producing dark silhouettes upon the pit's black walls, which only those with adjusted eyes could properly detect. There was an artistry to the dancing movements of these dark shadows, who were completely dependent on the trust of companions, and the flame whose extinction would point to a tragedy too difficult to bear. In the long hours of the dark, the blood and sweat was mixed with the dusty tears, which in turn cast its own shadow on the floors for the select few to see as it burnt away. And hands spoke of their own unforgiving bruises, their lines revealing traces of the fragmented scars that cut so deep they blackened the soul. It wouldn't take too much of a reader to decipher these simian etchings telling of hardship, suffering, defiance. Silted signs of ancestors whose tempter and desire were a testimony to the cold black conditions, which may only be forgotten in name.

Every day John would have walked past the towering black mountains. They were not just an integral part of the landscape. They were defining. But he would have been under no illusions about their content and character. Might he have even looked upon them with pride? A visible symbol of his manliness and a clear indication of the transference of his labour? Certainly, the only environmental concern held was to ensure he lived another day. Thereafter, he wished to return from his arduous work with all his working muscles and bones intact. Nobody needed a broken miner. And nobody cared what damage the blackness might have been causing. Breathe until tomorrow. Let the heart beat enough to prise the blackness away. John might also have marvelled at the way the mountains seemed to take on a life of their own. How they revealed deep cut paths in their surface, how those paths became deeper and wider when the rains fell, and how they would on occasions simply disappear from sight. The black mountains of the valleys became the image so often associated with its minerally abundant and yet sorrowful reality. Year later, they would become associated with a tragedy so devastating, it still casts its fateful shadow more permanent than any weather system. For what we called "the mountains" were no mountains at all. They were not the black mountains of the east in Powys and Monmouthshire, made of stubborn old sandstone, which stood so defiant in the face of the ice. They were moving waste dumps for all that was disposable, thrown out for all to look upon and nobody to see.

At the height of production, there were 53 collieries in the Rhondda. The seams ran between several feet to a quarter of a mile beneath the ground. The first deep cut into the soil of the valleys took place in the village of Dinas, in 1812 (it was called "Rhondda no. 3", following two previously failed surface-level attempts). It was sunk by Walter Coffin, who later became one of the wealthiest coal prospectors in the world. As expected, the first major explosion in the valleys happened there, taking the lives of 12 men and boys in 1869. The booming years also brought its own kind of explosions, money married with madness, death revelling with delight. A decade later, as "Coffin's Coal", as it become known (a phrase marked with its own tragic irony), had profoundly altered the landscape beyond all recognition, another 63 were killed there, partially buried in the darkness of its suffocating atmosphere. Nearly two centuries later, in 1990, the last of the pits closed in the village of Maerdy, which was already noted for its symbolism. The final piece of coal was cut, and the shaft was filled with stones and its entranceway sealed off from the world. The tunnels turned silent, except for the falling precipitation and channelled streams now creating their own internal weather system in the realm of the dark. Miners and their families left for one last time, walking back to the village through the mist and rain. Dignified to the end, yet knowing the future was lost. They would go to bed knowing the daylight had won, thereafter tormented in its visible presence. With the light of nothing having triumphed, it is understandable why many craved for a return of the darkness. Praying to the night that its hidden chambers might again be prised open and the flames on their candles relit. This pit however wasn't without its own tragedy. As the snows returned on Christmas Eve in 1885, an explosion killed 81 men and boys, some as young as John. Too many communities witnessed the burial of the many, valleys reduced to tears as lines of black coffins were all laid in unison, revealing through the mourning how they still found comradeship even in death. Maybe the philosophers are right after all. Death truly is the greatest of levellers, especially for those who already spent most of their lives underground.

A young child is staring out of the window. He follows the flight of a wayward roof tile that's managed to somehow break free, dancing in the wind before breaking into a hundred pieces as the fragile slate smashes into the asphalt on the ground. It sounds like broken glass shattered by accidental rage. These tiles would have arrived here from the northern parts of Wales, likely from one of the large quarries that was so integral to its industrial heritage. Their use dates back to the Roman period, which answers another question about what they ever did for us! Their dark grey uniform "tally" design was distinctive, as were the traces of its shards, which often littered the street with tenants scouring the rooftops to work out where they had fallen from. Replacing these stacked plates was important if you were to avoid suffering rain penetration and the build-up of mould that also toxified the lungs. The boy is already filled with boredom. He lives before the arrival of digitalisation and devices that abduct the senses, abduct childhood. Robbing children of boredom, we are robbing them of imagination and alternative futures too. The rain is falling, but he's already learned its patterns. He can detect its arrival and departure as sure as any meteorologist. And he still hasn't been beaten enough yet to remain a climate optimist. He pleads with his mother to be allowed out in the streets. It's only drizzling, which to his estimation is no rain at all. Everything is relative, it seems, especially when there's an advantage to be gained. He's told to wait and be patient. And so, he gazes back out of the window, dreaming of better times. Dreaming of when the rain will stop, so he can go out and survey the debris for himself and the damage it might have caused to the mountain den he recently built with friends. It's probably been destroyed, still worth a look anyway. But he knows the need to be wary. Streets can be hazardous. There are unforeseen dangers. For even when the rains stop, the chances of another undetected slate flying from the roof and setting its sights directly on him remains high, or so he reasons at any rate. His house was missing a few of these open quarried fragments, which he watched crashing into the garden a few months earlier. His parents however couldn't afford to replace them. They never could. Slates would be top hung, which meant they were prone to wind uplift and could reach speeds that rivalled any Olympic discus. Hardly ideal for these parts. Moreover, their aerodynamic design featuring flat surfaces and jagged edges could be all too easily weaponised by the indiscriminate elements, which have no concern for whom they assault.

The mines have now largely closed, but the ecological fallout looks much the same. Dirty water flows into the streets, and there's no way of telling where it will all end. I am eight years old, and this sight was familiar every time the heavy rains fell. The Penrhys estate is the same length of miles and years in the distance, hence no longer preoccupying my thoughts. Four broken slates are counted. Two seem to have come from the same terraced strip. Though it is difficult to tell, as numerous gaps are present. One chimney stack looks precarious, and if my suspicion is true, its impending collapse will certainly be a sight to behold. If only I could catch one slate before it hit the ground, maybe I could repair that leak that is damaging the superhero wallpaper in my bedroom? It's full of American characters that seem to have a more heroic relationship with the elements. Rattling tiles often keep me awake, encouraging me to look out from my bedroom window where the mountains reside. I see nothing but black. As dense as the most impenetrable void, it's strangely comforting all the same. There truly is nothing out there. The house is somewhat protected by allotment fields behind. Yet still the black waters find their way through, flooding the corners and intersections or making their way down towards the homes paraded at the foot of the hill. They already have the sandbags out covering their doors in preparation for another kind of war. A civil battle with nature, who was simply biding her time. She was always going to win. You could not wage this much damage and not expect a response. But as always, it's the foot soldiers who end up paying the highest price. Was the sacrifice really worth it? Gaia seems to have other ideas. And she will continue because the payback is great.

Frontal depressions systematically weathering these parts have now subsided, for a while at least. No sooner am I finally allowed into the street, several other children dash from their windows, appearing with one arm extended into their over- and undersized coats with a collective relief on their faces. This exuberant ritual might seem altogether synchronised to untrained eyes. One parent was all it took, before the rest wilted to the nagging pressure. Though there was always one child still sat at their window, head frantically rotating back and forth as they kept check on the location of the free runners, while pleading about the injustice of it all to stubborn parents. We always went to the mountains in packs. It was just more fun that way. And we always brought a football, in case a game was called for, which frequently happened once an argument broke out over who was the best footballer in history (which pretty much covered a four season window). Stood at the base of the mountain, our little feet are soaked by the stream of water, which didn't have too much difficulty finding its way through our holey trainers. I investigate the dark water and see the oxide film covering the surface. Yet another mishap befalls us, as we naively play in the toxic sediment of our abandoned time. Is "oxidental" even a word? Waters from the deserted mine still corrode the landscape, even if they add a certain warmth to the damp air. Orange-stained edges on the shale provide yet another sign of this valley's corrosion, which we will confuse with rocks of a more exotic kind. Maybe the ochre too can be applied to the skin to mask over the deficient rays? At least its metallic traces may make us more detectable once the technology catches up! I continue to wonder why there's no fish in these waters. If only one of us had studied the druids, maybe they could recount a poignant tale fitting for these adventures. Then again, we'd probably be reciting today the fable of "The Blackbird & the Rat".

The mountain is largely covered in rough grass and other determined fauna that would pretty much grow in hell. "That wasn't there before", one of the boys adds, stating the bloody obvious as the overgrown tip reveals a rather large black crack in its side. It was but a slipway only yesterday, barely wide enough to fit our malnourished legs without causing a bruise or two. Waters were gushing down it, so it was a perfectly sensible track to follow. We must have been out for less than an hour, and already we were sodden and covered in black dust. The dirt which accumulated on our hands as we climbed this unnatural ravine soon found its way onto our faces and into our hair. But we didn't give a damn! And we had long since forgotten about the flying hazards of Babylon. It started raining again. No worries. We were out now, and it would take some time before one of the attentive parents would track us down using intuition alone. Had somebody from the Magnum photo agency just so happened to be in the vicinity, they would have probably stood a chance of winning some award for capturing the essence of deprivation, as a band of "muckers" (a term once used to describe the low labourers who worked on the soil, but also used in the valleys for friends or acquaintances with all its evident earthly connotations) in their ripped jeans and broken-soled trainers appeared in the lens covered in multiple shades of distress. At least that's how it could have been presented, which was never a full truth. The mountains however tell a different story. They literally spoil every convenient narrative.

The black mountains were slowly covered, as a version of nature made its lauded return. We bore witness to this drama, though in truth never entertained its significance. It was as natural as any environment to us. It never looked like the catastrophe it always was, replete with its own toxic fallouts. While the coverage was never total as the dark patches remained, we always knew what lay just beneath the surface. Therein lay memories of last summer, which could be unearthed as easily as the pulling of moss from a stone. Some discussion was had on the planting of trees to accelerate the regreening. The forests needed a plan, after all, given the destruction they were never going to recover by themselves. Looked upon by the redundant who stared out of their windows waiting for the rains to end, the green valley romanticised by Llewellyn slowly made its heathered and windswept return. Yet despite its arrival, there was only muted fanfare, as a certain blackness still lingered. A blackness that now resided in the ecology of the mind. Still, for the children of these lands, the greening provided new opportunities. And as the seasons rolled on, the more we were able to slide down the grassy banks with our own wilful abandon, comradery and innocent pride. Winters were fun, but in the summer cardboard boxes prevailed. The laughter was plentiful, even if the grass-burns relieved a layer or two of skin. Parts of my DNA still remain waiting to be discovered on those grown-over tips which chapter my childhood years. How far have today's children of the valleys gone from confronting the reality of this black ecology, which was inseparably woven into the fabric of our destitution and delight?

John belonged to a fossil-fuelled time. His childhood dreams joined the hearts of men that were burning to an industrial beat. But the machines always triumphed, or at least outlived their suitors, until new machines were created to extract something new, something of value, something to be claimed. Despite the damages wrought, when John was laid to rest, his body still belonged to a geological age the scientists called the Holocene, wherein nature still retained its autonomy. Only now have we come to refine our understanding of the period in which he lived and look back upon all he stood for as a dark stain on history. Leonardo da Vinci's Vitruvius Man illustrated a body naked in ambition. Propped up by science and technology, it also placed the human at the heart of the world (or was it a tunnel?) he inhabited. This wasn't art, it was geometric engineering, a vision for the future fit for a time which learned how social engineering was also paramount. Generations paid the price for such delusions of grandeur, which only turned the masses into cogs in the wheel. Man would dig for men who had little concern with their dreams or humanity. Collectivised, their accelerated energies brought about a perilous exhaustion, in which the entire fate of the planet is now assumed to be on the line. If man can be spoken of today, it's burdened with the guilt of these black landscapes of neglect, which have thrown us into a new condition we have little time to understand, let alone reverse. What time remains is severed and stitched together, barely holding onto what memory permits. Thrown into a different anthropocentric disorder, the shadows of boys like John now provide further testament to everything that went wrong. Should we persist, the climatologist suggests, then surely a scorched earth event will become us all. Rivers will rise, and valleys will flood, landscapes will move, and peoples displaced. But where will they run to when there's no place to go? Where to take shelter when the planet burns like the sun? Such prophecies have taken over since the profits left.

And there is no recompense for the sorrowful, or those history would prefer us to forget. The Anthropocene is providing the script to this new geological calling. For an age in which humanity must suffer its fate. And it's calling us back to the black age of discovery, to consider the treasonous actions of those whose past now seen in the future imperils us all. But is this not another way of blaming the poor? Demanding they carry the stones like Sisyphus for us all? Have they not suffered enough from our wisdom? Are they not the ones we continually ask to fall?

What makes an ecology is not just the primacy of a visual aesthetic and its fields of perception. An ecology is an atmosphere marked by pressure and sound. Mining life was over-composed to the tune of mechanisation. Beethoven replaced by Brunel, the sonnet and symphony replaced by the industrial steam and the strident chants of unyielding progress. The boring of the earth was so intense, it would take the dulcet tone of a hundred choirs to have their spiritual voices heard above the metallic hum and machinic drum. The poetry of the bard that was once carried freely by the wind in the valleys always conflicted with the sounds of machines that ground and halted, creating false depths that could be erased from memory and place. As the blackbird lay dying on the ground on the banks of the Severn, the fall has ironically cleared its lungs. Often silent in flight, his last thought concerned why so many like him and associated with that colour are often muted and have their song taken from them at birth. Defiant until the last breath, the blackbird starts to sing to the chorus of "Myfanwy", as tranquil and calming as the comforting ocean breeze that's slowly sweeping his life away. The sounds of the sirens calling men to work, the perpetual noise of the rotational wheels, the screams of villages who lost their sons, the beating of the earth as ferocious as any war drum, are replaced by a haunting melody that is pulling deep from within the primordial waters beside. They revive a more eternal music, which accompanies the rhythmical bands of valleys life. But how can even this not be heard as a song of lament? Another symphony full of sorrow? The silence of the blackbird returns. The valley falls silent in turn. But there is no golden quietening in these parts. Indeed, sometimes the silence, like that of the blackbird before its fall, can also be the source of an immense terror. A silence that is only given meaning by the absence of a more important mechanical sound. Yet even here, not all is as it seems. For still there can be heard a tremble in the distance whose cry is like any other, reminding that in silence some things remain.

The subsequent "Greening of the Valleys" is widely touted by politicians and environmentalists alike as a model for landscape recovery. Some even call it a "green revolution". Hundreds of local reclamation projects have been initiated, along with substantial planting of coniferous woodlands to soften the mountainsides. Fossilised records also date these trees to the late-Carboniferous period. Conifers were once celebrated in Nordic mythology with the bird of Frey, who was associated with virility and prosperity — the latter most certainly would be welcomed here. One ambition is to resurrect a more idyllic vision of rural beauty that reflects better the twenty-first century. A return perhaps to our own garden of Eden with a warning about what happens if you eat the rotten black apple. A guiding principle of these efforts tells of how the re-sculpting of the rural setting will soon be mirrored back in a healthier vision of life, whose lightness of being lifts the body out of its unbearable sadness. But what is this ecology of suffering if it's not also about dealing with the remnants of a more recent and altogether visually explicit "Dark Ages" whose labelling would be far more resonant? One that wasn't to be associated with the fall of the Imperial project from Rome, but part of an Empire closer to home? Indeed, if the previous account of the dark ages of man that gave rise to what we actually come to know as Britain were widely overstated (not least in terms of overstating the cultural and literary significance of Rome that was by even generous accounts impoverished), the onset of this more overcast period that darkened the earth is a description backed up with a far greater wealth of historical memory, record and visual testimony of a monochromatic kind. There is a dark age of the valleys running from the early nineteenth century to near the end of the twentieth, and which continues to eclipse the ecology of life within its ravines. However, like so many of my contemporaries, this dark age coincides with my own family's heritage and is inseparable from many of the lived memories still cherished. Lest we forget, especially here, that the darkness and the black were not always associated with bad tidings, for it was in the repose of the night where we found ourselves.

Sixty thousand tons of rock fell, as the valleys once again held its breath. The landslide in Tylorstown in 2020 was another reminder that security has meant nothing in these towns. Another 300 they say, are still there on the slopes of time, waiting to fall. A million tons of cubic violence, abiding its tumble and recall. Let us return again to that phrase from which the spoil tip originates, *"espoilelier"*, which meant to seize by violence, plunder and take by force. Artificial mountains always had more freedom than the people whose labour made them possible, while the flood waters continue to spill into the streets from which the labours have fled. Not a year goes past when the valleys aren't filled with torrents of anguish, which according to the scientists are only going to get worse. When it rains, it pours, and here it rains more than ever. Maybe living in Penrhys might be advantageous after all? There is a vision of climate recovery, which imagines landscapes reborn, fish returning to polluted waters and woodlands breathing new air. But what of those communities for whom the green recovery feels like more of the same? There is no doubt a natural beauty once again to the Welsh valleys that is hard to deny. Yet like the streets emptied of its children, there's also a hidden story that's more complicated and forces us to look deeper into ourselves. There's an old Welsh word that was once spoken with some affection by the elders in the valleys. *"Hwyl"* was spoken of someone who was said to possess fire in their blood and poetry in their soul. A black *hwyl* has been coursing through Welsh veins for centuries. And it puts us in the valley directly in conflict with privileged types. So maybe we need a different kind of memory? Maybe it's not a contradiction to be critical of the extraction of the coal, but also retain a nostalgia for the Black? There's a need to be blacker than ever in the ecology of our minds? For it is within the void of our thoughts where we find truer meaning of who we were and what we can become. Or to paraphrase the last line to Llewellyn's tome, "How black was my valley, and the valley of them that are gone".

The fable tells of the most formidable tornado ever set loose by the vengeful gods. Cascading across the land, it reaches far into the heavens and is so powerful it cuts deep into the earth. Pulling everything into its swirling vortex of black dust, it summons all before as it builds its momentum, onward and upward and downward it falls. Its power is so immense it destroys nearly all living things on the planet. Only two remain. Both were carved from the same black rock in a more ancient time before time. If the storytellers were to be believed, it was said that the rock was laid deep inside the earth, encrusting the entire planet to keep the tormentors at bay. Those born of the rock were tasked with being messengers of the future, though very few could ever heed their warnings and even fewer could read their signs. At the very top of the towering column, in the faint white circle, there appears a single blackbird who has only managed to prevent himself from being consumed by flying as fast as the wind. At the bottom, in the darkest recesses of the earth, a rat is also scurrying as fast as he can, following the path that's been carved before its blackened eyes. Suddenly, the giant hurricane stops, and both exhausted creatures pause for breath. The bird looks down in envy, seeing the rat has time to rest on the ground and noticing he has found a scrap of food to eat. The vortex continues to swirl but now seemingly immovable from below. The rat looks up in envy, seeing the bird in the sky, sensing it could probably escape should it be able to muster enough courage. What the bird wouldn't give for some rest and a bite to eat; what the rat wouldn't give to taste the sweet air of freedom, just for one day. The blackbird becomes more and more frustrated with his predicament, and soon calls down to the rat to remind him how fortunate his life has become. The black rat shouts back, reminding the bird at least everyone else looked upon him with dignity. Nor should he forget that flying was the most craved-after thing. So consumed are the blackbird and the rat with their own misfortune, they are blind to what's happening around them. The hurricane at the top starts to pull everything down, while at the bottom it is pulling with tremendous fury the world into the sky. The dust collides. And with the mightiest of bangs the blackbird and the rat meet head on and are thrown to the side. After the dust has settled, all that remains are two overlaid shadows on the ground. The shadow of the bird, and the shadow of the rat. But the bird's wings are broken, and the rat's tail is cut. Slowly the rains start to fall and wash the excess dust away, leaving but one silhouette on the ground. The image of a young child appears, naked and bare.

A COLONY WITHIN

The marching men were cold and hungry as they walked through the impersonal, wintery streets of London's West End. They had been blacklisted for taking part in the General Strike of 1926, yet despite the hardship, they travelled over 160 miles in their worn-out nailed cobbled shoes from deepest and darkest Wales to have their basic rights respected. They were the denied. Political vagabonds who in the words of Idris Davies emerged in that "angry summer" — a time of soup kitchens and firebrand speeches in which the young Davies found his poetic calling. As these tired Rhondda colliers sang to raise their spirits, out of the shadows emerged a black Othello. Solidarity was found in harmonies; he identifying with the weight of history carried on their backs and recognising that their fight was the same that he carried across the Atlantic from the streets of New Jersey. The son of a runaway slave, by the mid-1920s Paul Robeson was a giant of a man, in stature and dignity. An international celebrity of stage and screen, he was also a wonderful orator and recognised as one of the finest American footballers of his time. Robeson was in London attending a gala, while performing the racially charged *Showboat*, when this chance encounter with the starved men occurred. Yet as he marched along with the oppressed miners, joining their chorus as a fellow human, the hunger was sated by a shared feast of unbroken pride. A beautiful friendship was soon formed, transcending the dramaturgy of racialised misconceptions which are still often applied to poor people the world over. It would also have a profound impact on the political life of Robeson, who became more strident in battling racial inequality. No greater a commanding version of

"Land of my Fathers" has been sung than Robeson's homage to the miners who embraced him as one of theirs. Such bonds were later fictionalised in the film *The Proud Valley*, starring Robeson and which was unlike Ford's adaptation of *How Green Was My Valley* in that it was actually recorded in South Wales and cast actors from its towns. Crucially, this friendship was never mired in claims about who suffered the most, who was the greatest victim of history or who had the greatest privileges to fall back upon in their shared conditions of destitution. It was built upon a passion to sing while still walking in the valleys of the shadows of death. Or to echo the words of one of Davies' finest poems:

"Who made the mine owner?",
Say the black bells of Rhondda
"And who killed the miner?"
Say the grim bells of Blaina.

Robeson went on to become a good friend of arguably the valleys' most famed of all politicians, the Tredegar-born Aneurin Bevan, who is credited with founding the National Health Service. But as Robeson took his fight back to the United States, he was caught up in the McCarthyite process of identifying the un-Americans in their midst. This resulted in the CIA declaring him an enemy of the state, which led to his blacklisting and his passport being revoked. However such restrictions didn't prevent him from participating in the Miners' Eisteddfod of 1957 held in Porthcawl, as Robeson called from a studio in New York and sang to the rapturous audience. The real-time broadcast by Robeson was made possible by the installation of the first transatlantic telephone cable the previous year. The concert also featured the Treorchy Male Voice Choir, who would express their support for the persecuted Robeson by dedicating at the start and end of the momentous proceedings their singing of the hymn "We Will Keep a Welcome in the Hillside". Robeson attended in person the following year after a petition sent by the miners of South Wales to the US Supreme Court. In that same year, he also told a welcoming audience of some 9,000 at an Eisteddfod in Ebbw Vale, "You have shaped my life. I have learned a lot from you. I am part of the working class. Of all the films I have made the one I will preserve is *The Proud Valley*." A legacy that would later have the valleys band, the Manic Street Preachers, paying their own respects to Robeson:

> Where are you now?
> Broken up or still around?
> The CIA says you're a guilty man.
> Will we see the likes of you again?
> [...]
> I've got to learn to live like you.
> Learn to sing like you.

Such a learning, however, as the spirit of Robeson continually reminds us, is not just about the future. It's about singing the historical present.

By the time Shakespeare had finished quilling his bardic tales on parchment using deep black iron gall ink, the Welsh had been fully conquered by their English overlords. They were firmly cast within a historical drama as a savage and unruly people who needed to be controlled. Much of this no doubt derived from Roman attitudes and their inability to properly tame the Silures of the forested highlands of Wales. Indeed, as Rome fell, as true of much of history, lessons about power were heeded as its Imperial spirit and the desire to conquer and establish a single unified authority (as first envisaged in the Kingdom by Emperor Nero) was the most powerful legacy that was retained. Britannia was now an idea that could be birthed within these Isles proper. Yet despite the calling of Britishness, the peoples of Wales, Ireland and Scotland have always known the Empire to be distinctly English, in which they were but a part of its expansive colonial geography. That doesn't mean to say the Welsh didn't contribute massively to the expansion of the British Empire; they certainly did through toil, sweat, blood and tears, often in far off lands. Still, this doesn't do away with the fact that Wales was the first colony to be forcefully incorporated and violently policed within the English Empire, as much as Ulster in Ireland was home to the first barbaric plantation systems, which would later become symbolic of how we visualise fields of colonial persecution today. Empires have always recruited their expendable fighters from within their oppressed ranks. Therefore, we can speak of Welsh history and especially the conditions of life faced by those in the valleys and how it connects to the power of Empire, while also speaking of an internal colony, which reveals some of the worst excesses of dispossession, human extraction, debt-bondage, denial of political rights, and cultural and historical decimation. Within the Principality, many colonial logics were forged, only to be later exported. This included the establishment of entrenched prejudices, which are still culturally reworked today, even if seldom considered in this age where privately-educated intellectuals refuse to speak anymore of white-on-white racism.

History arrived into my consciousness through familiar tales of glorification and lament. Studying in the early 1980s, we trudged through early settlements, before hopping, skipping and jumping around the decapitated heads of the lovers of Henry VIII, only later to be bombarded by the demands to learn the numbers and dates of World War II. What was learned of the Rhondda was part of a wider appreciation of our benefacting Isle, teaching us the importance of its place within the glorious Empire, while touching briefly upon the old revolution in order to remind children of need to be thankful we no longer had to work in the dire conditions of Victorian Britain. Simply put, history books proved our lots had stratospherically improved, since we no longer worked in those depths buried deep beneath the site upon which the school was built. Our school emblem was a phoenix emerging from the ashes, a reminder worn on the breast of each child that they now occupied a time after the coal. Very little made sense in school. Even my A-Levels in Politics and Economics commenced shortly after the Berlin Wall fell. Alongside studying all the constitutional dryness of Parliamentarianism and its flawed system of representation, while pretty much doing everything possible to evade sustained reflection on Thatcher and the miners, we were tasked with comparing America with the now defunct Soviet Union, working on the basis that the corpsed model was still somehow breathing as if held in some morbid suspension on an evil life-support system. All the while, the lived history we looked upon outside of the windows covering the prefabricated school's completely ill-suited post-modern design, read as cobwebbed as any teacher's badly fitting tweed jacket. The curriculum was distinctly ideological. We were taught how through the coming together of Thatcherism and Reaganomics, Britain and America were twinned in their optimism like never before, while the Soviet Union represented all that was oppressive and subjugating. Yet just as this study began, Thatcher was also slain, stabbed in the back by two Welshmen of a more conservative bent, who proved their credentials by coming across as English as possible. How many people in Wales knew the Teflon assassin Michael Heseltine was one of their own? Thatcher was politically dead, but in the valleys, it was met with a silence, for we knew the damage was already done. Politics lessons were scheduled first thing on Monday mornings. Back to Russia, whose historic ties with the Welsh were now as frozen out as the bleak winters we shared, there was a certain irony to mocking a system castigated for its queues and production methods, which it was claimed resulted in factories putting sawdust into bread to meet daily quotas, while having just done the walk of shame to collect free dinner tickets. Shame comes in many forms, though perhaps it's the shame of hunger that stays longer in the memory. Later I would take my studies home and eat sandwiches which were more than slightly wooden in texture, while pondering what comparisons and distinctions could be made. History and politics as educated in this way revealed the worst of curriculum design as it stripped away its all too human relevance and consequences.

The Silures were noted to be a people blessed with more a Mediterranean complexion, including possessing a thicker mop of dark curly hair. In the dominant English imaginary of the nineteenth century, this would be turned into another sign of deficiency as the Welsh, along with the Irish, were thrown into the same pit of anthropological subjection, which was systematically applied to all "inferior" peoples from around the world. The figure of the "Indian" was notably positioned as embodying a lesser species who inhabited a religious wilderness in the untamed "dark corners of the earth". Such attitudes were openly discussed in the seventeenth century, as evidenced in a London pamphlet, "We have Indians at home — Indians in Cornwall, Indians in Wales, Indians in Ireland". Such prejudices were not just about bringing the logics of race back into the colonial homelands. Pejorative attitudes towards the Welsh were already in existence prior to colonial expansion. While the Romans already sought to destroy druid culture, by the time the Venerable Bede wrote his *Ecclesiastical History of the English* in 730 AD (which is considered one of the most important texts in the history of Anglo-Saxon rule), prejudicial attitudes towards the Welsh were in widespread currency — a position consistently applied in the following centuries. Assumptions concerning the natural inferiority of the Welsh would be later backed up by a formidable school of scientific thought. For example, in his influential work *Races of Britain* (1862), once President of the Anthropological Institute (1889–1891) and Bristol physician John Beddoe argued that all men of superior race were orthognathous, meaning they had less prominent jaw bones, while the folk of Wales and Ireland were visibly prognathous. Being of Celtic stock thus made Wales inhabitants more closely related to the idea of the Cro-Magnon man, who for all intents and purposes belonged to a race of peoples distinctly "Africanoid". With Celts and Indian persons occupying a position of close proximity in the *Index of Negrescence*, both were distinct from Anglo-Saxons, who naturally possessed intellectual superiority. Racism then wasn't simply about the vision of "whiteness" as first imagined at the dawn of colonial rule by Johann Joachim Winckelmann, who many proclaim to be the founder of modern art and who consecrated a vision of superiority based upon a return to a pure and beautified Romano-Greek idealism. Prejudice has always been more subtle and deviating, regardless of whatever colour schematic was being imposed. Cultural implications were also telling and reaching, as most evidently revealed in the eighteenth-century children's nursery rhyme "Taffy was a Welshman", which stereotyped the population in terms of its thievery and moral depravities. Derived from the River Taff, the word "Taffy" would also be applied widely to Welsh soldiers fighting in the trenches, along with being a self-deployed cultural signature that only the Welsh might say to one another without a certain offence being claimed (not that it really bothered).

Near a century later, in 1934, G.R. Gair of the Scottish Anthropological Society carried these racial schematics into tableaus of Elizabethan Britain, reenforcing the positionings by claiming while its inhabitants belonged to the "tall, stolid, phlegmatic northern race", in the "western part of the British Isles we have a branch of the Mediterranean race" which was "marked distinction in mental outlook and culture". Five years after Gair's familiar words, a more revealing index of persecution was fought out in front of an audience of braying spectators. Joe Louis — one of the most brilliant of all black boxers — was making the first defence of his heavyweight crown. The fight was to take place in the packed Yankee Stadium, as 32,000 boxing fans would be present to watch what would be the beginning of the longest championship reign by any boxer in the history of the sport. The "Brown Bomber's" opponent was the "Tonypandy Terror" Tommy Farr, who was the son of a bare-knuckle fighter and was born in Clydach Vale close to the prized Cambrian Colliery. While the young Louis was fighting on the racially segregated streets of Alabama, Farr began his boxing career aged 13 and by the time he fought the Bomber had already taken part in over 100 gruelling bouts. Contrary to expectations, the fight lasted 15 rounds and the points decision awarded to Louis was mired in controversy. The winner doesn't really matter here. These were two fighters in the real sense of the word, brought together in a ring with histories that were more alike than dividing. Both were born of poverty and both knew all about discrimination. Both also knew that the conditions of coloniality never simply referred to "over there lands" beyond the riches and rewards of the metropolitan pale. Together in the centre of this gladiatorial arena, shared cuts went much deeper than geography. They were both part of the internally colonised, living destitute existences at its most capillary and systemically neglected ends. And equally true to form, they were set against one another in ways revealing once again of the most pernicious workings of colonisation. Divide and rule the poor, unto the death if necessary, for all our entertainment. Louis — a descendent of slaves — died as it all began, poverty-stricken and suffering from mental health issues that had also tormented his father. Farr died poor and destitute on St David's Day.

The history of boxing is intimately bound to the history of colonisation. The very rules by which the modern sport was governed owes everything to the 9th Marquis of Queensbury, John Sholto Douglas, whose upbringing was tutored on the colonised waters. He would also become rather infamous for his sordid role in the persecution of the poet and writer Oscar Wilde, who was having a sexual relationship with his son, Alfred "Bosie" Douglas. I have no doubt Wilde would have been accepted and found reasons to eloquently write of his encounter with the roughness of life in the valleys of South Wales as much as he did when visiting the miners of Leadville in Colorado. Sporting rivalry aside, there is far more to be gleaned from such human tales of sportsmanship confrontation and how it reflects upon history than any intellectualised spat concerning so-called culture wars. The bloody reality of colonised tensions has often been fought between those who stood nothing to gain or were fighting for the meagre chance of a brief respite. Yet, a colonised people possesses far a greater understanding of its history than those who sought to lecture in ways that invariably fall back upon crude essentialisations (the poor are inherently violent, the poor are inherently backward, the poor are inherently prejudicial and so forth) that in the end read as absurd as those who claimed a Welsh king named Madog may have actually found the Americas 300 years before Columbus, which led to bizarre searches in the United States for a tribe of "Welsh Indians". Despite all these attempts to impose a truth, what remains is the willingness to fight. This brings us to the tale of another John, who like the boy in the second chapter belonged to a different caste than the Marquis.

The town buried another of their sons on Veterans Day. He had been in a coma for over six weeks. Merthyr's people came out in their thousands to mourn the passing and celebrate the life of the local boxer John, or "Johnny" as he was affectionately called. It was raining heavily and the wind chilled the caravan of mourners, which included many local children. A Welsh flag draped over the coffin was lowered into the ground as the choir sang "Cwm Rhondda". In 1980, Johnny Owens fought the Mexican boxer Lupe Pintor in Los Angeles. Like Owens, who was born and lived on a council estate, Pintor was also born into poverty in a tough *barrio* on the outskirts of Mexico City. Although unlike the sense of community that protected and nurtured Owen, Pintor ended up being homeless having suffered physical abuse from his father, and hence needed to fight for his very existence. A ferocious battle ensued for twelve rounds, before Johnny was floored for the third time. Fighting should have been stopped two rounds earlier when it was obvious the boy from Merthyr was continually swallowing blood. A brutal right blow struck the head of the Welshman and left him out cold on the sweltering floor of the grubby and hostile ring in the City of Angels. He would never regain consciousness. The images are still haunting. With Johnny laying on the floor, as the *Sunday Express* reported, onlookers saw how the "Blood was spewing from his mouth, and his eyes were fixed in a glaze". Yet despite this tragedy, the world's focus was elsewhere. Ronald Reagan was swept to power that very evening and would make his own impression on the canvas of life here. Two decades later, Pintor solemnly walked through the forgiving streets of Merthyr town centre. He remorsefully moved arm-in-arm with Johnny's father as they unveiled a statue in memory of the fragile 24-year-old bantam-weight fighter. It was another rainy day and the Mexican looked genuinely saddened. This was as moving a sight as any this town had ever witnessed. And it was in that symbolic interlocking of arms, where humanity's ability to break through the violence of colonial worlds was shown. Together they revealed the fight and forces pulling and condemning the futures of its children. As one biographer noted, boxing "is really life whittled away to an ugly, simple truth". Or to echo the words of the highly respected sportswriter Hugh McIlvanney, who was writing as Johnny was still laying in the deepest of sleeps on that hospital bed devastatingly situated on Hope Street, "It is his tragedy that he found himself articulate in such a dangerous language". One of the greatest boxers, sportspersons, poets and indeed humans to have ever walked this planet — Muhammad Ali — sent a message to Johnny's family that was to be read out during his burial. Ali, for his part, would remain a vocal critic of colonisation and imperialism throughout his life. Many years later on the anniversary of his death, the heavyweight Mike Tyson paid a visit to Merthyr to lay flowers at the statute of Johnny in St Tydfil's square before honouring another local boxing legend Howard Winstone, who fought the Mexican Vicente Saldívar (who was also born into poverty in Mexico City) for world titles on three gruelling occasions.

Like Ireland and Scotland, the history of Wales is a history of battle, often against the enemy stood in the other corner of the geographical ring — the English. Such a battle has allowed many a nationalist to narrate the epic journey of this proud nation:

from the contested dates of its inception; through to the Silures and their successful warding off of the Romans; the arrival of the Anglo-Saxons that pushed the Celts farther into the reaches of the western part of the Isles and created what we have come to call England; the construction of a monumental ditch, or what is more officially termed "Offa's Dyke", named after the Anglo-Saxon King of Mercia, which marked the first physical separation between the English and the Welsh (literally named as the outsiders); that infamous date of 1066 and the arrival of the Normans led by William the Conqueror, whose excursions into the heartlands by all accounts led to the creation of Cardiff; the rebellions led by the Welsh princes such as the legendary Llywelyn Fawr of Snowdonia, which, mirroring the hierarchical structures of the invading forces, lent itself to the concentration of power and the promotion of aristocratic reasoning; the truly poignant ascension of Edward I, who was a notable crusader and tyrant, and who effectively brought about the end to any claim of independent rule, especially after naming his son the 1st Prince of Wales; the symbolic establishment during this time of a network of castles and strongholds for military and political occupation, which in terms of geographical density means that Wales remains the most fortified nation on this planet; the subsequent introduction of race laws, secondary rights status and the colonially punishing taxation systems that created a system of political and economic apartheid that was an internal experiment before it became a global export; the fifteenth-century spectacles of violence against the transgressive, which was part of wider processes engulfing the country and which effectively gave rise to the modern theory of Sovereignty as written by Thomas Hobbes, who we can now see was simply trying to rework the idea of a singular source of legitimate authority by once again vilifying the behaviours of the rebellious masses; onto the eventual Acts of Union at the behest of Henry VIII, who would demand and force political and cultural assimilation, including the imposition of his religious doctrine and the banning of the Welsh language. As the Laws

Act of 1535 read: "[The] Dominion of *Wales* shall be, stand and continue for ever from henceforth incorporated, united and annexed to and with this his Realm of *England*".

While violent acts of incorporation can be rightly seen as part of the initial stages in the formation of colonial Wales, petty feudalism and the claims to land alone were never sufficient enough to account for the fullness of its subjugations. Coloniality was far more pernicious and reaching than Medieval conquest. The ideas of two of the most brilliant writers on colonialism, Frantz Fanon and Eduardo Galeano, leave no doubt about the violence and the ways that colonised peoples end up psychologically embracing their servitude. Both writers also show how colonisation was born of an economic dream to extract as much material wealth as possible, and the political idea to control it. Closer to home, however, what we see in Wales is how, at its inception, coloniality wasn't just about racism — or at least racism wasn't the primary driver. Race simply provided the alibi to justify expansion for expansion's sake. Claims of inferiority were used to quell the resentments and dissatisfactions with the imposition of external rule, while sanctioning wealth accumulation through the dispossession of Others. If we therefore accept that the racism of the British Empire was already there and tested out upon peoples within its Isles of a different complexion and culture before it was exported elsewhere, this demands a more open conversation about the meaning of coloniality today. There is a need to address the suggestion that racism was brought back from overseas colonies as if it somehow fell like a Newtonian apple, or should we say Darwinian coconut, from a palm tree basking on shores beneath the blood red skies. Colonisation was always a multi-directional process. I should point out I have zero interest in claiming that since Wales was the original colony, that makes the Welsh the original victims who across the long duress of history have faced prejudice and persecution more than any other. There is nothing to be gained from such claims, except to fall into the contemporary trap of seeing victimisation as a competition to be traded about like a game of persecuted *Top Trumps* by a New Model Army of Twitter puritans. It would also draw unnecessary divides between the poor of Wales and the poor of England, who were also subjected to colonial rule. What it does demand is a forceful counter to those who flippantly throw around accusations concerning the relative advantages enjoyed by distinct and essentialised ethnic groups, without the faintest idea of the histories of violence and persecution faced by poor peoples irrespective of colour within the colonial model for human extraction and its processes of material enrichment for the very select few.

The valleys became the heartland for a new kind of colonisation. This is a colonisation we associate with the arrival of eighteenth- and nineteenth-century European Empires, who looked upon the world and its peoples like a master carver salivates upon a hung turkey which is deadened and ripe for plucking. He does so knowing the select guests' hunger will be sated. Or should we say, given a pleasant sufficiency, until the next feast, which largely turned every single day into a Thanksgiving for the master engineers of a new world order that was born of the ability to cut apart the flesh of the earth and plunder what lay beneath, while rightfully taking whatever else was desired — especially the bodies of young native women, boys and men, until such Imperial time as they grew weary. If the colonial model was about resource-extraction, in the valleys this meant a shift away from tax feudalism and the tyrannical grip of benefacted subsistence, to what we might properly call "The Coal Colony", with its demands to extrapolate all possible energies from the lands. While the iron industry was an important precursor to this, it was the desire to extract the black gold by any means necessary which marked the new dawn of colonial internalisation upon the peoples of South Wales, along with poor migrants from elsewhere who had no option but to sell their bodies for a shilling and a dime. Showing fully the intimate bonds that connected capitalism with colonisation, these desires resulted in a monstrous theft of wealth and life from the grounds of the valleys, only to service the appetites of a gluttonous industrial few.

While colonisation marked the psychic life of the colonised, leaving them to internalise their suffering as they learned to embrace their subjugation, there are enough visible traces left to map out its changing cartographies. If the valleys would be defined by its inward migrations — of peoples and ideologies — its brutal history is also marked by what would leave its naturally fortified walls. The hillside looks like something out of the most magical fairytale. The red castle that rises from the ancient beech woods of Fforest Fawr is amongst the finest examples of gothic splendour. Built upon a Norman fortification, the site was inherited by the Third Marquess of Bute following the death of his father in 1848. Designed by the eccentric Victorian architect William Burges, it would be rebuilt some thirty years later as a mere country mansion that also included Wales's first attempted vineyard. While the wealthy have been ritualistically drunk on their own merriment, for the peoples of the valleys Castell Coch (the Red Castle) that is situated just beyond Pontypridd has an entirely different symbolic meaning of passage. If you are going to dream of freedom and romance, then as the placement for this enchanting fortification tells, it surely lies beyond the valleys. The castle is also said to be haunted by the spectre of a white lady who never recovered from the loss of her young son who fell into a bottomless pool of dark waters on the site. She sorrowfully roams the grounds looking for the body of the lost boy. The Romans and the Normans built many fortifications in South Wales to subdue the masses and bring them under their administrative control. This castle on the hill overlooking the River Taff was no exception. Yet by the time the colonists of industrialisation arrived on the scene, their power was such that the purpose of the nobleman's fort became purely aesthetic. Or, as Americans believed, for the landed wealth-rearing aristocracy, their homes truly were castles. And their reconstruction was part of the new colonial design whose symbols of wealth, power and violence were intertwined. The most notable of these is Cardiff Castle, built again at the behest of John Crichton Stuart. Built on a site that revealed traces of this Romanic and Norman past, it was largely reconstructed by the Earl to become one of the most imposing and lavish Victorian palaces in the entire country. Many of its rooms would reflect wider colonial ambitions and the ability to appropriate ideas and artifacts from exotic outposts across the Empire's expanding geographical reach. This wasn't about warding off invasion; after all, the lands were now fully occupied by a force whose might was increasingly unrivalled. Often uninhabited, it was purely ceremonial, reminding the local populace they were outsiders living within.

I found myself occupying foreign territory. I had arrived. A land of intellectual and personal enrichment beckoned. I had no guide, and nobody from my family had even ventured into these terrains. But I wanted to be there. There is nothing that can prepare a child from poverty to enter the privileged setting of a university. A symbol of all that is great, it can feel as intimidating as walking through the doorway of any Medieval keep. Within its hallowed walls, which police poverty better than any other institution, there were a thousand hidden ways that reminded me of the past I so desperately wished to leave in those towns kept behind the gothic facades of that red castle on the hill. You have no idea of its culture; but you soon learn about its codes and exclusions. And you also learn of its intellectual batteries and assaults, which because you now occupied their citadel, meant the language of opportunity erased the memory of destitution as swiftly as any primary school teacher could wipe away the dusty chalk from a worn blackboard. A crisis of consciousness shapes the rules as you know you are lost within a milieu of promissory success. And still the ghost of poverty's child holds tight around your neck, knowing you feel his presence and knowing you hope nobody else can see him there. But they can. Especially others from poverty, who detect the apparition a mile off as they also desperately aspire to belong and not have their ghosts revealed. You look, but keep them at a distance, for they too know the fabricated stories you tell. All the while, you continue to exorcise that irrelevant past as you reinvent childhood memories out of existence. Besides, the chained apparition is of no real concern anyway to the socially sainted. Marx was dead. And it would remain dead, because nobody who was really setting the agenda wanted to redress centuries of structural decimation. Yet there were always ways in which the children of the wealthy could make you feel like you were the one most ethically compromised, and they were somehow the most experienced when it came to knowing the intimacy of neglect and the emotional pain of suffering. If there was a guilt to be carried, it was ultimately yours and should be internalised deep into your fortunate soul. You had arrived, hadn't you?

While it had already been part of the institutional fabric for over a decade, by the early 1990s universities were covered in a fair-trade blanket of colonial guilt. It was re-laid by the children of parents who wished they could have spent revolutionary summers in Algeria or Nicaragua, helping free the peasants, but decided the world needed their educated knowhow more. This was passed on to their vegetarian children, who buying chronicles, clothes, coffee and condoms from Oxfam, travelled the world during some "gap" in their lives to right the wrongs of the lesser active generations. They were the globally enlightened, and they had the holiday snaps embracing grateful African children to prove it. Testifying how they were really changing the world and really knew what poverty looked like beyond anything you could possibly imagine; a photo was all that was needed to prove their ethical superiority. The only place I had travelled was Magaluf on the Balearic Islands, surrounded by other Brits who were getting as copiously drunk as they did at home. And the only thing foreign I encountered was the radiant sun, which at least activated my hidden Silures genes. But as it still remains, so much of this missionary work (religiosity intended) to save the poor from themselves was just a performance. It was used to make others feel guilty, especially those who were under-privileged and couldn't possibly imagine taking a break from the reality of their lives. What was also evident during this time was how colonial guilt was profoundly different from poverty guilt. Poor people embody that penance. It shames us. Strangely and yet revealing all the same, I never once met a student who during their year of self-discovery went to any community project in the valleys of South Wales. They had more likely been to Timbuktu than they had Treorchy. At least my travels were more honest in their sun-kissed seductions, even if the cultural experience was altogether absent. But even the guilt has moved on as the poor of today are further recast into the unappreciative benefactors of history. Still, it's better to believe this fabrication and trade in compensatory solidarities of shared feelings that make victims of us all, than confront the structural depths of coloniality, which makes no sense unless we begin from raw human extraction.

A special place is reserved in the Welsh imagination for fantastical narratives redressing the injustice of conquest. While for centuries these myths remained just that — except for the romanticised heroics of our own veritable antecedent to Che Guevara (albeit without the photogenic iconography), the farmer-cum-guerrilla-fighter Owain Glyndŵr — it was when the Empire was at its peak that the people of the valleys showed what could also be forged from a revolutionary fire. Revolution needs its myths. And it needs to galvanise the imagination. This brings us back to the mythical birthplace of ideology, Merthyr Tydfil. If industrialisation began with the iron so necessary to producing the machines that the coal would animate with its steaming desires, the furnaces of Merthyr gave off the most potent heat. 1831 is a year cast into the smelting annals of valleys folklore. The poorly paid and exploited workers of the local Cyfarthfa Ironworks had enough of living with nothing and being asked to survive on even less, so they took control of the town. For the first time in history the red flag of socialism was flown, contrasted as it was by sombre, cloudy skies. The owner

William Crawshay (who was labelled the "Iron King") looked on from his own castle on the hill, replete with its turrets and battlements. As the protestors ransacked local offices containing records of debt holdings, they could be heard crying out "*I lawr â'r Brenin*" ("down with the King"). The Second Marquess of Bute, Lord Mount Stuart, who at the time was also the Lord Lieutenant of Glamorgan (a role first established by Henry VIII which designated that those operating in the name of the Crown would exercise full control over local militia) however soon responded to a request from Crawshay and deployed the army to bring order to the striking chaos. Hundreds were injured and some twenty protestors killed, their bodies left in the wet and muddied streets. Once the uprising was eventually suppressed using excessive military force, the 26 lead organisers were put on trial. Some of these were penally transported to Australia, while Lewis Lewis and a coal miner named Richard Lewis would be sentenced to death. While the former was reprieved and later sent to suffer in the heat of penal colony, the latter, now more commonly known as Dic Penderyn, was hung at 8am in a public spectacle at Cardiff market on August 13th. He was 23 years old. Inevitably, Dic Penderyn would became a martyr in the process, partly inspiring the later Newport riots which, also featuring coal miners, would in 1839 prove to be the last armed insurrection in the United Kingdom, leading again to many deaths, injuries and treasonous libels resulting in forced deportations. The lessons were consistent. When the threat of genuine resistance stirred in these mountains, the violence of internal colonisation reared its uncompromising head.

When the raw strength of iron met the unrivalled energy sources of the volatile coal, so the valleys were positioned at the forefront of the Steam Age (though we could invariably use the terms "steam" and "volatile" interchangeably here). This age propelled agrarian communities out of their pre-modern subsistence into a time of engineering defined by locomotion. With hindsight, it is perhaps no coincidence that the translation of the Spanish word "*loco*" is "crazy", which is said to derive from a US plant whose consumption drove horses insane. What we have also come to call the Industrial Revolution would be defined by these processes of mechanical reaction galvanised in mid-nineteenth-century Merthyr Tydfil. Once a sparsely populated hamlet, the dwelling place revealed some of the worst conditions seen during the entire Victorian era. The very first outbreak of Cholera in the United Kingdom in 1832 happened in the town, followed by another a few years later, killing over 1,600 residents. Inseparable from poor conditions, which some looked upon as as viral as the disease, markedly contrasted with the power of the town's English master, who was one of the country's very first millionaires. At the height of Crawshay's wealth and power, the Poor Law Amendment Act of 1834 was passed, which was in part influenced by the deeply racialised thinking of Thomas Malthus that sought to contain population growth, while justifying bringing the poor into the controlled conditions of the workhouses. The iron works in Merthyr would have a far-reaching influence in the Empire's expansions. Largely smelted for bulk production, it was in high demand for armaments that were essential to many of the wars during the period. It also found its way being laid on the railroads running throughout eastern Europe, and more troubling still, the iron from Merthyr was also used for those "pioneering" tracks that apparently "civilised" the American West. Crawshay himself invested over quarter of a million pounds in the American rail network. The Transcontinental railway system built in America during the mid-nineteenth century is often backdropped by depictions of Native Americans either looking in awe or travelling in opposing ways. That some of these irons, which proved so integral to the destruction of native life and were accompanied by tremendous lands thefts and well documented massacres, were forged in the valleys reveals how far the networked violence of coloniality spread.

Like all colonial projects, it was also understood that to control the peoples of the valleys, there was a need to wage a war for their hearts and minds. If the people were rebelling, it was a direct result of ignorance, at least that's what the politicians and newspapers like the *Times* maintained. Poor masses do not understand the weight or gravity of history, let alone its trajectory. The result was one of the most explicitly prejudicial colonial texts applied to the Welsh. A report into the educational deficiencies of its people otherwise critically known as *The Treason of the Blue Books* (1847), it professed that to speak Welsh and embrace its moral culture was the surest sign of a lack of civility. Conversely, to be part of civilisation, there was a need to speak, think and act as if one were English through policies masked in the objective pursuit of being educated. While never constituted into law as official government policy, like so much of colonial practice, its desired outcome would be instituted through cultured informal behaviours where the normalisation mandates are difficult to disentangle. Documents like *The Treason of the Blue Books* don't directly refer to the Welsh as being some kind of "inferior species", even though it makes explicit reference to their conduct (notably encouraged by the Nonconformist chapels that started to really thrive in the valleys) as being morally compromised to the point of verging on the bestial. Then again, very little of the Enlightenment discourse underwriting the intellectual basis for colonisation more generally specifically mentions what is needed to keep others in a natural state of subjugation. Implicit within its logics is a reworking of ideas regarding noble natives or savages, who through the enlightenment of education just may possibly join the order of civilisation. A pernicious accompaniment to this would be the use in schools of what became known as the "Welsh Not". Children who were caught speaking their native language were forced to wear a block of wood around their necks for the day with the letters "WN" inscribed in it as a public marker of shame. This would often later result in forms of corporal punishment. As the children of the valleys would learn, the spectacle of colonial violence can take many different forms and is often imposed by those who speak the language of sure progression. Indeed, it is precisely because of such progressive narratives that the colonist provisions their alibis. We should not also forget the pernicious and yet complex divisions in this Age of Empire, and how important the steam coal of the valleys would prove to be in maintaining the naval and military presence of colonies overseas, revealing further the powerful tensions brilliantly explained by Paul Gilroy in *The Black Atlantic*.

Idle men had been stood on the street corners for several weeks. Their anger only sedated by the boredom and melancholia that set in as the autumn leaves fell. Penderyn was now more a fable, seditiously whispered by mischievous grandmothers who spoke about his exploits to children before bedtime. Their stomachs also knew there was a need to demand more. Tensions had been rising since September, when 950 miners were locked out of the Naval Colliery in Penygraig. Following many redundancies that specifically targeted older and "less able" workers, miners were in further dispute with the owners, who were looking for ways to pay them less. Justifying this, workers were accused of being lazy and unproductive at the seams. A series of strikes ensued across what was termed the Cambrian Colliery network, which consisted of around 12,000 miners. They were organised, especially since 1905 when two major explosions in the Rhondda occurred, which included the Cambrian pit at Clydych on the outskirts of Tonypandy, resulting in 150 fatalities. What was to soon follow would be a pivotal moment in the political life of the valleys, as the power of religion that often pacified the locals by preaching about worthiness in the afterlife would give way to a new self-confident radicalism wanting salvation from misery in this world. A politics spearheaded by the likes of Keir Hardie, who was the founder of the modern Labour Party and became its first parliamentary leader in 1906 having been elected to serve the constituency of Merthyr Tydfil at the turn of the century. As the striking miners became increasingly agitated as their meagre demands were rebutted by the pit masters, in the near distance smoke billowing out of the operational pit in neighbouring village of Llwynypia was seen. Temporarily employing "black-leg labour" from outside the valley, it inevitably became the focus for picketing locals who marched demanding its closure. In the autumn of 1910, the miners had reached tipping point. The valleys had already seen a large influx of paid-for-hire police from constabularies as far away as Bristol and Gloucester as the owners sensed a growing resentment. Batons would now be wielded as they drove the miners back into Tonypandy Square. The following day, the miners were repeatedly attacked by the police, who corralled and charged at them, continuing their assaults as the miners fought back with redundant hands. An evening of rioting set the market town ablaze. Much of Tonypandy's main street the morning after looked like a warzone, as shopkeepers proceeded to board up their damaged windows with sheets of corrugated zinc and broken strips of wood taken from the floors within. Such preparations for worse to come would later become a common feature as the villages feared German aerial bombardments. The village was now in lockdown. Residents were under siege. But from whom exactly? Regardless of who threw the first stone, the riotous behaviour of the mob continued, making it clear the police had lost all control of the valley's streets.

Folklore tells that the only shop spared was the chemist owned by Welsh rugby legend Willie Llewellyn. This is yet another endearing tale speaking to the valley's respect for sportspersons that come from within their own ranks. Sporting aspirations aside, as far as the coal colonists were concerned, there was a need to re-establish order, with a request sent to Westminster to help restore the rules of the game on the preferred uneven pitches. The Home Secretary, Winston Churchill, sent a further 500 police and more controversially a cavalry of 260 Lancashire fusiliers, who, already based in reserve at Cardiff, arrived on horseback in the light of day to pacify the local rioters. This was not the first time troops had been sent into the Rhondda — in the

1893 hauliers' strike the military was also deployed to quell demands for better workers' rights. The conditions faced by the hauliers were amongst the worst of all the miners, often living in clouds of dust thrown up by the trams and ponies. But this was different. It was more of a spectacle and the political message it conveyed was more determined. While Churchill's summoning of the troops in Tonypandy remains a bitter point of contention for many people in the valleys, it is nevertheless fully in keeping with the logics of coloniality and the recourse to military violence once the masses become too troublesome and can no longer be contained. Admirers of this elder statesman have continued to maintain his role was more conciliatory, and besides, subsequently helping to defeat Hitler and his army of fascists who sought to turn Europe into an entire colony pretty much gives you a get-out-of -jail-free card. However, given Churchill's willingness to use whatever means were necessary when tasked with putting down local uprisings elsewhere in the British colonies, locals who insisted he ordered the troops to directly attack the miners, resulting in hundreds of casualties and one known loss of life, seem far more believable. The military would retain its occupation in the valleys for a few months after. Whilst this event no doubt galvanised local militancy and would have more protracted political effects, including being deeply influential in the introduction of a national minimum wage, the riotous miners, for their part, would slowly starve into submission, relying on handouts once again from the chapels. Nevertheless, they would soon be brought back into the fold as the demand for coal became a national priority following the outbreak of World War I. Many years later, Churchill would be given the freedom of the City of Cardiff, which was another means of separating valleys people from those in the city.

Two years prior to the Tonypandy riots, the Welsh politician David Lloyd George (who the lauded economist John Maynard Keynes referred to as being a "Welsh Witch") lamented the utter contempt with which the English looked upon their neighbour. Less officious but no less demeaning, in the same year as the Rhondda riots, a book would be published under the pseudonym "Draig Glas", later revealed as being one Arthur Tyssilo Johnson. While providing a quintessential example of how publishing was becoming more sensationalist, *The Perfidious Welshman* spoke to the bigoted attitudes prevailing within the English aristocracy. As the book begins:

> No people were ever less fitted to call a country their own and themselves a nation than the Welsh. They have not a single essential factor for the making of a nation. Indeed, many authorities contend, with good reason, that Taffy is none other than a low-bred mongrel of Mongolian origin, that he is allied to the inhabitants of the Basque provinces of Spain, to the Magyars, Turks, Tartars, and certain inferior types of French Peasantry.

Such groupings of perceived lesser humans were commonplace in colonial literatures. But there's a more sinister logic to these negative relations, for the real enduring strength of any colony was proven to be its ability to divide. Getting the colonised to fight amongst themselves was crucial. Shortly after the Tonypandy riots, another more unsavoury episode happened in the valleys that demands our attention. By 1910, dozens of Rhondda towns were home to many immigrants, including Italians who set up cafes and ice cream parlours, along with Jewish refugees, such as the wonderful artist Josef Herman, who were fleeing antisemitism elsewhere in Europe. Indeed, by the early twentieth century, well established and thriving Jewish communities were evident in Merthyr Tydfil, Brynmawr, Aberdare and Pontypridd, as elsewhere. A notable resident of the latter was Gerald Baron Cohen, whose son Sascha became an internationally celebrated comedian. But valley folks were not in any way immune to the violence of scapegoating, and on one particularly troubling occasion turned their anger upon a marginalised group who were closer to hand as they sought to make sense of their desperate plight. The Tredegar riots of 1911 are a harrowing example of how a community can be divided and turn upon itself, as hundreds of young men marched through the streets and proceeded to loot Jewish shops. Such destruction also spread to other communities; though whether this was driven less by race and more by economics is still open to question. Whatever the reason, on this occasion, an even more racially charged incident took place on the Cardiff docks several years later, which was led by disaffected soldiers returning from the horrors of the Great War and remains one of the most deplorable acts of racial violence the country has seen.

World War II was a watershed moment in international affairs, which resulted in a profound transformation in the balance of power. The sun did finally set on the British Empire and its calling would soon be replaced by a glossier version made in the US of A. Politics would become trademarked and the Yanks could be presented as saviours of the "free world", including all that could be bought and consumed in her name. That the Soviets suffered the greatest toll and were probably the ultimate reason why Hitler was defeated was fully written out of this script. But the lived effects of history are never so easily bracketed, which at least is my excuse for never remembering dates in school when memorialising the past. Time seeps through the cracks in peculiar and unpredictable ways, revealing in the process the complexities of cultural reckonings. America had already arrived in the valleys by the time the pendulum of war was in full swing. Tom Jones recalls how the stationing of black American soldiers in Pontypridd before the D-Day Normandy landings had a profound impact, exposing him to its varied genres of music and confident styles of dressing, along with giving to impoverished families all kinds of exotic, processed foods. During the war, some three million American GIs were stationed in Wales, and many departed for the final assault in France from Barry docks, which in times past was key to coal exports. Only two generations later, America revealingly arrived into my home as a result of commodity envy. A neighbouring "butty's" uncle visited the country and brought back a gleaming red and blue fighter jet, which seemed just as futuristic and capable of warping hand-held speeds faster than any of my *Star Wars* toys. This strange land called America was the future, and we would no sooner be crying together as Apollo Creed was slain by that evil Russian. Many years later, we openly embraced aspects of American culture, including the arrival of Public Enemy and NWA, who I hold responsible for the explosion in highly flammable shell-suit tracksuits that turned us into "chavs" long before the term was publicly debated amongst the London set who invariably need to claim to have discovered everything. *Fear of a Black Planet* certainly resonated far more with my contemporaries, many of whom really identified with hip-hop culture, than "Ice Ice Baby", which we knew was a domesticated imposter and nothing but a superficial upgrading to "don't worry, be happy". But there was still much history to work through before Americanisation and its sugar-coated seductions took hold to further rot the teeth of children already addicted to cheap pop (I am referring here to both the music and the stomach-colonising fizzy drinks). For the decline of the Coal Empire that we watched in real time in these towns was a more protracted and drawn-out separation, which countered the speeds of a runaway world of globalisation with a resigned standstill by a people who were now waving white flags, hoping that somebody, anybody, would liberate them. Maybe this slowness alone explains why our ruins have more permanence?

Seven young boys are huddled together on the cold tombstone at the edge of the ruined church. Winter has arrived, yet they would rather be playing here than sat indoors, whatever the weather. They had been hiding and seeking within the partially destructed stone façade beside the belltower of the once prominent English-styled building. The rubble of its blackened stone was scattered as if destroyed by an earthquake. It was getting dark, so they figured it was better to be in closer proximity. You never knew who might pay a visit to these overgrown grounds. The Church of St John the Baptist was built on an ancient religious site dating back to at least the sixth century. Following the collapse of a Medieval upgrading, its current iteration was constructed around 1845. One of the most prominent events to take place there during its glory days was the marriage of the daughter of William Abraham — commonly known by his bardic title "Mabon" — who was a powerful trade union pioneer and the very first Member of Parliament for the Rhondda constituency. As the night descends, six of the children huddle closer together, while another surveys the dates and inscriptions of the neighbouring headstones. Many have been broken with the weight of time, others barely readable due to the erasure of the elements and the loss of a few of the leaded letters that once stood prominent. Several are well over a century old, likely the earliest settlers from when the town and its population were developing. They seem to belong to another world, yet the names read all too familiar. "Jones", "Davies", "Evans", "Thomas", "Smith", possible descendants whose history were seldom now entertained. Opposite the church a handful of elderly villagers enter the imposing Bethesda chapel, which once attracted thousands of religious revellers. Its congregation is now fully dependent on these few staying alive. They encourage the boys to join them, though are met with a polite decline. There used to be a notable social rivalry in the valleys between the church-going and the chapel-going types, with the former believing they were the more respectable and the latter more frequented by the commoners. Yet as the well-dressed elderly and the dishevelled young boys exchange their courteous words across the street dividing these once mighty institutions, it seems that order in social and economic standing had been reversed. The church once stood proudly within the extended local district delightfully called "The Hundred of Miskin". This contained several parishes, including Ystradyfodwg, which was the name previously given to what became the Rhondda. It was closed in 1979 and soon turned into a makeshift playground for these spirited trespassers.

In the frosty twilight hours, the boys started to do what they always did on such occasions — try to scare the life and wits out of one another. On this occasion, the eldest of the rabble assumed the floor and began to tell a story. He was identifiable by the black-taped armband on his worn winter coat, which could easily have been mistaken for a symbol of mourning, as he played amongst the cracked open tombs of the dead, though in truth it was more tasked with keeping the mottled lining inside his sleeve. He told of the ghost of the White Lady of the Bwlch Road, which led over the mountain pass at Cwmparc and across to the westward valleys. According to his version, the White Lady would be waiting at the roadside at the top of the road in the dark hours looking for somebody to stop and offer a lift. She was mostly ignored, but the sighting alone was enough. Somewhere along the journey, as the driver looked back into the rear-view mirror, they would see her apparition sat in the backseat and upon gazing into her eyes, she would scream out causing the car to career off the road. No sooner was this boy reaching the dramatic crescendo, which invariably involved the wild screeching, that another boy whose father had vanished over a year ago interrupted and killed his Academy Award-winning moment, much to his derision. He had it on good authority (namely his alcoholic mother who now only speaks in the language of bitterness), that the White Witch was far more vengeful. He explained how she would appear in a beautiful white gown with parts of her body exposed, seeking out male drivers. Once they let her into the vehicle and were charmed by her seductions, her kiss was deadly as their mouths would lock, and fate foretold. The travellers' eyes were drawn closer and closer into a harrowing and fixed intimacy, gazing upon the purely white surface of the witch's eyes. All the torments and misery that would later come to pass would then be projected as they continued to stare into the absent abyss of those terrifying orbs. Distracted in this briefest of moments by the vision of pain they cause to loved ones, the car was forced to fly off the road into the ravine below. Rumour had it that the White

Witch was a local girl who discovered on her wedding night the adulterous behaviour of her husband, and so fled to the top of mountain and threw herself off into the basin, causing her body to break apart on the jagged stones and immediately turn into white dust. Her spirit was petrified in a rock. She has since been looking to enact revenge on any man proven to be unfaithful. No sooner had a third boy disgustingly rebuked, "Well, they must be stupid. I wouldn't kiss a ghost", the silhouette of an eighth boy appeared from behind a larger standing tomb. As he comes closer, it is clear he is only wearing a worn grey t-shirt and old ripped jeans that cling so tightly to his matchstick legs they could be mistaken for denim paint. The boy's t-shirt features an image of a fight against the devil on top of a large boulder in the underworld, accompanied by the words, "Run to the Hills. Run for your life." This Iron Maiden classic released a few years earlier sang of the colonisation of the Americas, but this chorus had a different meaning to this child. He strikes a familiar resemblance to another in the group, though the spark in his eyes has been replaced by the prominent deep-set blackness of his pupils. He looks drugged on destitution. Surrounding those empty holes is pale whiteness covered by an aged mist and abandoned resignation which belies his years. The rest of the boys are slightly perturbed as they sit quivering, with their sleeves extended to cover their frost-bitten hands and coat necklines pulled up over their chapped, freeze-dried mouths, while this boy seems at ease, even if his lips are a whiter shade of blue. He sits beside the boy who had just finished his more promiscuous adaptation and says, "I have a story to tell".

A town was once so removed from the world that its clocks stopped moving. All its villagers lived in deep holes in the ground. They were slaves to a powerful overlord who was never seen in person. Yet they knew of their master's presence because of the invisible chains they felt around their legs. It also threw meagre amounts of food into the holes every night. This stale bread provided just enough energy to continue cutting their holes, deeper and deeper, in the quest to reach the centre of the earth. Overtime, however, the villagers began to secretly organise, and they even called upon the fire of a dragon to help defeat their punishing master, allowing them to briefly emerge from the depths. No sooner was the master defeated, another and even more powerful one arrived with a ferocious army that drove the villagers back into the depths. As the years went by, the master grew weary and tired of searching for the centre of the earth. So, one by one, they allowed the holes to collapse in upon themselves, killing those who were caught inside. The rest escaped and set up new homes on the ground above on the abandoned lands left by the former master who died from consumption. They soon forgot about the holes, which were now covered in grass, except for one that lay at the far reaches of the village. Something terrible was however unleased when the earth finally trembled, and the bells of a local church stopped ringing. Rumours started to spread that the adults in the village were disappearing, leaving their children to scavenge for themselves amongst the broken buildings where the stale bread was once made. The whispers were true and eventually every adult had vanished, and only the young could be seen cowering in the nearby woods where they fled. They feared the woods because they were haunted. But they feared the hole more, which from time to time could be heard crying the most sorrowful of songs. One late summer's afternoon, a young boy who was about to turn 16 lost his bearings while following the flight of a blackbird and found himself in the far reaches of the village. He could hear the cries from the hole, and how it was now calling his name. As he stood on the edge of the bottomless pit, he saw a white fiend emerge from the blackness. Shrill and risen, it was covered in the blood of the villagers, whose faces could be seen carved into the infernal walls with their surnames etched below as a prisoner would carve theirs in the hope of being remembered. The boy was frozen in horror. Unable to flee, terrified to fall. As the fiend drew closer, he recognised her face. She reached into his heart and snatched away time itself.

Margaret Thatcher arrived at a moment when the Coal Colony was already crumbling at its seams. Even before she came to power, the mining industry in the Rhondda was in rapid decline. Post-war nationalisation had resulted in many closures, while those remaining in production struggled to find willing and able men to recruit and follow in their fathers' footsteps. No sooner had she taken power, "Going Underground" was less a calling than an anthem for a lost generation, suitably b-sided on its 1980 release by the "Dreams of Children". In many ways, Thatcher simply accelerated a process that had already been taking its toll and was reaching its inevitable conclusion. And we should never forget the hardship of a life working in the pits. It would be wrong to say the valleys was some utopian place of industrial glory, which during the 1980s was sent into lasting oblivion. Its people have always known they were cannon fodder. But in such communities, her war on the unions was seen as a war upon a way of life, however hard it was and however difficult it was to sustain. This was not just an assault on the present, it was an assault on the lived memory of the place. Throughout the twentieth century, despite the pain and suffering, the valleys were a hotbed of political activism, nurturing caring and supportive communities. People truly left their doors open. And they would take care of their neighbours. That all changed with Thatcherism. With the radical landscape slowly decimated, she would sanction the dropping of the mightiest bomb and make no apologies. There was no such thing as society, after all, she maintained. The fallout can still be seen today, as many of its once thriving main streets are full of boarded-up and ruined premises with little prospect of being rebuilt through some reconstructed effort. There is no Marshall Plan for these parts. While the valleys largely escaped the bombing campaigns of World War II, they also learned that sometimes a catastrophic event takes a longer time to appear. Like the earlier story of the young miner, it's not just about the explosions, but a slower and yet no less brutal consumption. Thatcher waged a war upon society, and it was the people who were already exhausted by the fight which felt its effects the most. Whatever lifeblood remained was brutally severed like the unwanted child of a prostitute thrown into the desolate streets. We were those orphans of Thatcher and the lives of our parents pulled further into the darkened abyss.

Thatcher's disdain for the Welsh as an independent people would resurrect the spirits of Edward, Henry and Winston, while arming them with new capitalistic purpose. Places like the valleys, in her eyes, were no longer to be appropriated and its human capital extracted. Worse still, having been exhausted of their potential, they would now be abandoned and left to rot in their own containment. There was nothing to be exhumed. No autopsy was necessary because no crime had been committed. History had taken its course and the final pages were written. There would be no concern then for the unemployed as much as there would be no concern for the voice of a people who desperately needed a different kind of politics. Again, this was predictably upheld by a wider cultural apparatus in which the Welsh and the valleys people would be presented as some inferior, uneducated and backward race. These attitudes would be concentrated on Neil Kinnock, who also like Bevan was born in the valley town of Tredegar. The son of a coal miner, Kinnock was leader of the Labour Party and Thatcher's dispatch box nemesis. He was often ridiculed by the cultural bourgeoisie of London, and seen as unpopular because of his uncouth dialect and verbosity. We even bought into the media-driven hype concerning Kinnock's "unelectability", which was another way of saying we'd rather perish than be governed by a Welshman from the valleys. A sentiment also held by the middle classes in Wales, who were all too aware of his loutish "boyo" heritage and what that meant for social standings. This was apparent in many newspaper headlines and stories in the build-up to the 1992 election, which proved to be the last under his leadership. The *Daily Mail* referred to Kinnock as a "brawling how's-yer-father boyo from the Welsh valleys", the *Sun* as a statesman who when the going gets tough will revert back to "Taff the Lad", while the

Telegraph depicted him as the "wild man of the valleys". All this culminated in the *Sun*'s headline on the eve of the election, "If Kinnock wins today, will the last person to leave Britain please turn out the lights". As the newspaper's previous reporting on Hillsborough showed, this mouthpiece for Thatcherism, which was fully intent on continuing her neoliberal legacy, despised the working classes, even if it constituted its largest readership. The 1992 election was the first I could have voted in. I conscientiously objected. Unified in the year of my birth, the Rhondda constituency is the safest Labour seat in the entire country. I was doubly disenfranchised, knowing that a red Smurf was more likely to win than a candidate of any other political colour, while also knowing there was no way a boy from the valleys could go on to become Prime Minister, especially in these declining industrial times.

Thatcher opened the already exhausted veins of the valleys to the unrelenting pull of globalisation. If the welfare state provided some comfort, fortunes were now cast adrift on open shores while bodies landlocked in ways that accelerated the need to escape. Our mountains of the mind felt more incarcerating than ever, while each day another structural remnant of the mining past was boarded up or turned into a fast-food outlet. Working men's halls became unworkable, progressive clubs vacated, libraries turned into cheap housing, chapels home to the heroin demons. So by the time Tony Blair eventually arrived on the scene in 1997, the valleys had been gutted without renovation. "Things could only get better", right, as their D-reaming anthem proclaimed? After all, wasn't this a Prime Minister who was opening the doors to working-class kids like Noel from Oasis? "Cigarettes and Alcohol" certainly reverberated in these towns, as did the Stereophonic beats of our new rock and roll poets. Who could not be seduced by the coming of Blair? An Oxbridge-educated man, who was finally down with the people, Blair brought the promise of devolution to the Welsh. Yet in terms of their economic outlook, Thatcher and Blair really weren't that distinct, and as we would later learn, neither was their appetite for war. And so, despite the rhetoric, the valleys were continually ignored and left to their own misery while the gentrification of previous no-go waterfront areas in the capital continued apace. Is there not a more tragic figure than the colonised who are so eventually disregarded that they become altogether ignored by all potential masters? While some may argue Wales had already emerged out of its colonial condition in the early to mid-twentieth century, pointing especially to the grand structures of national importance built in Cardiff as proof of this liberation, these arguments poorly appreciate how the economic drives of control have always proffered token gestures. The construction of a Civic Hall, National Museum and Library meant zero to the people of the valleys. They were just another reminder that power laid elsewhere, as much as the construction of the Senedd National Assembly building that was opened by the Queen on St David's Day in 2006 at the cost of millions was a further reminder of a Regally-bound past. Henry VIII was known for robbing the gold from the ceilings of the churches, but now the valleys people looked on, having been instructed many years earlier to replace their beautiful slate-tiled rooves with a more durable and nondescript composition, only to see this new monument to national beauty gleaming on dock of the bay, dressed in the most refined quarried grey stone. Another hidden symbol perhaps of the ways the valleys people can be trodden upon in plain sight without anybody recognising the significance of the act for what it represents.

The mist is rising on this cold new year's morning. A red starry flag is flying in the distance as the poor children once again smile in my direction as I climb down from my makeshift bed and empty my shoes. It's New Year's Day and for once I don't have a hangover, though I am anxious all the same. It's 2006 and I am a world away from the valleys. Why had I travelled to the other side of the planet to try and make sense of violence, when it was always there on the doorstep to my life?

Was I seduced by colonial guilt, as I ventured into the Mexican rainforests and sought refuge in the welcoming embrace of the Zapatista communities of Chiapas? Maybe we need to keep violence at a distance? The poverty endured here was different to what I had known. Yet their fight for dignity against global forces was all too resonant to the world I knew. I had ventured to Chiapas in the hope of doing my bit as a global citizen. In truth, I was a tourist, of little value, especially for all the books I read. Like poor people I had known back home, they didn't need somebody like me teaching them about violence and oppression. They lived its devastating effects every single day. They knew the sting of those scorpions I was fearful of discovering in my boots, as much as they knew the slaughter the indigenous throughout the Americas had faced for centuries. But as I looked upon that flag blowing in the wind backdropped by the dense forest, while greeted by the curious smile of a young seven-year-old child so fittingly called Emiliano (his namesake was the leader of the Mexican Revolution in 1910 and from whom the Zapatistas took their naming), I felt the comforting spirit of those men in Merthyr. Poor people don't need to read Marx to stand up for what's intolerable. Nor do they need some educated intelligentsia lecturing them on the meaning of coloniality and what true oppression looks like. They intimately know when they are appropriated by systems that will dispose of them when they are deemed to no longer be of value. The stories told by those in the valleys of South Wales and the valleys of the Lacandona Selva rainforests are part of the same jigsaw their spokesperson Marcos wrote so eloquently about. Though admittedly, the giant silk structure holding all manner of moving objects located just behind my ramshackle wooded cabin, which has been the cause of many sleepless nights, has me thinking that the web of life may just be a more appropriate metaphor. Never did I overcome arachnophobia.

The Zapatista insurrection was in direct response to the signing of the North American Free Trade Agreement, which came into effect in 1994. It was endorsed by Blair's American liberal peer Bill Clinton. The parallels with NAFTA and the Treaty of Maastricht (1993) that led to the formation of the European Union were telling, not least the ways in which it was primarily driven by the desire to have profits and goods move seamlessly across nations. Much less concern was invariably paid to the migratory potential of poor people. But the impoverished always somehow find a way to have their voices heard. That people in the valleys turned and voted leave the European Union by some margin in that fractious Brexit debate, for example, was not incidental. They were taking direct aim at the new entitlement model for politics, which many saw as profoundly middle-class. I am writing this as somebody who fully recognises the importance of the political idea of Europe as a way to bring lasting peace to the continent. I am also writing this knowing its lasting economic effects will be calamitous as it makes us ever more dependent on America. But I am also writing it knowing it is arrogant to assume people of the valleys were simply duped into voting Leave by unscrupulous leaders, who encouraged them to live out jingoistic fantasies. Such explanations ultimately fall back upon the idea that the uneducated, like children, cannot be left alone and trusted to act upon their own political intuitions. Sure, migration was horrifyingly politicised, but it wasn't the only reason. Being European meant nothing, if the offering gave no solutions to lift a people out of a century of misery. Many in these towns don't own a passport, let alone find something to rejoice in the fact it would no longer need to be stamped. I am not saying holidays don't matter; on the contrary, it is precisely the politics of everyday life which proves far more valuable than petty concerns about "sovereignty". The people of the valleys forced us to confront a different question that nobody wanted to pose. Namely, what becomes of a once colonised people when the machinations of industrial exploitation have passed, and they slip into wasted lives? Very few pundits wish to talk about the valleys as being part of an internal colony today, even if they try to reckon with the decades of neglect its people have endured. Yet to fail to grasp this is a failure to grasp the suffering and neglect, the anger and resentment, which is also finding its paths into the heart of contemporary politics like tens of thousands of mini volcanos all waiting to erupt upon an island that believed itself to be finally dormant.

It's now nearly two decades since my travels to Chiapas. The counter winds are blowing and the entire world — well at least social media — is awash with discussion on decolonisation. I stare blankly at an officious email about the need for us all to better decolonise educational practises. I have some sympathies, but not through these kinds of impositions. I have been teaching the thought of leading anti-colonial thinkers, including Fanon, who I introduced into the curriculum at my university. Not a single person in the email thread mentions anything about the colonised peoples of Wales, Ireland or Scotland, let alone elsewhere in Eastern Europe. Coloniality is now distinctly colour-coded, pure and simple. Whatever happened to essentialisation? Once again, I think about Mexican caste paintings, which made so painfully clear the racial hierarchies created in the name of civilisation, especially the way some natives were completely left outside of the schematic. We were not simply adapting to inverting this logic? There is also much talk about micro-aggressions, which are being presented in ways that trump the lived experience of actual physical violence. I get drawn into a discussion with some who have taken umbrage with my criticism of white privilege. I still don't know what it means, except for allowing middle-class intelligentsia to place third-generational colonial guilt firmly onto the backs of the poor. I let the whole micro-aggression survey slide, sensing my points about how confrontational language in poor communities is frequently used not to perpetuate violence but to disarm assailants will get lost in translation. I anticipate it will be read as another example of my uncultured aggressiveness that those who grow up in poverty know all too well, and so I will confirm some toxically masculine stereotype they suspected. I also let the white privilege debate go, knowing it makes no sense to those who cannot be blamed for how they have come to know the world and figure it is better to let black and other scholars of colour provide the necessary counterpoints. I do fear however for students caught in a cultural melee, which is cheer-led by social media academics who have made a bonfire of the terms solidarity, criticality and the radical. So I reflect, especially on what I have betrayed about my past. Surveying the university landscape and its fetishization for a particular vision of coloniality, I never felt further away from the realities of the kids I grew up with on the streets of the valleys. How did we get to this moment in our conversation? Might I have contributed with my own extended narratives on psychological violence to such a shameful inverting of history? Where was Robeson when you needed him?

ONE HUNDRED YEARS
OF DEPRESSION

The first signs of significant economic decline in the valleys of South Wales can be traced back to the summer of 1924. While unemployment was typically figured around 2% in the coalfield areas in the spring months, by the end of the year it increased five-fold to 12.5%. Then by August 1925 it had risen to a staggering 28.5%. Part of the problem was the valleys' reliance on the coal-export market, which was hit because of the financial settlement from the Great War. The Treaty of Versailles in particular had a marked impact, with Germany needing to provide coal as part of its reparation payments, which effectively undercut the profitability of South Wales's exports. This was further exacerbated as the coal mines were now back in the hands of private ownership and all the wage agreements and union protections secured before the war had been abandoned. These economic conditions were further compounded by the global market shift in fuel preference towards oil, along with a turn in the United States towards coal producers in the Southern Americas, and by the time the Wall Street Crash hit in 1929, the valleys had become one of the most depressed places in the entire industrial world. Unemployment was recorded to be close to 45% of the entire population. What has become commonly termed the Great Depression was felt greatest in these mountains. And its people would learn their first lesson in the unforgiving nature of globalisation and the punishing nature of its forces, which were beyond all local control. Moreover, as these changing economic fortunes effectively reversed near 150 years of unrivalled industrial growth, the structural conditions that took hold would have lasting effects. The depression here didn't just last for a number of years, or even a decade. It has lasted a century.

Considered reflections on the Treaty of Versailles often consider the harsh conditions it imposed upon a broken nation, which would soon turn into resentment and give rise to the horrors of the Third Reich. Through this, many have reflected upon how the inter-war years were more a temporary break in the cessation of hostilities between competing colonial powers, which in the end, turned all of Europe into a barren wasteland strewn with untold devastation and its people ravaged by the pain of such savage loss. Seldomly, however, is the focus attentive to the impact the Treaty had upon the colonised peoples of the Welsh valleys and what this meant for the region's decline. Partly as a result of German reparations, the selling price for Welsh coal fell by nearly 50% in the aftermath of Versailles. In the years between 1921 and 1936, there were 241 pit closures in South Wales, with the number of miners falling from 270,000 to 130,000. Unemployment became a way of life, which was to be subsequently bookended by the two most violent episodes in human history. The desperation of these times was captured in the photography of Helen Muspratt Dunman, who, upon returning from documenting the hardship of life in the Volga in the Soviet Union, turned her lens upon the unemployed miners who could be seen scouring the hillsides for loose pieces of coal to warm their homes during the wintery months. Governments became as paralysed as the unemployed mind. Inertia became the principal logic of political rule. Hoping to ride it out, doing nothing became a favoured policy choice, despite the economist John Maynard Keynes' reminder that in the longer run we would all inevitably be dead. Yet still the local people of these towns tried to voice their resistance. During this period the valleys were becoming notably more militant, as witnessed by the riotous responses in Mardy (1932), Merthyr (1934) and Tonypandy (1936), culminating in 100,000-strong marches in the Rhondda later that year, which occurred shortly after the start of the Spanish Civil War. This dress rehearsal for World War II grabbed the attention of many socialists (it was publicly spoken about by union leaders at this rally), including George Orwell, who found some resonance between the miners he wrote about in Wigan and the partisan fighters in Catalonia. It would also connect these distanced lands in other ways, including through the photographs of Robert Capa, who not only captured some of the most iconic war images ever seen (including the now infamous falling soldier from the Spanish Civil War), but who came to document the lives of the miners in the Rhondda the year after the release of the motion picture *How Green Was My Valley*, in 1942. Orwell joined the International Brigade of intellectuals, poets, activists and organised workers who went to help fight for the "last great" socialist cause. Of the 174 Welshmen who joined the ranks, 122 were from the valleys of South Wales. Primarily from the Rhondda and Merthyr, they constituted the largest single group of British volunteers, 33 of them dying on foreign soil. Spanish Aid Committees were also set up in many valley towns, helping to raise material support in the form of food and humanitarian supplies in the fight against fascism despite the terrible hardships felt by those who could barely survive themselves. Such generosity from a people who desperately wanted to be shown the same kindness is something I would witness time and again in these lands.

My grandfather was born in the midst of this devastating time. He was thrown into the life of the valleys in the year following the first hunger marches, 1927. Like many children of his generation, his early years were marked by watching his parents fight for their very existence. They weren't alone. While they did have homegrown vegetables from a small allotment holding, the children were still dependent upon food provided by the local soup kitchens, which although doing their best, resulted in widespread malnutrition and the continuation of hunger. With the family rented home situated in the village of Pentre, every day he waited in line at the local Salvation

Army or British Legion, which was manned by former soldiers. Broken-booted and cracked-lipped, he wore a gaunt expression of unassuming denial. With a soldered Tate & Lyle tin in hand, he was normalised into thinking this was simply how food was meant to be provided to the quivering queues of the young. Most families lived well below the subsistence level, so charity was a matter of life and death. At least they were better off than those families who could only provide the extra sustenance of bread and a dripping of lard, which waged its own assault on the arteries of life. He was second oldest in a typically large family of seven children, who all lived in a small, terraced house, which had limited gas lighting and featured gaping cracks in the front door. With his father unemployed from what he thought was permanent enough work and a guaranteed income (however lowly and meagre) in the local pit, there wasn't enough to provide for any of the basic necessities, let alone heating the home, despite the abundance of coal still in plentiful supply in the depopulated tunnels beneath their lost feet. While illegal levels were dug into the mountainside as miners sought to take matters into their own hands, extracting further coal became a treacherous enterprise. Unemployment benefit was provided as a result of the Unemployment Insurance Act (1920) that replaced the Poor Law, but it was soon subjected to stringent means-testing. Those who qualified were paid 15s. (75p) per week for man and wife and 5s. (25p) for each child. According to the British Medical Association, a family of two adults and three children needed at least 22s. 7d. (£1.12) for food alone per week to provide the most rudimentary nourishment. All the starved children, who suffered in varying degrees from rickets and other forms of bone and muscular deficiencies, slept together in the parents' worn bed, which became a petri-dish for bronchitis, pneumonia and other contagious ailments that thrived in such squalor. A number of outbreaks of scarlet fever were recorded, resulting in higher infant mortality rates directly linked to the worsening economic conditions. If the streets were cold and wet, much of the house was damp, rotting and infested. The air was full of soot that seeped down from the disused chimneys, which would be thrown into the heart of every room when the ferocious winds spitefully brought its revenge upon infants who committed no crime. The toll upon family life often proved unbearable, especially for the women, whose physical and mental health was the worst affected as they went without for their children. Time was also brutally marking. Poor people know the importance of time better than anyone. Every second can be intimately felt. My great-grandfather felt it acutely as he stood waiting as part of the growing army of the unemployed outside the pit each morning, hoping in vain to get just a day's work. A sign reading "No Men Wanted" was backdropped by a gated closure. That didn't stop him walking on those marches with barely enough strength to carry his aged body. Dignity was bookended by the experience of dead time, as he returned to stand in the dole or food queues, which publicly shred whatever pride he held. A condition further compounded as he walked several miles down to Tonypandy to visit the distribution centre that provided aid parcels of clothing, which were sent from relief campaigns set up in the City of London and still provide so many of the quintessential images of poverty experienced during those desperate years. Life was marked by the constant presence of a time that crushed the present and pained the future. Whereas his wife tried her best to keep the children free from infections without any defensive protections. How can you possibly keep a child clean and healthy when there was little soap, no hot water and nothing to replenish a deficient soul? This was a slum of a more rural kind, as people endured a cramped and suffocating existence. Such conditions would age the body and the mind long before the years had intended. Still, the children played in the muddied streets and derelict homes as the start of our lasting abandonment began and the permanence of a depressive state took its fated hold. It also gave rise to a black-humoured spirit, which was so characteristic of those born into such times. "Keep smiling", my grandfather constantly reminded, even when already overcast skies became darker.

If the boom years of the coal industry were marked by mass migration into the valleys, during the 1930s this process was notably reversed. Estimates suggest around 440,000 people left Wales between 1921 and 1938, with some 85% of those leaving the coal-producing valleys. Those who stayed had no option but to remain, it seems. This resulted in the familiar pattern of long-term unemployment, matched by a certain fatalism as the lived environment also began to reflect the collapse. Outward migratory processes were actively encouraged by the British government's Ministry for Labour, which persuaded the unemployed to be more mobile, setting in place a lasting idea that to be successful, one needed to leave these blighted towns and head for the cities of England. Dreams of depopulation have also lasted a century. Prosperity lay elsewhere. Hope was located beyond the here and now. Rainbows always landing outside the valley's natural walls. Left with an aging population, many of the young and able fled having been inadvertently seduced by the government's only solution to local depression — population transfer. When stasis becomes part of the depression, flight is an act of survival. An even more harrowing twist of fate could be detected, which rest-bit the misery during this period in the valley's history. A brief cessation to the local conditions of everyday struggle would be realised as Europe was back into the machinations of war. Miners again became valuable and their productive energies in high demand as the war gave renewed energy to its industry. If South Wales steam coal was looked upon as one of the most important resources by the navy to secure victory during World War I, so its capacity to motor the machineries of Total War remained of the utmost importance in the follow up, which was even more demanding of energies of destruction. War became industrious, one more time, as the army of the unemployed could be redeployed and asked to give their fight on the home front for the sake of a future. World War II provided economic salvation. Unemployment fell to non-existent levels. Cracks of depression were plastered over, so the destruction could commence. Productivity was a call to arms. Coal as important as conscription. Clear evidence of this could be seen when the government took full control of coal production in 1942, paving the way for the subsequent nationalisation of the industry and establishment of a National Coal Board in 1947. War also led to the liberation of the female workforce of the valleys, from clothing factories of the Rhondda tasked with producing military clothing to manufacturing what at the time was the world's largest arsenal in armament factories at Bridgend. The coal-industrial complex and military-industrial complex were inseparable in this moment. We can only imagine however what harm was done to the psyche knowing recovery was tied to such horror, then again the call to war can often be seductive, especially if it offers the guarantee of gainful employment in communities where it has been painfully lacking. We can more accurately say that sentiments no doubt changed when the war was declared over, and the mining families started to realise that the salvation was temporary and the predictable collateral fallouts would soon return to mark them once again as the disposable of history. Did they believe that finally things would be different this time, and their efforts at last would be appreciated and valued?

During the breakout of the war in 1939, there were some 2,000 mines operating in the United Kingdom. The life of the miner in each of them was caged. They were also bound and tied to mechanised dreams, which began with chains that lowered them into the ground. As Rousseau had ruminated a few centuries before, there were so many invisible ways those chains held. Yet despite ideological claims of progress, miners crawled through tunnels on their hands and knees, cutting into the ground illuminated by naked lights. A post-war autopsy of the pits revealed them to be in a dire state with terrible working conditions. Nationalisation was to be the cure. Yet despite large-scale investment in technological modernisation, whatever optimism was there in the valleys had also long since migrated. Machines were in fact seen as the problem, as much as they were the destroyers of worlds. Life and fate in the valleys would nevertheless now be overwhelmingly tied to national politics, which, in the end, provided to be the last laceration upon an already sacrificed body. Many fathers (like my great-grandfather) didn't want their children in the mines. They knew the hardship. They knew the terror of the descent into the darkness. They knew its romanticisation came from those looking down into the black from above. Everything was eclipsed below, even the shadows cast into the footprint of the darkness itself. Yet they also knew there was little alternative and that casting some shadow was better than none at all. So, if the sounds of the morning call to work from the billowing steam hooter were always met with trepidation, the muted sound of its denial, the quietening of the fighting spirit, brought a greater fear to these parts. Nothing is absolutely silent. Beating hearts still persist even when exhausted. But what becomes of this heart when the sounds of a dignified life are replaced by the silent cries of hunger? How long can it beat when its blood is bled dry into the bottomless abyss below? Were you to swim around the subterranean tunnels beneath the valleys today, you would be swimming amongst waters possessed with the lost hope of generations. A truly infernal network of waterways, which would have every nonbeliever cowering at the presence of something so tremendously fated its atmospheric power could never be denied. We don't see those waters today. Maybe we prefer to forget their existence. The problem however is those still waters have with time turned into the deepest wells of depression. Unseen aquifers saturate everything above in the towns of South Wales. Sometimes I dream of those tunnels. I can feel only the waters, they offer no reflection. Their weight is something I cannot describe. It pulls me down. And there is a blackness like no other I have ever seen. I am submerged in a forgotten wilderness with no visible exit. They say nothing. That's what frightens me the most.

Should I be so inclined, the next thirty pages could provide a flood of miserable statistics from the post-war years, the subsequent and some might argue all too predictable decline of the industry, along with the economic fallouts of the soon to be forgotten political promises, to send the most sceptical into a state of provable submission. I could back-up my own elaborate theory of social depression and ritualistic decline to not only prove how educated I was on a subject both my forebearers and I had lived for so long it had become woven into the sequencing of our shared DNA. It could also show I was a bona fide voice rightfully joining in professionalised talking-head debates on matters of abjection and its intellectual concerns. Such a tragic irony in presenting the self as an "expert in poverty". Though it does seem to be one of the only areas for social commentary today where authenticity is not demanded. Everybody seems to have the right to talk about poverty, its embodied consequences, especially those who have never experienced it beyond their slumming experiences at university. For every single year that passes, things only seem to get worse for many in these towns. Generational unemployment and addiction are the only inheritance left by those who too often die too soon. Lasting wills and testaments merely providing debts of misery and inescapable loss. I could go further and pull the heartstrings by focusing on the plight of the valley's children. Continued malnourishment and widespread neglect might be recounted. Elaborate details could be offered on various indexes for calculating childhood deprivation and correlating proficiencies in the children's lack of any such attributes. Statistical measures may be served up on the lack of opportunities, which feeds endless debates about whether this is all about educational failures, bad parenting or a form of structural violence. None of this would however capture anything remotely human about the realities of living in a place that endured 100 years of depression.

Far too much time has been wasted in the company of social scientists of every ideological and radical badge-wearing stripe, who insufferably compete to be authentic voices for things nobody should experience. Suffering should not be a prizegiving pursuit or an accolade to be a further source of extracted value. Armed with elaborate formulas, too many theoretical saviours have carved out careers by promising to find the holy grail of insight into the unrequited meaning of social deprivation. Underwriting grandiose theories on the one true cause of it all, findings speak with a determined authority on behalf of the underclasses. None of which has made any lasting difference to the communities of neglect I intimately know and couldn't possibly hope to capture in a number or single theorem. There are thousands of inventive ways for conjuring approximate measures for despair. Often, they are set by moralists, who, equipped with well-intentioned rescue-the-world smiles or a healthy dose of bourgeois radicalism, conceal a new kind of saviour complex that fixates on rescuing the poor from their own wretchedness, invariably by following the moralist script that too often also depends upon seeing the poor as uneducated dupes. Economic suffering has its means and measures, there's no doubting this. It counts. Seldom, however, do they come from spreadsheets. I am not saying poverty is immaterial. On the contrary, the very basis for life is learned through the means of one's own destitution. Nor am I suggesting nothing meaningful can be said about the reality of economic denials. It should be a starting point for any conversation regarding so-called "privilege". What I am saying is 4.56 tells absolutely nothing about how a mother feels, how my mother felt when she cried holding her eight-year-old son who had taken 20 pence to buy a bar of chocolate, and instead of getting angry because she couldn't afford to buy potatoes for the next two days, reassured him that it wasn't his fault, even if the consequences for the family were significant. Nor can they capture what it meant for the same mother to walk in the cold and ask with tears rolling down her face the owner of the local newsagents to pay the small gift in instalments in the coming months, so I wouldn't wake up Christmas morning with nothing but that piece of black coal, which would have indicated I had misbehaved too much to receive anything that year.

Home was now far away from the estate. Still we lived on the cheapest street due to its proximity to the abandoned pit. Due to its situatedness on the side of the steep incline, the foundations of the last row of terraced houses cut into the mountain slopes with their elevated fronts accessed by a steep porch. This created an angled hollowed black space beneath the ground flooring, where streaming pools of water and rodents of various kinds gathered, whose peculiar noises I soon learned to identify. Peering through the cracks in the floorboards was mirrored by thoughts of what was peering back through the darkness. Damp was a permanent problem, especially in the back of the house. The terrace had three small bedrooms, though only two were occupied. There was no heating except in the living room which had a floating Cannon gas fire, and the character-building benefits of an outside toilet. It was resident to several very large arachnids, who conspired in their locations, ensuring the young child was never fully able to see them all without frantically scanning each of the far corners of cobwebbed stone and slate hut. Various methods were tried over the years to avoid their detection, from slowly opening the door and creeping in, to entering and trying to relieve as fast as humanly possible. Dark nights in the heavy rain made this an entirely more traumatic affair, especially when strong gusts of wind blew under the open-bottomed door and extinguished the candlelight. The weapon of choice for the clean-up was fittingly the *Sun* newspaper, which was cheaper and more lasting than the most coarse and rudimentary toilet rolls. From the outside, the home's only distinguishing feature was the red worn paint that surrounded its aged stone gables that was contrasted by a black, slowly rotting front door. We lived in number 13. Unlucky for some, they say. The home was sparsely populated with handed-down furniture and showed little sign of being part of the modern world. Only the living room was carpeted, though the stairs did have an eclectic mix of sample cuts acquired when my parents convinced the local store on several visits that they couldn't make up their minds on which to one buy. Carpet on the stairs was a luxury they couldn't entertain. There was a newly fitted bathroom at the back of the ground floor that was installed following a grant given to poor families as part of a government scheme aimed at improving hygiene and better sanitary health. It was situated behind the kitchen, which featured a single basin sink and a rented fridge and cooker. Both rooms had exposed concrete walls and varnished concrete floors to seal in the dust. The main downstairs back window was boarded up due to a large crack in the glass, which shattered during a storm and which my parents couldn't afford to replace. A broken pane on the backdoor was also covered in a cardboard-filled binbag, which, held in place by Sellotape, frequently blew off during the heavy rains. Without heating, winters were bitterly cold, and I would often wake to discover my thin net curtains stuck to the frosted windows. Much of my wintered childhood was located on the broken wooden staircase, which was the warmest part of the house, directly connected to the only room with any warmth.

A well-rehearsed cliché says children in poverty don't know they are poor because there is nothing to compare it with. Whoever repeats this has never lived in poverty, like those who say language hurts more than physical harm have never been punched to the ground and kicked repeatedly in the head. I won't go back there. Poverty is first felt as a microscopic division. Those who have barely anything are made to feel thankful they don't have nothing at all. It finds ways to shame those without, especially the young, who from their inception learn the relative torments of want. I was eight years old when poverty-consciousness knocked. And it arrived through the thing I then loved most of all: football. I was now old enough to try out for the local team at the boy's club conveniently situated at the end of the street. Although a year younger than other kids, I was selected due to my speed, which owed everything to my slender frame. But while already a seasoned pro when it came to the organised chaos of street football, I had no idea the move to a professional grassy game came at a cost. One notable benefit, however, was that for the very first time I could look forward to having a weekly vitamin infusion, which was charitably meted out in an indulgent way during half-time. Segments of oranges were provided, meaning I had my one portion a week. Fruit and football would be forever twinned in the mind of the unexpectant child. There was, however, a more pressing concern. Who was going to buy the boots? And why were some mocking the attire of others? I soon understood the pain. Having borrowed a pair from an older cousin for the first three matches, which were at least two sizes too big and to my estimation the reason why I hadn't scored any goals to date, the arrival of the Dunlop black leather shoe with moulded soles marked my passage into class warfare. Being the cheapest on the market, they tore both into your ankle and your pride every time you walked onto the pitch. I even unsuccessfully tried painting three stripes on the side of them to disguise their branding. Of course, I wasn't alone on this relatively poorer pitch of life. Others would also walk off the adult-sized parks, sodden from the rain, ankles and feet bleeding as the unforgiving leather left its mark along with the worn studs of the brutal defender from the opposing team (there was always one who took a particular dislike, cheered on by some over-eager parent), yet still armed with a beaming smile if the result went accordingly or game not lost. As the decade developed, the branding of everything continued apace. And for those of us who had walked onto the pitches of existence, the reminder was spectated by every footwear, winter coat, torn jeans and items never possessed.

The constancy of poverty is to weave feelings of shame deep into the fabric of time. It invokes peculiar measures those who seek to quantify its effects seldom discuss. As my mother meticulously carved the potatoes into exacting numbers of equal size to ensure we were all fed the same, I looked through the cupboard to try and find that sachet of sauce retrieved from my grandmother, who knew a woman working in the chip-shop. We never ate out during those years, nor did we even have the ability to buy takeaway from the fatty food outlets that provided their own Malthusian service by adding to the obesity and heart-attack rates. But at least we ate as a family, sat together in front of a rented television set, though anxiously consumed by the impending fear of the vanishing affordability of time. The appliance had a rotational dial on the side which started to click when the money was running out. Rented TVs were an early form of pay-per-view, which was amplified by the fact the electrical supply was also on a paid meter. As a family we therefore had to work out to the second what programmes to watch during the week to ensure there was enough banked in both to meet the demand. We tended not to watch anything during October and November, as we saved for the Christmas period when all the best things on television would be shown. Together we enjoyed most watching comedies, from the *Carry-On* films to shows such as *'Allo, 'Allo!* and *Cannon & Ball*. Kenny Everett was also a family favourite, having us sat on the sofa in shared fits of laughter as he paraded in drag and jived his brotherly love. Everett was brilliant at cutting through prejudice, all in the best possible bad taste. It is a shame he ended up supporting Thatcher. Time management was however an inaccurate science, often leaving us badly miscalculating and viewing pleasures cut in crucial moments. Being plunged into a complete darkness (physically and metaphorically) due to financial outages were very common, even if the grid was working perfectly fine.

When Thatcher arrived, we were already destitute. Her shame was to make poverty feel a million times worse. The leader who famously insisted there was no such thing as society, left the deprived with little but the desire to be rich and famous in towns marked by a permanent denial. The recession of the early 1980s (which was recorded as being the worst since the 1930s) had a devastating impact and would dramatically widen the income and wellbeing gaps between the rich and the poor.

Social security was savagely reduced, as inflation continued to rise, albeit less severely than in the discontented winter of 1979. Everything that could be privatised, would be privatised. Hence with social welfare seen as a market distortion; those who existed beyond the pale felt most the pain of its effects. Cuts in benefits were also matched by a change in culture. Despite the fact my father was medically declared incapable of working due to the severity of his physical and mental health, he would still be constantly subjected to humiliating means-testing to prove he wasn't fit for anything. This was demeaning for a man who wished nothing more than to live a dignified life. What does it say about the compassion of a state when parents are forced to fight in front of their children not to have what little they are provided taken away? A situation I sadly witnessed too many times, and which still pains me deeply to recall. I will never forget the suspicious ticking of that officious plastic wall clock on the interrogation room wall. I will never forget the condescending look on the sweaty, bearded face of the worker wearing that badly-fitting brown suit. And I will never forget those hopeless tears my mother cried as she left the Department for Social Services building wondering how we would get through another week, every week, knowing circumstances would never change. Policies were far more pernicious than agreeing whether or not to provide meagre levels of invalidity benefits on account of whether some bureaucrat agreed with medical opinions beyond his job grade. Frequent visits were made to the house to ensure the family hadn't accumulated any saleable items (such as televisions, etc), which might prove we were somehow defrauding the system. Installation of a fake exterior burglar system was enough to have the benefits suspended for a week based on the notion something inside was worth stealing. Why else would you need such a deterrent, despite the sharp rise in house invasions due to the growing heroin and glue epidemic blighting the village? We were meant to conform to the expected image of poverty, including the demands to sell items gifted, for this was a way the state could save money as its frontiers were allegedly rolled back. Having removed the record player from sight, my parents frequently hid behind the sofa when the inspectors were spotted peering through the windows of those we shared our destitution with further up the street, while asking the children to be silent as if they were playing some game of hide and seek with the watching state.

Cross-generational forms of insecurity are defined by lasting dependencies. Like a people cast out on the treacherous oceans of an unforgiving world, knowing they are going to be hit by wave after wave and unknowing if the next one will be even more ferocious, what's required is for somebody to come to the rescue. Ideas of social security, which can be directly traced back to the problems of the valleys, promised to do this. Yet how quickly the demands to help the vulnerable turn into a burden. Dependency is not care. It creates relationships of false hope. Dependency is an anchor. Not one that allows the castaway to find a sense of rootedness again. It pulls the dependent down, while they cling onto its chains with more and more desperation. Dependency turns everything into a transaction. Those who speak the language of dependency do so with a cold officiousness, even if the dependent is so marked with emotional scars that they can barely contain their feelings. Watching my parents trying their best to not beg for support revealed the inner-most workings of a politics of insecurity manufactured to make people ashamed of their plight. Dependency is opposed to dignity. It turns children into financial obligations, which in turn has the vulnerable internalise the weight to assume the very position of the anchor that's sinking deeper and deeper into the bottomless black ocean. So as the dependent learns, the anchor is no real security. It pulls everybody down, turning everyday life into a battle for togetherness and not allowing self-pity to freeze you and others from within. And as families learn, the normalisation of cultures of dependency can create cutting dynamics, where the very bonds of family and friendship are emotionally transacted because the victim has become us all. I will return to this later. Those who would have us believe a doting father who carries a child on their shoulders as they walk down the valleys streets see them as a dependent, would also be the same who turn love into sacrifice and marriage into a legal contract. We may rely upon one another, needing to be carried from time to time, but never in a way that creates bonds of unpayable debt that turn the desire to see the world from a different vantage point into a painful chore, which so often turns into anguish, resentment and doubt. This is not in any way to suggest there shouldn't be measures for social protection for the needy, based upon a truly ethical sense of care. People of the South Wales valleys need this more than anything. But it is to insist that if such protection strips people of their dignity and makes them wholly dependent upon the official coldness of power, it is no protection at all, for it merely adds to the descent. I recall the first time my young mother was asked to fill in the section on the form concerning how many children were in her loving care, provoking a response which could be both a question and an answer to all that was painfully wrong with the system. "Excuse me sir, what is a dependent?"

Dependency transacts suffering into a quantifiable assay with all its waits and measures. Means-testing in our reality meant paying the bare minimum. During the first twelve years of my existence, this qualified in numerical terms to a weekly benefit amounting to approximately £65 for a family of four. Mortgage payments each month were £130 for a house my parents purchased for £3,600. Leaving aside the essential running cost of electricity, gas and water rates, rental costs for appliances, along with clothing. To have some perspective, the cost of other goods at the time included the *Sun* newspaper (toilet roll) 10p, a weekly loaf of bread 28p, frozen chips 60p, pint of milk 18 ½p, cornflakes 57p, Maxwell House coffee 84p, orange squash 54p and tinned beans 19p. If the family was feeling completely indulgent, they might save a little for six chocolate biscuits, which were 29 ½p, or a packet of jelly at 25p. This didn't include any thoughts about home improvements, birthdays, Christmas or holiday breaks, which during this time was largely confined to daytrips with local chapels and clubs. Some items at the time were however beyond all reach, such as a kilo of bananas, for example, which cost in the region of £1, and small joint of beef around £3. A black-and-white television in 1980 would have cost £110 and a colour set around £250. The quarterly phoneline rental was £13.45, which we couldn't possibly consider. More importantly still for a child of those times, Patrick trainers, as worn by many Liverpool players, were £14.95 for the most basic pair. They remained the stuff of dreams. I had a poster of one such pair on my wall with the mail order label strictly guarded just in case (who after all knew where this so-called money stuff really came from?), alongside *Shoot* magazine posters of Diego Maradona, Kenny Dalglish and one I had acquired from a magazine I found on a train featuring the Phantom Flan Flinger from the hit television series *Tiswas*.

Like the apparition on my bedroom wall poster, poverty is often hiding in plain sight, just waiting for the right time to strike. And that's what makes it so senseless. I still struggle to make sense of it. It truly makes no sense. How can we step back from it, observe its effects and still rationalise its presence? Still, it lingers. And still I carry it around with me, knowing it defined me more than any other identity, even if I delude myself into believing I have left it all behind. For poverty creates an inescapable economy of feeling that is crystalised by an emptiness that can never be learned from any textbook. It can only be experienced. Yet there is no definitive explanation. Nor could I possibly begin to properly do any justice to its lasting condition in a thousand essays. What I can say is poverty has cast a fatalistic cloud across the towns of South Wales without any silver lining; covering over stars of the future as it weathers a torrential system of neglect that promises only more of the same. Poverty has its children believe the world has no reason to ever want or need their presence, and that the only identity they really possess is one defined by an inescapable shame. We learned to embody that guilt, even as we learned to laugh in the face of our shared plight. Poverty has parents weeping at the altar of hunger, reflected their exhausted tears back in a shattered infinity mirror full of broken glass. Poverty has the impoverished raging with an absent silence, knowing nobody listens to the simple cries of their hearts. Poverty pushes families into a nervous system of hopelessness, where the pain is only sated once the world is sedated and has given up. Poverty condemns a society to a permanent state of want without wanting, teaching its inhabitants to be obedient to almost nothing, nothing in fact which is less than barely at all. But the social clamour of this is more pernicious still, as it condemns the poor for being unread authors of their own plight. For poverty tries its best to violate the very bonds of togetherness, savagely turning the poor into imposters of the self. Poverty creates intractable geographies of wretchedness, internalising the trauma as abandoned bodies are cast out on despondency's shores. Poverty kills any sense of the promise, the wishful, the dignified; leaving its victims to simply imagine living as a somebody, anybody, elsewhere and outside of this forgotten land. And poverty infects the minds of its claimants, it is a viral depression whose infectious hold is seldom cleansed and whose daily stories are seldom less ever told. I feel the weight of these stories behind every closed door. I know the weightful neglect shared, for mine and ours was a story every single one of my childhood friends might recount.

Evidence of clinical forms of depression are all too evident in the valleys. My father suffered more severely than most. His life was especially tough. Thus far, all the ancestors I have referred to belonged to my mother's side of the family. I know less about my father's side and have little care in finding out. I know his grandfather arrived in the valleys at the start of the mining boom and worked on the railways, helping to lay the tracks that took the coal and profits out of the Rhondda. He was killed by a passing train while working late at night. The rest just has me dwelling about what happens when a character becomes so dominant in a family that even the prospect of talking about them still creates anxiety and trepidation. Not all tyrants are seen the same, because they often treat people differently. Some are awfully kind to those they favour, while being awful to others. Nobody's life is universally felt. Dominating personas know this better than most. I struggled however to watch someone I deeply cared about trying to gain approval but receive nothing back. I found this even harder to come to terms with, for it was a situation I couldn't relate to, having grown up in a condition that was at least rich with love. Still, there is no better place to start learning about politics than one's close surroundings. What I witnessed provided a lesson in strict patriarchy of the worst possible kind. One that still had descendants looking to praise and shed tears when the cold body turned colder. The valleys were populated by many like this, as much as they were home to the dignified and gentle. And the marks they left could last a lifetime and beyond the grave. Before his illness which struck when I was two years old, my father was already emotionally damaged. After the procedures, he was thrown into state of deep depression. Part of the move to the new home was to help with his condition. Still, he was unable to leave its walls for around three years, later taking weekly steps to find comfort in one equally marked house, then one determinably cut street at a time. He remained wracked with guilt. The guilt of being ill. The guilt of being unable to provide for his family. The guilt of not being loved. The guilt of being born. The guilt of fearing death. From the age of eight, my father wouldn't go anywhere without my company.

But the depression here is not simply individual, even if it reaches deep into the psychosis of every living child. It's collectively shared. While the region's dependency on antidepressants has reached epidemic levels and has frequently captured the deriding attention of national media outlets, mental health charities and local advocates continue to remind of its links to the lasting economic conditions. Depression in the valleys is marked by an ecosystem of abandonment, loss and neglect. Manifest through an ecology of suffering, the withering sense of psychological decline is held down by a weathered permanence. The depression that continually casts its shadows over the people of the valleys is one of a slow catastrophe. The Romans never managed to conquer the people of these parts. Yet while we look to them now for guidance in terms of the fall from glory, from Empire to ruination, the same tale is played out here in the ruins of a landscape far from where monuments to Caesars reside. The deep, black cracks that gave the valleys its identity now appear like a wound in time. They have become an empty cavern, into which nothing meaningful is added. What after all becomes of a people when hope is fully extracted from the earth? Yet what I have since learned is that the losses reveal traces of a past, and how the simplest sign of decay is another memorial to a decayed passage of forgotten time. Each time I return, I see further signs of this slow catastrophe, time lapsed only by my absence from the place. Another store boarded-up, another chapel vacated, another public library closed, another factory with its gates chained, another small business failing like the rest, another promise fallen by the wayside, all signs of ruination as painfully normal as the rotting doors at the garden ends of most terraced homes. Cracking paint tells its own story. The slow corrosion of life has become more than a metaphor for the violence of post-industrial times. There is a seeping pain also corroding the oxide blood of a peoples whose thoughts on finding salvation are battered every time the winds bring yet another volley of rain down through the vale to cut with sure repetition whatever dreams remained. Depression thus reveals itself here to be an ecology of pressure and a lingering sentence of recognisable doubt. This may sound all too contradictory and intellectualising. Yet, as anybody who lives in the valleys knows all too well, what appears to be a contradiction is often just the way things work in the absence of any resolution. Indeed, we often embrace the contradiction, for not only is it the way things were intended to appear, but through its embrace we are at least able to break out of the dogmatic certainties all ideologues impose.

The 1980s were kickstarted by a recession born of another energy crisis in Iran a year earlier. While the subsequent national decline resulted in many inner-city riots, including Toxteth and Brixton, and a notable increase in unemployment in all poor areas, especially the valleys, the period would also be defined by further geopolitical concerns that left a local impression. I will return to Argentina later. It was the summer of 1985. A number of us were playing on the disused and rusty machinery just up the mountainside adjacent to the boy's club. It was a death trap with inner spaces replete with large rotational spikes, which made it all the more compelling to explore. There was a bright red button with the label "danger" attached, which we could never get to work. I believe it may have had something to do with crushing, cleaning and sorting the surface coal, which given its focus on saving things of value would have no doubt meant we would have been utterly doomed had it been of working order. We were inspecting the carcass of a dead lamb, which we figured must have escaped and got trapped inside. The stench was unbearable, but we toughed it out. Maybe we were all just kids to the slaughter? Another local boy from the street appeared in the distance frantically waving his arms. He was a good kid, though prone to unexplained violent outbursts from time to time. We were born in the same month, which he tried to convince made us brothers of a kind. On many evenings after school, he could be seen walking the streets. Neighbours worked out an unofficial rota, concerning whose turn it was to feed him. He would just enter, sit and eat as if it was the most natural thing in the world, while never failing to ask if there was a biscuit to be had at the end of the meal. His mother was a cheap alcoholic, by which I meant she drank whatever was the cheapest and made her forget. She could barely speak, having drank bleach one forgetful night. I would say she was lucky to be alive, though she probably didn't see it that way. She was both manic and depressive, both at once on occasions. Still the boy had a smile on his face. He was sent to remind us it was time to go on the expedition. Or should I say, to begin our charity walk for the emaciated children of Ethiopia. I had managed to get the sworn pledges of nearly £2 (which was an enormous amount by my estimation) should I complete the arduous task. In truth, it wasn't really a test at all, for all we needed to do was walk to the top of the mountain through the well-trodden valley where the Maindy Colliery used to reside. It was around 4km to the abandoned school bus at the top of the old mining road pass. I've no idea how that got there, though we did reason that a bunch of kids plotted an escape one night and simply vanished and were never seen again. Given I had already run 12km in the local half marathon only a few weeks prior, this should be a breeze. Besides, we were committed as there were starving children to feed.

Around 40 adults and young boys set out on this humanitarian march. While some grown-ups were sent to accompany, they were the ones that really needed keeping an eye on as a number started sweating profusely only five minutes into the climb. Another local lad who was probably the toughest person I have ever known and who I learned recently passed away spent most of the journey performing like Freddie Mercury with the sleeves of his white T-shirt rolled up over his shoulder. The entire street had gathered around to watch the Live Aid concert, which had taken place the previous week. It had a remarkable impact, which is easy to be cynical about today. Even then, we knew he stole the show. The sun was blazing and two of our guides decided they should stop halfway and keep look out. Typically, however, as we started to get nearer the top, the familiar presence of the ominous grey clouds rolled down the small valley, which prompted the tough Freddie, for reasons still unbeknown to me, to take off his top and start bellowing out "I want to break free". Genius. Right on cue the heavens opened, and a debate started to rage about whether we should carry on to the summit or call it a day. Nobody would after all know if we didn't complete the task. Besides, what kind of person wouldn't pay up given the cause? A number decided to summon a retreat, though a few of us decided we needed to plough on. Observed from a distance, there must have been something quite beautiful to the sight of a group of malnourished and dishevelled children led in unison by a tough Freddie Mercury wannabe singing in the rain as they optimistically thought about helping children on the other side of the world. The poorest are often the most charitable and hospitable. I had made this walk a number of times. But in that moment in time, my eyes set on a powerful natural relic I have since found to be so poignant to the life of this small valley. When the rains fall, the mass of water tends to accumulate on the top of the mountain, which eventually finds its way down through a waterfall and the river that once ran through the mine. Because of the fractured nature of the earth, however, some of it continually seeps through the sides of a vertical stretch, which has been cut and shows its deep, black face. The boys carried onto the bus. I stood for a while staring at the weeping wall. Who was she crying for? The lost children of the valleys? The starving children of Africa? I walked past her again in January of 2022. She is still weeping tears for the forgotten of this world.

Endless government and thinktank reports tell the same story of the valley's economic plight. With near 200,000 persons living in the most desperate conditions, very few areas match the scale and depth of its destitution. Close to a quarter of its inhabitants exist in a permanent state of social depression, affecting every aspect of life, from an impoverished cradle through to a premature grave. Those who die here, tend to be born here. That is another defining feature of no-go areas. Depression and death, both tragedies render a people immobile. And the only thing successfully regenerating is the cycle of despair, for a largely white community homogenised by deprivation and a manufactured vulnerability from elsewhere. The vast majority of the most deprived wards in all of Wales are found in the southern valleys, and national comparisons are perhaps most readily made with the most rundown areas of Liverpool, which, as noted, the people here still share political and social affinity with. With an estimated 10% of the working population having never found any gainful employment, it also shows some of the highest rates of permanent illness and disability in the United Kingdom. A sickness is out there and is slowly eating the people from within. Whatever the measure, the valleys appear close to the top of all the metrics gauging social "under-performance". Are they the left behind? Or merely left to rot? School-leavers with no qualifications are staggeringly high in number, while those working in professional roles is minimal by comparison to nearly all other areas in western Europe. What the valleys have tended to produce abundantly is elementary school teachers and nurses, which along with solicitors and doctors remains the most secure employment in the region. All of which are fully revealing of the character of the local economy — one that continually needs to care for the young and attend to the chronic conditions of lasting depression, while attending to those who invariably fall through the cracks in the worn face of the depressed earth.

During the Great Depression of the 1920s, traces of what would later become termed Ghost Towns would appear more prominent and lasting. But what exactly was being haunted in such places? Did they require the complete absence of people? And do we not invoke the term to save us from the real truth of the nightmare? The Ghost Town label has most often been applied the world over to former mining and single industry villages, who literally have the life sucked out of them and show no prospect of recovery. We wander through the ruins of entire ways of living, knowing they belong to a history whose spirits have also been defeated. Yet what if we turned this around and see the past itself as walking among the present? Dereliction is a key symbolic indicator for these sites stripped of all vibrancy and vitality, spaces where all that remains are traces of a severe rupture or trauma in the very productive fabric of existence. But what of the people who followed? Are they not defined by a wound they can no longer even explain? By a tragic loss that runs so deep they can no longer put it into words, let alone locate? Traced only by memories of a time that was once chronicled, making them the ghosts of history which now forgets to record they are even alive. Often, as with the valleys, the process begins with the appearance of idleness, notably by men who feel disempowered and emasculated. Empty tunnels deep beneath the earth become metaphors for soon to be hollowed-out lives, emptied existences, which will eventually only leave a presence to unsettle landscapes of the present. While the start of the exorcism of valleys towns began in the 1920s, with lost men occupying the streets, stood around as if they were taking part in one perpetual Sabbath as they awaited some kind of divine intervention or at least economic redemption, slowly the collective bonds withered, and their fading shadows left to haunt themselves. But the haunting was already there. Shadows of an economic mire produced an army of displaced souls, trapped in a moment that offered no escape. There was nothing to do, all of the time. So as the streets of Merthyr, Tonypandy and Treorchy slowly emptied as the twinned diseases of depression and decay took hold, so the social and the psychological became entwined. Yet much of the tragedy remained hidden underground. It's hard to imagine an absence when it cannot be witnessed with naked eyes. But other signs are all too visible. While main streets in local towns managed to recover for a while and return to some kind of normality, slowly they would succumb to external forces and find themselves unable to compete with the monopolising powers of the free market. Today the main street of my town is a pale reflection of what it was even in the 1980s, when the decline was accelerated beyond all measure and recovery. Despite the hardship, valley streets were once bustling and full of independent traders, from "Bracchi" Italian cafes (named after the first Italian family to settle in the Rhondda and open their establishments), local fruit and vegetable stores, working men's clubs, community halls and libraries, sweet shops, newsagents, post offices, high street banks, iron mongers, butchers, repair shops and other locally essential conveniences. Very few towns have retained any of these and their memory is quickly fading. When a haunting becomes unknown, it cannot be easily lifted for if there is a memory, it's a reminder of an unnameable loss. She who can no longer be spoken, except named: Rhondda. She whose spirit is now permanently left looking out from behind the weeping wall. As long as people can remember, the valleys have collectively experienced what can only be called the psychic life of abandonment. And it has been so debilitating it was only a matter of time before both the elderly and the young started to permanently fall into the shadows. Living apparitions in these ghosted towns would become altogether more fatalistic.

School was unbearable that Monday morning. A weight of sadness burdened the air as the terrible news greeted the children arriving, unaware of the pain the young boy must have felt. Never before had so many children in this school cried in such a collectively grief-stricken way. The sense of trauma was visible in the shaking hands of those who kept frantically running their fingers through their mottled hair, as they tried to excavate from their minds some kind of explanation. Two of his close friends started fighting each other in the playground area away from the gathered crowds as new tides of the disbelieving arrived. Normally a ritualistic daily sport that had the watching spectators baying for blood and gravel-marked battle scars, today we knew this fight was different, so we ran over to separate them and remind them it wasn't what he would have wanted. Frustrated and guilty punches turned into inconsolable hugs. One of them apparently made a joke about the incident. It wasn't sick. The sickness lay elsewhere. Humour was just a familiar way of coping with devastating loss. So much confusion, it hardly seemed real, even if we knew it would have a marked bearing. So many questions, which only he could answer. Why would such a popular and jovial boy take his own life? I had hung out with him only a few weeks earlier, as we bumped into each other and spent the afternoon chatting about nothing. The nature of his death only added more to the sense of tragedy. Yet maybe by taking his own life in such a public way he was telling us something more about our own plight? Or maybe he had simply just had enough of it all? Numerous pupils from the school had died prematurely before. Though to our estimation they were mostly drop-outs and troubled souls, who once in a while we cautiously came across sniffing glue or whatever else they might decide to consume in a place where other forms of consumption were limited. Their deaths were never mourned. It simply meant there was one less hazard to contend with at the local train station during the night. How providing the means to sedate those who wish to forget the misery of their plight so often appears the cheapest cure. But what were so many really crying for that Monday morning? Was it for the boy who would become part of a new depressing chapter in the life of the valleys? Or was it for themselves? Maybe they were both linked in some way? His suicide touched something I still cannot fully explain.

Like many problems in the valleys, as the years wear on things tend to get worse. The realisation these communities were facing a suicidal crisis of epidemic proportions captured the international media attention back in 2008. Focus centred on Bridgend and the tragic loss of so many young teens in quick succession within a ten-mile radius. Whatever we think of the causes, some of the British press rightly caused outcry in local communities, as they sensationally wrote of the devastating losses with headlines such as "Death-Cult Town". Enough evidence was provided to refute any such claims. If there was a fatalistic cult of contagion, it wasn't located in a small teenage pact. The rise of suicides in the valleys of South Wales is one of the most difficult subjects to deal with as its personal effects are known by everybody. For better and certainly for worse, it is nigh-on impossible in the valley towns to be "not known" and your fate is public knowledge. Suicide is also amongst the most urgent problems, especially given the prevalence, which predictably means the valleys again appear near the top in national statistical comparisons. But what does this reveal about the history of the place? We know it is easier to say the disproportionate incidence of suicide among the young here is "complicated", and while there are patterns, ultimately each case should still be considered as another indication of an individual's ability to deal with significant mental health issues. And yet, do such explanations provide yet another example of reducing complex social problems to questions of individual psychosis? Hence, in the process, this precludes the necessary insight to deal properly with the psychic life of power, especially for those who feel they have none and are left to take this one final devastating choice. Mindful that suicides among young girls (as in Bridgend) is a growing problem — indeed I have lost two immediate cousins this way — what's blighting the valleys is the exponential rise in young male suicides between the ages of 16 and 44, which by far account for the largest single grouping. How else should this be accounted for, if not the crisis of masculinity? It's all too easy to say men of the valleys just need to "speak about their feelings"! There was a time when talking about one's emotions were more a private affair and suicide was never such a problem. What has changed today is a social system in which young white men are struggling to find any meaning in a world where everyone is asked to talk about identity, but theirs is denied; a cultural system in which young white men are being asked to embrace their vulnerabilities, while stripping them of the very qualities that might allow them to deal with difficult times; an economic system in which young white men are continually being told they should aspire to whatever, knowing full well that to be born in the valleys means the chances are less with each rotation of the clock, which reminds them of how static the empty time of social depression can truly be; and a political system in which the very idea of community has been supplanted by new media technologies, which promote a vapid individualism and only exacerbate the hyper-anxieties felt about all perceived deficits — which for the peoples of the valleys are the only thing they have in any abundance. Faced with these conditions, is there any surprise desperate young men in these towns try to find a lasting way out?

"We love a good drama," the people of Rhondda can be heard crying on the streets of their terraced confinement. We have befriended pathos, finding comfort in the darkness of its embrace. It's hard not to be fatalistic. We have endless charts projecting the bleak truth of our lives. But things could be worse, the mothers of the valleys continually remind. Depression is met here by an optimising sense of the tragic. Children versed in cemetery rhymes, we continually wear black armbands, mourning the fated passage of time. Stoics of a unique kind, finding something of meaning in the complaints of the soul, mastering stories that laugh without lamenting the open wounds of a cracked heart. Maybe that is why we still find so much comfort in narratives of blood. It's never about purity or God-given rights. It's about a raging desire to release a passion that refuses to die. We remain a passionate people, that much can't be denied. Too passionate some might say, but that's their own version of the crime. So still there remains some defiance, despite all the odds. A fatalism is there, but it's never totalising or complete. A fight for dignity still remains, even if it looks defeated all the same. A battle against the sedation, which has for as long as I can remember told the people to accept their inevitable and natural place. Yet, I remind myself now, I am an outsider, again. Looking down upon a valley that is coal-tinted and still there. I am caught between two lenses of a tragic romanticism that eventually fades to black. So, I am a walking contradiction. I was made that way. And I still carry some of that depression inside of me, knowing its presence, yet thankfully until now keeping the shadows at bay. But I know the dangers. And I feel the concerns. What I don't want to become is another extractor, feeding like others off the real pains of hunger, which still persist and gnaw away at the bodies of many who live in the valleys today. There is nothing worse than an outsider who becomes a seller of suffering. And nothing worse than a trader who benefits from the plight.

Temperatures had never been higher in the valleys. A searing heat was revealing of a time when everything was burning. The march of progress was matched only by the warmth of the people. Any cold was sated by the embracing winds carried across the mountainous pass. Even the skies seemed to be raining fire as the stars looked down with a heavenly mix of envy and pride. What made a people so determined? What made them laugh in the face of everything nature had conspired to send their way? They were truly triumphant, collective masters in the crafting of existence. This would be the warmest day on record. I am not referring here to the thermostatic conditions as marked by the science. But the temperate state of life, which was scorching the earth, leaving alight footprints in the ground. But this invariably came at a price. The heat could be felt, but it was impossible to see. The barometric compression of the white heat covered the landscape in an impenetrable fog. Every now and again, monochromatic silhouettes could be made out in the distance. They moved and shapeshifted in unison, but each knew their place and purpose as if guided by some inexorable force. And what was that force, if it wasn't some kind of destiny? For even the fires appeared to have absorbed all other colours as they enacted their ascending fiery dance. This could be heaven; then again, it could be hell. The young child needed to escape.

Guided by intuition alone, they made their way past the felled trees and through the open expanse beside the last remnants of the ancient woodlands. Eventually they reached the summit, emerging out of the smoke line which blanketed the now hidden valley below. It was as if being above the clouds. In the near distance, an elderly man was sat on a jettisoned stone. He was familiarly dressed, with dark trousers that were held up by black braces, which partially covered his white vest. His flat cap matched his shoes in the tattered and worn department. The child thought they recognised him, though it was difficult to tell now his face was clean and the deep marks of history were more visible on his welcoming face. The elderly man invited the child to come and sit beside him, as he pulled out some leaves he'd gathered earlier from beside the railway track and gently loaded them into his smoking pipe. In leaner times to come, the desperate locals would refer to this as "*Bacci Dai*". He was ahead of the times. As the child looked across the horizon, they noticed how the clouds now appeared like a calm and tranquil lake. Its white was so dense, it was reflecting back the deep blue sky. It seemed like all colours had returned. And the lands themselves were doubly blessed in reality and promise. "It's going to rain soon", the elderly man spoke with the confidence of somebody who knew how to read the signs, "and it will feel like it's never going to stop". The young child continued to rock back and forth their dangling feet, which were hovering over the smoky lake, as they kept looking into the distance. "It's always been raining here", the wise sage added, "do you want me to tell you why?" The child politely shrugged their shoulders, hoping the man would indeed tell his tale of the eternal rains.

Chronos the God of Time realised his majestic red dragon needed a place to rest. So he set about carving a deep wound into the earth, far away from all sources of danger. When a dragon sleeps, they do so for centuries, so it was important to ensure the balance of nature was maintained. Unbeknown to Chronos, however, Plutus the God of Wealth had instructed man to invade his lair. One notable profiteer was especially determined to capture the dragon's fire, so set about chaining it to a single magical stone that was connected to the centre of the earth. Instead of awakening with rage, however, as the profiteer had expected, thereby enabling him to capture the essence of their fire, the beast slowly started to vanish from sight, until one day it finally disappeared. The profiteer now became mad with rage and set about chaining his fellow humans, commanding them to breathe fire. Knowing this was impossible, he set about to harvest their energies in more demanding ways. What the profiteer didn't know was the dragon had simply allowed itself to be absorbed into mother earth, leaving only its oily, black veins visible beneath the surface of the ground. But he couldn't tell anyone about this, especially Chronos, who he knew would be truly vengeful. Still alive, the dragon continued to breathe, which slowly covered the land with permanent clouds. Since the dragon's breath helped the beast regulate its fire, it was full of water and thunderous cries. The chained dragon thus cast an unintentional curse, which explains why it will continue to rain and the black veins of the earth continue to weep. According to the legend, the curse will only be lifted once the dragon is released and given back to Chronos who, still searching for the lost beast, has frozen the place in time. It is said this will only happen when a child who is born of tragedy stands upon the chaining stone and sings with the most angelic voice "The Song of the Valley". Fearing, however, that this story would be lost to time, the chained villagers instructed the secret society of poets to paint from the colours of the mountains an image of the dragon on worn pieces of cloth. They were to be flown for all to see as a secret reminder of the dragon's and the peoples' fate. The young child stood up upon the stone and smiled at the elderly man. They whistled a merry tune and descended back down into the clouds. The rains began to fall.

THE WAR AT HOME

The sound of the incendiary was deafening. A murderous breeze accompanied its plaintive reverberation, swiftly followed by the particles of a blackened cloud rising from the earth and eclipsing the sombre light guiding these grounded souls. All that could be seen in the near distance was the glare of a hundred men's eyes, peering through the dark and into the desolate nether lands beyond. They were camouflaged by a permanent nightfall, which had descended over all existence, across all time. What hope was there really for a life caught up beneath the wings of the angels of history? How many explosions would be felt by these men from forces never properly located? Still, the siren rings out, yet another in their unit has been taken by a senseless loss of life. They heard the wailing and the screams, knowing immediately who had their limbs broken by that indiscriminate engine of worldly destruction. And still the eyes look onward, fixed on the invisible roadway ahead, waiting for a signal, for at least a sign meant that not everything was lost and there was something to be recovered. A silence descends as sure as the spirits of the takers have been awakened. The only noise heard was the sound of their heavy breathing and the beating of their veins. They know he is dead, but who amongst them will have to tell the children? But even in death, there is the possibility for the ordinary to appear extraordinary. Out of the distance she rides, majestic and strident, carrying forth on this savage terrain the body of their fallen comrade on her back. The appearance of the burning white horse in this world of blackness, overlooked by a respectful wall of a hundred white eyes, still stirs the imagination and says something quite magical to raise the spirits of these dejected bodies cast down in this God-forsaken hole. The heat has been unbearable, but suddenly a coldness rises. The temperature of a moment is inexplicable when death returns. In the shadowing breath of this wild, only the horse speaks, and it speaks to the language of an ancient fire. Her ancestry could also be traced back to the earliest Celtic times, roaming the highland moors as defiant and yet reliable as any companion that once strode the molten earth. But the men here are fluent in her verse, knowing her tragic lines as intimately as the depths of their sorrows. There is a sublime quality to her movement, proud and defiant, even if she is also beaten by time and suffering the same as these poor men. As she passes, each man bows his head, but seeing everything as only those who live in the dark truly know how to see. She looks beside and down upon them as they kneel, silhouetted like a murder of blackbirds respectfully mourning the lost crimson hope of a forgotten sun. Or is it a congress she sees anticipating the next deliverance? How many of them will fall this way? How many will be shot through by bullets that rain from a merciless storm? Too many of them can already see their fate as foretold by the ideological profits who have determined their cause. All know they will eventually die in this town.

One of the strange novelties of the Welsh valleys is the relative lack of World War II memorials. Cardiff was bombed and Swansea mercilessly blitzed. But the valleys were largely unscathed. Unlike elsewhere, not every grandfather in these parts had heroic tales of what they did in foreign lands and the part they played in World War II. It wasn't that they were absolved from duty nor compelled to show their allegiance. While the call up for men during the early years of the war led to labour shortages in the pits as a few thousand signed up for the cause, by 1943 the situation had dramatically altered. Workers were even contentiously brought into the valleys, causing a notable rift between the locals and the later awarded "Bevin Boys", who benefitted from better supplies and working equipment, along with having more favourable roles away from the trials of the deep seams. Yet even those conditions were undoubtedly full of dangers. Some were also forced into the pits due to their conscientious objections, which created its own toxic climate as much as it did on the battlefields for those who refused to shoot enemy soldiers who were recruited from the same underclasses. At least one in ten eighteen-year-olds would be subsequently drafted into the mines instead of carrying out military service. For the able-bodied men of the Rhondda who were free from injury, their national duty was to be served, like every other day, fighting at the face. Coal was essential to the war effort and so the men had to stay behind. There are very few plaques or memorials to remind us of this. No medals for bravery handed out to them. And yet, while the soldiers that left those ships at Barry docks ended up on the blood-soaked beaches of Normandy, fighting to the death to claim distance on the ground, the miners kept digging for their yards down below. Like young men who waded on their stomachs through rat-infested and flooded trenches, which cut into the surface of the earth, those at home still endured the same conditions out of sight in the tunnels of South Wales. Both thankful for having survived just another day, living in fear of the toxic clouds that could arrive to remind them that terror truly was ecological, shell-shocked by the climactic sounds of explosions, scarred by the fate of history, slowly losing the will to live or to fight in conditions that seemed like they were living a hell on earth. But for the valiant men here, there would be no end to their predicament. Life was a daily struggle and the logic of violence part of the everyday fabric of mere existence.

The valleys have a long and perilous relationship to the history of war. At the start of what was arguably the very first modern conflict — the Napoleonic War — the town of Merthyr Tydfil proved to be strategically vital to the effort. Recognised at the time to be the iron capital of the world, the town was noted for having the most squalid and violent living conditions in Victorian Britain. This would invoke comparisons with conditions of life on plantations in Africa and elsewhere.

As the renowned pacifist Gwynfor Evans, Plaid Cymru's first elected Member of the British Parliament and former President, observed during this period, "Little difference could be discerned between her economy and that of a colony". The Napoleonic Wars ran from 1803–1815. It was the very first war in which soldiers were recruited from Wales to fight in a battle for some external cause, which had nothing to do with them whatsoever. Following Napoleon's model, mass conscription soon became a reality on the continent. It was also war that entrenched the idea of "Britishness" as a unifying concept forged in the theatres of overseas lands. Like the iron produced in Merthyr, Pax Britannia drew its strength from the molten earth, while leaving its people to battle within their own minds between the forces of poverty and patriotism. Coal was already in high demand during the period for smelting the iron for armaments. While Napoleon took control of French coal production, the first pit in the valleys was sunk in 1809. Its strategic importance within the military diagram for power should not be underestimated. War fuels war. And it would increasingly rely upon that which was born from and could return a blackness to the earth. The steam engine also arrived in 1811, which, although having little impact in the war against Napoleon, would be key in the conflicts which followed, most notably the savagery that tore Europe apart a century later. Thousands from the valleys would perish in World War I. Again, for reasons which had very little to do with them. This war was ultimately still a battle between competing colonial powers. True to form, it recruited en masse those who were seen as utterly disposable to the ruling classes. Millions from the underclasses of society perished, slaughtering one another for a cause that would have little benefit to their own lives and desperate living conditions. For the mining soldiers, they faced the further indignity of arriving home, finding either there was no longer any work for them, or their jobs had been taken by others. Still, the call to Britishness was effectively mobilised in the name of protecting smaller nations from aggression, while workers of the world were divided like never before. While the effects of these divisions amongst the workers on the battlefields of Europe are recorded in the 40 million casualties, divisions within the valleys were no less fractious. Keir Hardie was a notable here in his conscientious objection to the war. Hardie brought his message to the streets of the valleys and was cheered and heckled in equal measure by crowds who saw him either as committed to the socialist cause or a treasonous man who should be imprisoned. Hardie was following the pacifistic lead already set in the valleys by certain non-conformist leaders who spoke out against conflict. The chapels would later change their position on the war. It was said Hardie died a broken man, one year into the conflict, in 1915. By 1918, miners from the valleys were being conscripted, hundreds of which were imprisoned for their refusal to fight. What could possibly be salvaged from this barbaric tempest? If the rumours were true, perhaps the most evocative image of that entire devastating affair — the mythologised football game at the Christmas Day truce of 1914 — would have featured boys from the valleys as part of the Welsh fusiliers, who were on the front that particular day. Did they find some solace of humanism as those darkened skies cast a long shadow, which meant the sodden valley playing fields would never be the same?

The interwar years began with a remarkable flourishing in two distinct visions for society: the artistic and the technical. Indeed, while the period was notably tough for many in places like the valleys, for others the 1920s were roaring with a newfound optimism and bourgeois sense of confidence about the future. If European art would give us abstract expressionism, the technological world truly ran apace, notably inspired by the profound transformation in the mechanical organisation of production, which was later titled by the Marxist Antonio Gramsci as "Fordism". But as the decade wore on, the plight of the underclasses spread and the technological vision for human progress challenged by those who recognised the myth connecting technology with human betterment.

More technology either made humans alienated from the means of production or redundant (which was always destined to be the endpoint), while the owners of the industrial means saw their personal fortunes increase exponentially. The impact on war was also telling. World War I was all about bodies. It was fought on open fronts by men whose numbers alone made a difference. World War II was a different beast. Of course, it still required the expendable bodies of the masses, who could be brought to the slaughter. But it also ushered in the shift towards a kind of Total War made possible by industrial mechanisation. Bodies of men cavaliered around the world by the unrivalled might of the coal-powered Naval frigates were less important than the machinic power of planes, tanks and bombs. How ironic the very war that gave rise to the demands for accelerated technological advance would, in the end, prove to be fatal to the livelihoods of the miners in the valley. While the war economy saved the valleys for a while, it also gave rise to a desire to fully mechanise productive capacities in the name of better working conditions. This appealed to a galvanised belief in the wonder of technological pursuits. What looks progressive to some, however, often appears as a kind of dangerous and uncompromising fanaticism to others. When it was over, the war that gave us Hiroshima and Nagasaki didn't result in a deep and lasting reflection on the head-long rush into some technologically-driven vision of progress, which was waning during the Great Depression. It gave it new momentum. In fact, the naked appeal to technological advance was increasingly presented as the surest, indeed the only, way to alleviate the most pressing social problems, all the while it made more and more of the men from the valleys less productively relevant. There is still a strange quietness surrounding this history of technology and the valleys today. Still, it's easy to understand why people are seduced, especially if the shiny lights of progress emanating from commanding machines promise the future.

Despite the demands to stay and work in the pits, a significant number did lose their lives fighting overseas in World War II.

It's likely many signed up as they simply didn't trust the return to some kind of coal salvation, even if they numbered much less in comparison. But this was a war where the very idea of the frontline was turned inside out. Britain was being attacked and the country facing the prospect of being invaded and conquered by another colonising force. The War at Home thus took on many novel features, even if the idea of being colonised by an external enemy wasn't entirely alien to the ancestors of peoples in these towns. The blackouts must have been felt rather peculiarly in the valleys. Many there were used to the darkness. But the aerial threat was all too real; indeed, we might argue it was the defining feature of the war. The covering of windows and absence of light at night would be complemented by the appearance of sandbags for the first time. They would be deployed on many occasions later in battles with a more natural foe. Because of the aerial nature of the threat, however, internal suspicions of outsiders became more pronounced. A notable impact on populations in the valleys would be the rounding up of Italians, notably families like the Bracchis, who had become a well-integrated part of the local community. One of the most tragic outcomes of this policy would be the sinking of the *SS Arandora Star*. This former cruise ship was requisitioned by the military and deployed to transport Italian and German civilians to internment camps in Canada in July 1940. She was sunk by a German U-boat off the coast of Ireland, resulting in 805 deaths. 53 of the fatalities were Welsh, with many coming from the valleys, who had been declared to be "Enemy Aliens" of the State by the British government. While some could rightly point here to the ways in which war tends to collapse neat distinctions in the theatres of battle, for the people of the valleys the home front has always felt like a conflict zone.

Battles between the artistic versus technical imagination have deep roots in Welsh-Celtic traditions. Poets have always fought those of a more calculating and technical persuasion. Earlier bards understood it was far easier to destroy a culture if it was codified in books using printing technologies that merely replicated the word, than spoken to memory in a poetic verse. That doesn't however mean to say that all technology has been met with suspicion. One notable technology openly welcomed during the 1920s was cinema. Many big screens appeared in the valleys at this time, like the one installed in the landmark theatre and Workingman's Institute, the Park & Dare in Treorchy. Already notable for hosting grand theatrical productions, it began screening silent films shortly after to help bring some kind of humour to communities dealing with the Great Depression. It would also later screen *Pathé News* broadcasts, including one by Churchill during World War II, which despite the circumstances and the support for the effort, was still met by a barrage of boos as the memory of Tonypandy lingered. The icon of the 1920s, however, was and remains the incomparable Charlie Chaplin. And his films would be continuously showcased throughout the valleys during the interwar years. How much did Chaplin's Tramp resonate with the people of these towns? The story of a nobody, who means something because in so much of the industrial world he embodied everybody? But Chaplin's Tramp was slowly being killed the moment the "talkie" film arrived in the 1930s. Indeed, the more the silent brilliance of Chaplin faded, the more the power of the televised orator rose, who spoke an entirely different language. None more so than a tyrant born in the same year as the comedian, Adolf Hitler. Might we not see the death of Tramp as symbolic to the loss of a dignified life, which despite the hardship, believed in the virtues of all too human production? Of men, who find their voices silenced as the televisual spectacle renders politics all too explicit? A death then of a respectful appreciation for tragedy, which would soon be displaced by the fetishization of all manner of technologies that promised thereafter to save us from ourselves, including the destructive machines we had already made? If only we could take as much pleasure from laughing at tragedy instead of trying to kill it? Reminiscing about the genius of the silent master, I occasionally amuse myself as I imagine Chaplin's Tramp boxing Hitler in a re-enactment of that wonderful scene from *City Lights* (1931), which would be the last film he made before the Führer came to power. Is it any coincidence that his next movie, *Modern Times* in 1936, provided a scathing human critique of industrialisation that was being fully embraced by the world's most notorious failed painter, who was now putting artists on trial in Germany while running apace with vast programs of mechanisation, and resulted in a mutual early show of collaboration, support and respect between the fascist and Henry Ford?

War is written in many different ways. Those of a more conventional kind, which notably feature soldiers on battlefields, are easy to define. We know when they begin, and we know when they end — or at least that's what the politicians and historians would have us believe, even if lived experience challenges these assumptions. But there are wars, battles and everyday conflicts which rage in more undetected ways. Sometimes they remain largely silent, though from time to time, the silence is punctured by the most violent of explosions to reveal what had been simmering for decades. This has been the basis for socialist ideas concerning class warfare, which all seemed in the West to rather die out in 1989 with the fall of the Berlin Wall. And yet before that happened, maybe the last stand for those who firmly believed in this idea of a civil war were the miners of South Wales, along with other communities in the United Kingdom. Those who first flew the red flags and became the frontlines of a war for social equality and justice, found themselves defending the last pieces of productive territory. What perhaps made Thatcher so disliked by the miners was that she was the last General in command during a civil war upon an entire way of life, which she ideologically despised until her final breath. She would not appease, negotiate, call a truce or seek out some lasting peaceful settlement. Her strategy was one of obliteration. And she won. No denying her victory. It was another kind of total war which totally ended unionism, collective bargaining and industrial production in the mountains of South Wales. But while it was celebrated the world over by champagne-popping yuppies, the post-war settlement for those on the frontlines was simply a reminder of the defeat. You could see it on the faces of militants and those mining families who stood on the lines for that final time. You could feel its pain even as the proud marchers in Maerdy walked in a final dignified parade. And you could hear its fallout, as the streets went quieter and quieter, retreating back into a post-industrial state of disorder that left a people totally defeated. Little wonder then, like tempered conflict zones the world over, that the valleys are home to so many non-governmental agencies and charitable organisations still aiding the recovery. I would say the death of Thatcher brought celebration to these parts. That would be a lie. Similar to the handouts now given to people exhausted by history, there was simply tired relief.

It was the summer of 1990. A turning point in my life had been reached. I had spent what I thought was my last day in school. Fittingly or tragically ironic, my final GCSE examination was in Geography. What was I now going to do with the rest of my life? The first task was to ceremoniously cut my school tie into shreds. I truly felt I was never going back. I figured I should just enjoy the summer. I had already been working for a number of years teaching karate, which gave me some money in the bank. It must have been a difficult feeling for my parents seeing a 15-year-old child bringing in as much money as the state was providing for all of us to live. While I had been crowned Welsh *kumite* and *kata* champion on a number of occasions, I had however lost all interest in the martial art after a good friend who I really looked up to was killed in a car accident the previous year. We ran karate clubs together in a number of venues throughout the valleys. A few years older, he was high on drugs and hit another vehicle head-on after leaving the notoriously rough Hillside nightclub on the outskirts of Trebanog (which was as wild and fractious as it sounds), leaving his shattered body on the road having shot through the windscreen. He was due to join the Marines. But it was only a matter of weeks before I was completely bored. I must have spent the following three weeks or so going back and forth the local job centre, but as usual, like the hopeless congregations there who also looked at the little advertising cards written in illegible letters on gender-specific shelves worn down by a thousand men's stares, there was nothing suitable. There was nothing suitable for anybody, it seemed. Just hundreds of peering eyes becoming more and more dejected as they scanned for work, knowing they stood little if any chance of securing an interview. I wondered whether any of these jobs were real or just a way to prove some theory or other. The local job centre at the top end of the village of Treorchy was a cramped, sweaty and uninspiring place, which left one feeling altogether dejected at the prospect of finding a tomorrow worth considering. In marked contrast, and conveniently situated directly across the road, the recently opened joint Army, Navy and Royal Air Force recruitment centre was a spectacle of unrivalled opportunity. Its windows glistened with photographs of exotic lands populated by photogenic bodies, which were far more compelling than the local travel agent's magazine cut-outs of Benidorm. A few soldiers had visited the school in previous years, but I paid them no heed or attention, still perhaps thinking the world was probably going to swallow me whole long before I needed to find some kind of work. Treorchy comprehensive has since become the very first school in Wales to have a Combined Cadet Force attached (established in 2007), which is part of a wider drive to boost recruitment from disadvantaged areas and instil properly the types of militarism more prevalent in England. Upon entrance, I was reassuringly met by a young receptionist girl in smart and fitted blue attire, who was gleaming with optimism and a delicate smile. She invited you to share a cup of tea, before the immaculately dressed and well-spoken officer appeared, sun-kissed and radiating confidence, who assured you there was certainly a place in the forces for somebody of your talents. At least that's how I felt on my first "chance" visit early in mid-July. How lucky was I they just so happened to be there when I needed direction in life?

The local job centre was often fractious and prone to incidents of violence. Persons working there were frequently subjected to abuse, while threats were made to others should they have the audacity to apply for a position the threatening party stood no chance of obtaining. Part of their training was to have the wherewithal to help find the already disqualified some kind of hope, matched by an ability to deal with alcoholism and raging frustration. I don't know if I was intimidated more by the prospect of work or the drunken men who paced around like uncaged bears. This became more pronounced during the 1980s, when the redundant needed to prove their willingness to work. This often meant being willing to put yourself forward for whatever ropey prospect was unceremoniously placed on wooden rails, which held the uninspiring placards in check with their own strings of systematic neglect. Clinging on a display that simply reaffirmed how precarious everything had become, this often meant you were reluctant to take them off in fear of damaging the pitiful infrastructure. What was being played out here was a spectacle that revelled in exposing every kind of personal deficiency, the failures of a life painted on faces whose gaze mastered abjection. This "take whatever was on offer and less so" office of statistical manipulation (the government was primarily concerned with massaging the unemployment figures), was situated up the road from the Abergorki Hall. Founded in 1915 and paid for by a weekly levy donated by the miners who worked in the nearby colliery, which at the height of its production had over 2,000 miners digging in the deep shafts below the village's ground (it was previously known as the Abergorki Workingman's Institute), it was once another hub of social activity just a mile away from the imposing Park & Dare venue, which also included its own 503-seat cinema. Nearly every town had institutes of this kind, all paid for and maintained by the workers themselves. In the post-war years it also become home to the Ystradyfodwg Art Society, of which my great-grandfather was one the original founding and notable members. In the early 1980s, the top floor of the largely derelict building was taken over by a family member who turned it into a renowned local gymnasium that developed a reputation for the widespread use of anabolic steroids. We might say the shadowing of the arts by a mass body index of enhanced anger and social emptiness, matched by the alternative spectacle of emasculation for a generation told the only muscle truly now worth exercising if they were to have any ambition was the mind, made the location of the military recruitment outpost strategically convenient to say the least!

Within a week, I was invited for a further interview in Cardiff with somebody more senior in the Air Force recruitment. I still have no idea why the RAF appealed more. Maybe it was because I just wanted to be sure I was getting away and that I'd summarily dismissed the Navy due to my innate fear of the waters. Maybe it was because I was still traumatised by that Irish ferry crossing the year previous when the waters were so ferocious it took us an extra 12 hours of being thrown around by a merciless force before docking. I had been in Ireland representing Wales in the British Karate Championships. In the same waters where some many have lost their lives, for the first time in my life I truly felt afraid of dying. It would also be the last time I would see my friend alive. Going for what I thought was an informal chat, I left the Cardiff HQ, which was in close proximity to the castle, having been told I had "passed" the initial aptitude test having apparently evidenced the right attitude. I don't remember much of the interview except the rather quizzical question: "Do you know anything about Iraq"? I had no idea, after all my geography was primarily learned through football and the nation was completely off the World Cup radar. I managed to bluff my awareness, saying I believed it was a place that was "very important" to the world. Why else would he ask, I figured? In truth, I had no idea whatsoever, nor anything about a professional career, let alone the military. My mother since told me she had sleepless nights when I was a young child, worried that I would never work because my disabled father had no contacts or employment history in the local factories. There was a dedicated adviser in school, who was just as defeated by the years of offering advice, knowing most of it meant he was being a monumental fraud. The kids also knew he was largely going through the motions, so as we waited in turn to have our fortunes shred, elaborate ambitions were devised to either entertain or get him even more aggravated. He simply shook his head and called out "Next" with due resignation when I explained I wanted to be an astronaut. Two weeks later, I was sent a letter saying I was now welcome to move forward with my application subject to passing the mandatory fitness test, and to my utter surprise proving that I passed three of those recent examinations I had taken with little effort or care above grade "C". So those exams now mattered? Why didn't anybody tell me? Despite my lack of effort, I was relatively confident of scraping through. Finally, it seemed, I could plot my own great escape from the valleys and my real life could begin. Or at least I believed, until the fates and furies of war and peace decided they had other plans in store.

Boys from the South Wales valleys were now being asked to fight in the deserts of the Middle East for another black source of energy. When Saddam Hussein invaded Kuwait in August 1990, the drumbeats to war were already sounding across national television channels. The media, I have since learned, play such an important role in normalising the inevitable. Crucially, for the valleys, the world had now become dependent on oil, so those idle bodies that were spending most of their time thinking of being somebody else in the elsewhere regions of the planet, once again had a value and purpose. They had little care if that purpose was primarily about liberating the very thing which sent them into lasting destitution. The fluidity of the black liquid would become an apt metaphor for the liquidity of the declining industrial age. Everything would become increasingly fleeting, except the poverty and misery. The bonds which held communities together would be uprooted, but then left to be tossed around on the winds without any safety nets to catch them when they inevitably fell crashing to earth. Like the post-industrial wastelands across this island, which was fast becoming a land of broken colonial dreams, zones of abandonment like the valleys were prime spots for militarism. There was a seemingly endless supply of young men in particular, who all had dreams of escape, who all desperately wanted to reclaim something meaningful in a world that denied them any masculine claim, who were tough and just needed to channel all that aggressiveness which had been coursing through their frustrated veins for as long as they could remember. A strange kind of patriotism thus started to take hold in the valleys during this period, which become more vocally expressive in its scapegoating of unknown peoples in far-away lands. So that is where Iraq was, I learned. The political classes have always learned how to divide people, so the cause of their plight is placed upon the shoulders of others who they have far more in common with than the benefactors of such divisions. A painful reminder of this was revealed as I entered the still thriving open market in Tonypandy in the September of 1990. As the elderly woman was dragging the weight of her anguish through the gravel and rain, she turned her attention to the some of the market stall-owners yelling with a deep bellowing resentment I hadn't witnessed before. "Iraqis Out", she called out, over and over. This market hosted a wonderful mix of traders, who provided an array of goods from cheap leathers and fake clothing such as two- or four-stipe trainers, to fresh fish and meat, which brought notable energy and life to local towns on scheduled market days. Some of the stalls were run by local persons, others by immigrant traders from Cardiff and elsewhere who knew there was an appreciative market for their cost-saving items and more exotic foods and spices, even if they had no idea what to do with them once they were purchased. "Madame, Madame", the polite Asian responded as she continued to yell for all to hear across the partially covered marketplace. "I'm not an Iraqi, I am a P*ki", he cried back laughing at the absurdity of it as she continued to drag her bag of anger along through the puddles that couldn't have been more ecologically different to the dusty market streets of Basra. While the latter is no doubt revealing of how derogatory phrases also mark lines of self-identification, in that moment many locals just laughed with a strange kind of humorous solidarity with him. Things, however, would only get worse over time as the racial demonisation grew.

While the international political environment was becoming increasingly concerned with the rise of a buoyed political Islam and the national scene by the violence of the IRA, our concerns were of a more local kind. The Welsh knew the "Irish problem" was a continuation of its fight with the legacy of English coloniality. Indeed, while there was less sympathy for the violence of the paramilitaries, the cause resonated with many. I recall a number of very heated arguments in the local pubs in the latter part of the decade between vocal Welsh nationalists and those of military families. There certainly wasn't any outrage when the IRA attempted to assassinate Thatcher in Brighton in 1984, though I do vividly recall many who were pleased at the release of the Guilford Four following their wrongful imprisonment for a bombing in the Surrey town in the year of my birth. The same sentiments were all too apparent following the highly televised release of the Birmingham Six a few years later, which resulted in a rather violent skirmish I witnessed between the elder brother of a friend at the time (who was by all accounts serving in the SAS) and a local man who kept yelling in the local wild saloon, "Justice for Ireland". In truth, very few believed in the legal idea of justice here. We knew the rules were written in favour of the rich. If the English had to deal with the violence of the IRA, during the 1980s the young of the valleys had to navigate the marauding street gangs, which soon built "avoid at all costs" reputations. In our valley, this began with gangs such as the CLA (Cwmparc Liberation Army), which had no guns, no ideology and no agenda, except to bring an indiscriminate beating upon whomever they fancied. I never actually bumped into any of their clan or kids associated with "Ystrad Skins" (which was abbreviated for skinheads), but you knew of their existence through white, painted graffiti across the upper valley walls. While every single random assault would be pinned upon them, their reputations far exceeded their activities. Still, during this period, there were some dangerous gangs around, which often had one or two shaved-head members who wore visible National Front insignia. Painted NF slogans would become more commonplace throughout the 1980s in the valley. The most vocal would often be the ringleaders of a motley crew who would only engage in violence when the pack was all together. One of the leaders of a clan from a neighbouring village was the son of a leftist militant, who was locally known for his toughness. I can't help feeling there is such a thin line between the failed leftist militancy and right-wing fascism. Leaving aside the more diverse cultural heritage of the skinhead movement, which was deeply rooted in immigrant music and style, the real contradiction of these gangs was how they largely terrorised other white people. White terror begins in the valleys by terrorising itself. Though invariably they would also target the very small minority of immigrants from the Asian continent too, notably stores owned by persons from Pakistan and China that became an integral part of the local food economy.

While some of the gangs of the valleys were by-products of the years of deep depression culminating in the Winter of Discontent and the subsequent shift to Thatcherism, which brought further problems such as the heroin epidemic and the fundamental breaking apart of all social cohesion, seeds were planted during this period that would open the doors for a more intolerant sensibility towards immigrant populations. Some explanation is needed here in terms of the complexities of the Thatcher years, including the shift away from identifying an external enemy in the guise of a Slavic industrial strongman, which the people of the valleys more often found affinity with instead of decrying, towards threats that could be presented as a fundamental attack on the very freedoms defended during World War II. Freedoms, we might say, which are always mythologised yet historically contested in these parts. Still, it remained the case that the fight against fascism and unelected tyrannies continued to compel a certain allegiance, especially if that allegiance could be represented as a response to aggression. The Falklands/Malvinas War of 1982 would be a litmus test for this commitment and would shoot another militaristic arrow into the valleys to quell somewhat the growing resentment against Thatcher. Or at least that was partly the case until her domestic war on the miners became undeniable. Since the war against the Argentinians reaffirmed the idea that defending Britishness still mattered, it inevitably extended the symbolism of Welsh soldier deployment in Ireland. Soldiers from the valleys would be an integral part of both conflicts, helping the Kingdom preserve the last remnants of its fading colonial past, while embedding further the logics of militarism so central to the post-ideological wars that would soon arrive and change the entire face of international politics. Though it should be added that protecting freedom would continue to be a rallying call for those who found security in the Union. It's remarkable to think the war for that outpost off the coast of Argentina only lasted two and a half months. Victory was decisive. Were it a more prolonged affair, who knows what impact it might have had upon Thatcher's premiership and the battle of attrition with the miners. I often think about the vexed history at play here. For if the military propaganda was true that many a valleys man wanted to join the forces in the immediate outbreak of the conflict, I wonder how they might have psychologically fared had they confronted on the battlefield Argentinian soldiers from that Patagonian region, who may have been descedents of Welsh emigrants fleeing the nation back in the nineteenth century? Fighters, in other words, caught up in wars of division, rooted in the colonial ambitions of Britannia, which would also see boys from the valleys (who were recruited into the Royal Welsh fusiliers) looking into the eyes of the angry natives in areas such as Bogside in Londonderry from 1969 onwards.

With hindsight, we can see how the Falklands War was mobilised by the British political classes to paint Thatcher in red, white and blue and mythologise her legacy by bestowing upon her a Churchillian moment. That far-away island was less important than the political capital it generated. In reality, while the war was raging, despite the jingoistic press, the public in Wales was largely disinterested. As the most famous survivor of the war, Simon Weston, observed, "The world did not stop for the Falklands War. It hesitated, perhaps, for five or ten minutes each day as people switched on for the latest bulletin." Weston, a Welsh Guardsman, whose badly burned body and face provide a lasting visual memory of the conflict, was a working-class boy from the valley town of Nelson in the borough of Caerphilly. The bombing of the ship *Sir Galahad* upon which Weston was stationed became the most iconic image of the war overseas, depicting the incident that resulted in the largest single loss of life, including 31 Welshmen. While the harrowing images of Weston alone should have been enough to warn us all about the dangers of warfare, the victory galvanized Thatcher and enabled her to position herself more confidently on the international stage. Indeed, it is revealing that the most memorable image many associate with the war featuring Thatcher in a tank was triumphantly staged four years after the conflict. Exact details were less relevant than the construction of an image of this modern-day Boadicea. The confidence the war gave her administration and the subsequent election victory it permitted enabled her to build a stronger partnership with Ronald Reagan in his fight against the "Evil Empire" of Soviet communism, which would also have evident local effects. Socialists the world over could now be directly fought in every village, every household and every industrial setting. In the process, the War Cabinet would for all intents and purposes become part of the Home Office and the Exchequer, key in provoking an assault on any claim to sociality throughout the political body of the nation. To many, the narrative could be presented as a seamless continuum. But as already suggested, the attitude in South Wales even towards Argentina was more complicated than a straightforward militaristic reading of history would suggest.

I am reminded again of myself in 1984, weaving with the ball around nonexistent Englishmen in the valley rain, dreaming of Maradona.

The conflictual and at times contradictory overlaps between class, race and nation that swept up the men from the valleys in the violence of the twentieth century, reveals further the complexities of identity politics. Farther back than the tensions caused by the wars that captured the attention during the 1980s, there is no doubt, for example, that World War II had a marked impact upon national identity and probably set back for many years claims to Welsh independence. Famously, the only political party to make a public stand of conscientious objection to the war was the at the time much lesser-known Plaid Cymru, resulting in the open vilification of many of its members. This raises another important point, which has become altogether more fraught within the towns of South Wales today. While many in the valleys many have harboured anti-English sentiments, for the proud ideological miners and their families, the fascism that emerged during the 1930s was a far greater threat. A notable example of this would be when Oswald Mosley's Blackshirts were literally run out of Tonypandy in 1936, having been met by fierce anti-fascist crowds who prevented them from speaking. It would later enter local folklore by socialists as the Battle of De Winton Field. This would be the very last time the British Union of Fascists tried to hold a rally in Wales. But invariably, as the ideological currents were moving away from concerns with coloniality, so a space was opened to embed deeper a sense of "Britishness" born of this new collective struggle. The complex lines of claims to be British after the defeat of Hitler's fascism would take decades to properly untangle. Indeed, we might say that as the power of socialism subsided during the long and difficult winters of the Cold War years, so the power of militarism increased as the ideology of the miner was displaced by the symbolism of the soldier. Both of which sought to create communities of togetherness through the power of mourning. "Lest We Forget" would become less and less about those who died beneath the ground and more about the black carriage processions and acts of mourning for those who were tasked to fight in lands far beyond Europe's now peaceful shores.

Communities are often brought together through a shared sense of mourning, struggle and public grief. While it may be presumptuous to say the valleys invented this at the birth of the modern period and the onset of its catastrophic reckonings, it has some truth. But what happens when the mourning takes place for the very idea of community itself? There has been no funeral procession for the loss of the valley community tied to the mining industry. Its death was so long and protracted, that when the end finally arrived, the mourners were too exhausted and defeated to march to the cemetery and speak to the good of what was lost. In a place where the very bonds of togetherness were torn apart by an ideological war that attacked the very notion of community with a rampant individualism, for individuals marked only by their deficits, vulnerabilities and denials, it's easy to recognise the appeal of a military life. But ever since Churchill sent those soldiers onto the streets of Tonypandy, many in the valleys have been less willing to give themselves over to military solidarities and its vision of togetherness born of some tragic loss of life. World War II is unique in this regard, as many in the valleys stood together in the face of the killing machines of historical fascism. What comes after, however, was a more complex affair, firstly bound to the rampant British flag-waving jingoism that accompanied the war against Argentina, then overshadowed by the very real presence of a victorious war against the underclasses. With the socialist alternative firmly dead in the ideological trenches, by the time we arrived at the so-called "New Wars" of the 1990s, still in rather familiar former colonial outposts, conditions were ripe for alternative forms of fascism to emerge. With its roots already forming in the groundswell of social malaise during 1980s Britain, one of the triumphs of Thatcherism was to create the conditions that normalised intolerance and enabled far-right sensibilities to thrive in working-class minds. Turning the immigrant and the outsider, who had previously been welcomed into these hillsides, into the scapegoats of history would be integral to this. Populations were now encouraged to fear those who were said to be enemies to an entire way of life; despite the fact that the way of life in these towns was killed off by the very ideology we were encouraged to defend. Who after all really believed that Treherbert would be lost to some invading iteration of the puritans from Afghanistan? Nevertheless, the conditions made it easy to racialize politics, from without and within, which would even lead to an essentialised defining of these communities in terms of racial intolerance by those who spoke with familiar socialist tongues. Bourgeois radicals marked by colonial guilt would be equally complicit in this, which, as I will mention later, cannot be divorced from the shift towards an individualised politics of victimisation, which is far removed from the daily realities of structural violence. Such individualisation that proceeds in the name of solidarity and community represents a further triumphant outcome of Thatcher's civil war, turning the original inventors of the ideas into the problem.

Thatcher was no Churchill. He was just a wartime leader who proved to be rather ineffectual when it came to domestic politics. She waged a successful campaign on both foreign and home soil, instigating her own revolution that would truly decimate the system left in her wake. Inspired by the military General Augusto Pinochet in Chile, Thatcher understood how it was possible to impose a free-market mentality while also ruling with an iron fist to brutally suppress those who may dissent. Key here would be a return to ideas of renowned economic thinkers such as Milton Friedman and Friedrich von Hayek, who allowed her to make the political and economic case for her attack upon the faltering yet still defiant remnants of socialism. The latter thinker would be crucial in recasting the very idea of oppression. Erasing from memory the history of socialist struggle against fascism that was so evident in the valleys, Hayek argued in his most famous book *The Road to Serfdom* (the title alone could be reapplied a thousand times over to those who walked the valleys streets) that socialism was not opposed to fascism; it was its most vocal and strident expression. Political thinkers have ever since been debating these connections, while trying to portray the one true reality of fascism, from socialism as fascism, capitalism as fascism, onto the more recent and fashionable explanations that fit in with the identity politics of the time, notably: concerns with right-wing politics as fascism, radical left-wing intolerance as fascism, white male patriarchy as fascism, Islam as fascism, the list goes on. All of which contain a certain element of truth. Thatcher was also an astute reader of history and a formidable strategist of the contemporary moment. She was already guided by the Baghdad-born brothers Charles and Maurice Saatchi, who famously came up with that 1979 poster "Labour Isn't Working", showing the lengthy dole queues so familiar to these parts. She was also in the company of Bernard Ingham, who was her press secretary and became non-executive director of one of the oldest public relations firms in the world, Hill & Knowlton. Thatcher understood that optics was everything. Indeed, in an increasingly televisual age, which was matched by an explosion in advertising, marketing and public relations, she understood fully the power of the media spectacle. Having heeded the lessons from Churchill, Thatcher learned that if you were going to wage a civil war at home, the main lesson is that it shouldn't look like one! So instead of sending in the troops to quell the miners' uprisings, she effectively weaponised the police and turned domestic officers into frontline combatants for the State. Furthermore, through privatisation, it was possible to add lasting depth to militarism through the onset of a new private economy of arms production and procurement. As the economy moved from mass intensive labour towards a more "skilled" workforce, so the country as a whole positioned itself as a leading arms manufacturing base, which invariably tied the support for militarism to everyday livelihoods in more subtle yet no less entrenching ways. Many in the valleys would now try to join the army of more than twenty thousand in Wales directly employed in prestigious arms manufacturing and defence companies outside its basins. In the post-industrial period, Britain has since become the second most profitable arms warehouse for the world. But who can really blame those who simply turn to find employment in such secure industries? War continues to remain profitable and seductive, especially in an age when the free market creates enough demands for disaster to thrive. And it would certainly be remiss for any British academic to take an absolutist moral stance or condemning position against those who accept employment, knowing full well that the entire university sector, its pay, pension funds and its buildings have since their inception been deeply invested in the war economy. Very few areas of life in this Kingdom are completely autonomous from the investiture of war.

Two certainties exist in times of war. Profits and casualties. For many who have left the military, often the trauma lasts a lifetime. It is well-documented how many ex-service personnel end up struggling with life outside of the military. This often leads to chronic depression, imprisonment and homelessness. Like many poor areas, the valleys have relatively low levels of homelessness. That at least is one of the benefits of living in an area where most of the housing is classified as "affordable". But what of its veterans who return broken? Those whose bodies are mentally scarred by the violence of a different kind? Many of these fighters would leave the valleys hoping for a better life. But what happens when that life proves to be worse than they ever imagined? While the exact figures are difficult to establish, according to various mental health and homeless charities, the numbers of ex-military personnel who suffer from PTSD or find themselves on the streets and in prison reaches into the thousands in the South Wales region. Some prefer to sleep in ruined buildings as it reminds them of warzones. Others turn to drugs and alcohol, which only exacerbates the problems. Too many are unable to switch the violence off, because, well, war is never that way. A number end up on the streets of Cardiff, Swansea and Newport, as it's easier to survive among the many. There is a real tragedy at work when thinking that the town synonymous with the Chartist movement of 1839, which remains the largest single armed uprising against the British State and led by the coal miner Zephaniah Williams from the village of Blackwood, would become home to former soldiers who had been discharged of all obligation. Some, it seems, only have use when it comes to killing for those in power, ending up as disposable as anybody else once the duty is served. True to the way disturbances have always been dealt with in the South Wales valleys, the working-class Chartists were met by overwhelming violence, with Zephaniah and his accomplices the last to be sentenced in the Kingdom to be hung, drawn and quartered. Following a national outcry, this sentence was reduced, resulting in forced transportation to the overseas colony in Van Diemen's Land (now Tasmania). What might he say to a homeless veteran on those fractious streets of Newport today? Maybe he would remind them how tragedy has a way of blowing back across time, from the deserts of the Middle East to the broken ruins and abandoned holes, which mark a new kind of mental gateway in between earth and hell.

Dawn is breaking and I have just finished my early morning run. I had completed several lengths of the bay, despite the low visibility. I would only later learn about the beaches and surrounding area's history in training soldiers in the aftermath of the British defeat during the Boer War in the colonialised lands of Africa. Aside from the sand, there seems very little else to compare. Unexpectedly, my parents had just acquired a small caravan. It was the first week in August, and this was the very first time I had been in the seaside resort of Porthcawl during this time of year. The last week in July and early August were officially designated "miners' fortnight", in reference to a period after World War II when the pits shut down for annual maintenance, and all the workers descended en masse to either Porthcawl or Barry Island. Entire valley streets were vacated as neighbours went away from it all, with everyone they knew in close proximity and part of the same expedition. Like roasting lobsters, they would be more tightly packed on those beaches than in the tunnels below. With colliers' demands to stay in those aluminium-cladded boxes at their peak, the prices during the "miners" were at a premium, even if the weather was never guaranteed. As a result, we had been unable to afford a visit during those weeks. We had, however, enjoyed a few daytrips to both places in the years previously, well organised with sandwiches to match by the working men's clubs. My first memory of Porthcawl appears sometime during the early 1980s. Alongside the toffee apples and beach donkeys, which seemed just as overworked as those in the pits, my thoughts are marked by running battles on the seafront between gangs of skinheads, punks and rockers, who would be the source of ruination for many traveling visitors' leisurely dreams. Since the 1960s, Britain's coastal resorts became a hotspot for the violence of dejected youths known as Generation X. It arrived slightly later in Wales, but the violence was no less ferocious. This would however soon morph into less cultured and more territorialised battles between the unholy trinity of Cardiff and Swansea City football fans, mixed in with boys from the valleys who had divided allegiance, though really just wanted to join in the ritualistic bank holiday melee of Candy Floss warfare.

It's only 6am and the beach is empty. Traces of distant life can be made out through the sandstorm, including a stall-owner frantically running down the promenade trying to catch a wayward silhouetted inflatable shark moving at impressive speeds. Sat on these windswept beaches, you were often hit by flying objects of a blown-up kind. I think back to that evening in the autumn of 1981 with my parents as we sat on the sofa and watched *Jaws*. Television truly was an event in those days. A year later we day-tripped here and many still seemed to be reluctant to go into the murky sea, fearing the appearance of some Great White. I doubt any film has had such a powerful psychological impact. I faintly see the outline of the Water Chute landmark in the distance, which would later need to be pulled down due to its rotting timbers. Visibility all around is limited, as the mist rolling in from the ocean has blanketed the cove and surrounding areas. I can hear the faint retreating of the waves in the distance, but I am unable to see them through the dense fog. It made the earlier activity quite exhilarating, as if running into a complete unknown. Towards the cold waters I walk, leaving my wet footprints in the sand behind. Eventually I reach the water's edge, but now find myself completely submerged by a white mist that has surrounded my body, restricting my visibility to a few feet in each direction. The gentle waters start lapping at my feet, and I have never felt more conflicted. Having the good fortune of being in the seaside resort for the summer, I found gainful employment in both the local fairground and a bar on the caravan site, which was a favourite amongst the elderly. The evening was often finished watching the entire venue of drunken geriatrics further intoxicated by the ocean breeze singing as loud as they could some Vera Lynn anthem. Dual employment meant some days I was in the company of local tough kids, gypsy families and various outlaws, who were often down from the valleys on the run from the police, while others I was in the company of a group of wealthy kids, who spent the entire time chatting about surfing, dance music, foreign lands and what they were going to study at university. If there was such a thing as coming of age, this summer would be that moment. I also had my first serious liaison during that time (in the sense that it lasted more than one month), who was obscenely wealthy and had an addiction to match, but at least she got me interested in clothing. She was also the first serious drugs "casualty" I knew, to invoke the familiar language of the time to describe those who often ended up walking around in a shellshocked state due to their recreational usage. This was the summer of C+C Music Factory, MC Hammer and Technotronic. It was also the summer that saw the illegal raves of Acid House culture sweep across Wales, which eventually came to an end with the Criminal Justice Bill in 1994. My first night out with the sophisticated bunch from the ocean town was to a gathering at an abandoned warehouse in Swansea, which for a Cardiff fan such as myself was once considered enemy territory. For all the drug problems associated with those chaotic attempts at filling derelict spaces with the energy of glowstick-waving, semi-naked youth who wanted to dance to a different repetitive beat, at least it tempered the football hooligans, until they become more organised and brought their casually dressed menace into the dance music scene. The Acid House revelry also attracted its own paranoic violence, resulting in targeted turf wars of a gun-toting kind, as the culture and music became less important than controlling the profits from the illicit shadow economy, which were as organised as any military outfit. From Bogota to Bute Town, Kabul to Kenfig Hill, the lines of the drug wars were rapidly breathing in the dust of a naked and alluring global angel of a more terrifying, blooded and seductive kind.

Stood by the rolling waters with my future lapping before me, for the very first time I truly felt I could be the author of my own decisions. This was a revelation. Those cool and infectious kids made me realise there was another escape from it all. Soldier or dancer? Fighter or fashionista? Did I really want to go to the Middle East? Why not education? Slowly the haze started to lift, and I could see the ocean waters and the beckoning distance. Perhaps this morning's run had a different purpose than ensuring I passed the RAF's fitness entrance requirements. Was it the mist or the personally impending fog of war gently easing away? Maybe it was all just perspective? What I do know is that I would look at the humbling ocean differently after that morning alone with my thoughts. I just needed to convince my parents I should be the first in my entire family to even consider university. And of course, hope I now gained the requisite five "C" grades the school required for me to stay on for further study. My parents and I struck a deal; the grades would decide. Let's just say I cut it fine, or as I told myself at the time, I got those five with the only flying royal colours I now desired. If life is indeed defined by moments, what do these moments say about the contingency of my life? Had I not spent that summer away from the hills, might I even be alive today? What luck was involved so I could become the master of my own destiny, instead of letting a rather determined fate decide? How close was I to becoming the very thing I would later spend so much time critiquing? What would it be like to stare into the eyes of my 50-year-old hardened military self? Who would be more set in their opinions? Would his thinking on violence really be different to mine? Would such a conversation show just how spontaneous and cultured opinions are? And how close are the conflicted paths for those who simply want to find a way into the unknown? Whatever the answer, back to school I went, with the ambition of becoming a fashion designer. That however soon faded as sure as my wardrobe, which now at least aspired to better fitting shades of black.

Whilst I didn't appreciate those waving arms of togetherness at the time, looking back I find myself deeply moved by the real sense of pride shown by those elderly women and men, including my grandparents, singing Vera's hymns. It wasn't jingoistic, more a celebration of a time they managed to somehow live through, despite the pain. How sad to observe the demise of those coastal towns, which perhaps never fully appreciated how their history was fully intertwined with the lives and fates of those raucous men that invaded each summer, whom they often referred to as "valley commandos". We embodied violence in so many subtle, different, yet publicly acknowledged ways. And this too marks the lived memory of valleys life, as sure as the marks of demonisation inscribed upon the body of the underclasses has always been. But memories are often fraught, contested, and as I have appreciated, prone to change. It would take a special kind of monster not to feel saddened by the terrible loss suffered by so many during the Great War. And whilst peace and non-violence were never properly given a chance, it would be hard to find anybody from the valleys (especially the surviving older generations) who weren't deeply affected by the horrors faced by soldiers during World War II. The problem, however, would be the subsequent collapsing of all conflicts into the increasingly less than silent reflections of those previous battles, which were fought for entirely different reasons. Since those times when men from the valleys were willing to fight the forces of twentieth-century fascism, British forces have been constantly engaged in conflicts around the world. Mindful of the contentious nature of these interventions, those who have sought to promote a wider militaristic agenda realised the benefits of fusing this violence into the memory of those past glories, especially due to the emotional hold they still possess in the popular imagination. Remembrance Sunday was notable here as it moved away from simply remembering the two World Wars, which conscripted their soldiers from the masses, to commemorate all those which followed, including the more contentious battles fought by armies of professional soldiers from Argentina to Afghanistan, Ireland to Iraq. Observance in the valleys alone reveals these tensions. There is one final point we should address as we think about the swirling sands of colonialism, whose timeless grains speak to a worn memory of falling sedimentation strangely still connecting the history of Porthcawl with places like Pretoria, shadowing debates that have never been so divisive. Countering this from both sides of the identity divides, some might argue the presence of Welsh soldiers from the valleys contradicts the internal colony thesis. Was Wales not a benefactor of colonial wealth? Colonial projects have however always recruited from within as much as they have built lavish palaces and civic buildings upon colonised lands. In fact, we know of no colonial dominion within the British Empire, for example, from which its forces have not been replenished and profits used to pacify the favoured. To say the existence of men from the valleys fighting in overseas imperial wars invalidates the notion they were also colonised, means saying the presence of commonwealth forces in World War II, from Africa, Asia and the Caribbean, is revealing of colonialism's passing.

The wintery months of 2022 had arrived. A familiar bleakness resumed. People were already exhausted. And once again, the cold winds from Siberia were blowing across Europe. While the war against the virus was slowly fading from concern, a familiar older foe replaced it in establishment eyes. The people of South Wales once looked east with comradeship and respect. That history was however gradually undone, including replacing the calls for solidarity with the devastating words of Solzhenitsyn. Europe's gas chambers shown in a sisterly embrace with the bitter love of the gulag and its policy of equalisation. I recall the red flag flying on the mountains of Merthyr. Not like this. Never like this. Russia invaded Ukraine. A new version of the "evil empire" had returned. The claim had some merit. But this was not the Cold War. Those ideological battles had long passed. My problem was I didn't trust NATO or the United States either. Hardly exemplars when it came to respecting sovereign integrities. I look elsewhere and can't stop thinking about the author in all this. Solzhenitsyn wasn't alone. My mind turns to another from the region, whose book was deemed so dangerous it was also literally "arrested" by the KGB. Vasily Grossman was born in eastern Ukraine in 1905. His first job was to work as a safety inspector in a pit in the Donbas region, before writing his first novel that focused on the miners there. Its title, *Glyukauf*, which translates to "Look Up" and was the phrase the miners said to each other when arriving back at the light of day. Having subsequently lived in Moscow and worked as an acclaimed war reporter (he was the first to report on the horrors of the concentration camp at Treblinka), Grossman has been rightfully recognised as one of the most compelling authors from the Soviet zone, sitting alongside Dostoyevsky, Tolstoy and Chekov. Indeed, his *Life and Fate* (the second work to be officially arrested by the Russian secret police) is arguably the greatest book ever written on the complexities of war in the twentieth century, providing a stern reminder of the need for basic humanism in our deliberations. It is also offers a brutal insight into how a revolutionary movement ends up eating its own, especially those who have the audacity to speak truth to its power. "I don't believe in your 'Good'", Grossman reminds, "I believe in human kindness".

As mediated images of war dominated every platform, how quickly the very complexities Grossman was determined to have us think about as we try to salvage something of the human out of the wreckage of war, had given way to immediate soundbites and memes, which filled the air with a digital noise that couldn't be further away from the authorship demands that plagued Grossman. The tragic beauty of *Life and Fate* was to show how our humble uniqueness as individuals can work against those who would condemn a life through political and moral certitude. It is a testimony to the power of imperfection and the search for a deeper truth to existence. Dwelling upon this message, I couldn't get out of my head two classical artworks from Russia's past. They have always resonated, probably because the valleys and that faraway nation's past have been so intertwined. There is something truly revolutionary about their very poetic existence in this world. Creativity always manages to find a way, even in the most oppressive of states. Everything is in the eyes of the beholder. Besides, have we not witnessed too much violence? Ilya Repin's *Ivan the Terrible and His Son Ivan* returns with such devasting resonance. The tyrant and his murdered son, the Tsar whose anger killed the one he loved. Ivan's eyes are filled with torment, anguish, delusion and pain. They speak to a past, but also a deranged future that awaits. Nobody has quite captured that moment of madness better than Repin. But how many Ivans have we looked upon and continue to fall into their suffocating embrace? Oligarchs, pit owners, Imperial monsters and legitimised thieves, they all eventually kill what is within their closest possession, thereby killing the future as it might have been. It could be hung in any Imperial palace, though it is better suited on the ruined walls occupied by the dispossessed.

Europe resumed slaughtering her sons. The spectre of Ivan returned. Some were deeply pained. Others turned away from the terrible sight. Who can stare at Repin's work and not be traumatised by its horror? The shadow it casts offers no escape.

And who can gaze into his eyes and not fall into the madding abyss? What have we done? What will we continue to do? Others still had their own agendas, reminding us of others, reminding us of them. But there still are profits to be made. And somebody should make them. A tragic inevitability in a world in which suffering competes for airtime. Yes. White men can be victims too. The Angel of History hasn't afforded many in the million no such privilege. I recall the artwork's appearance in dramatized television spectacle *Chernobyl*, released a few years back by HBO, which retells the tragedy that befell the place in 1986. There are some places where devastation is so pronounced, their very name invokes a sense of the tragic. We have our own such place here. This series narrated the historical bonds connecting these two fractious nations in a catastrophe that was still about energy. It's always about energy. Those who master movement, after all, master time. And those who master time control the history. Disposable miners would at least be remembered in this drama, recalling those subterranean men who gave their lives in the hope of saving Europe from an unprecedented disaster and who had largely been forgotten. Four hundred of them from the Donbas (where the war had been raging) and Tula dug beneath the contaminated earth, knowing the chances of a premature death were considerable. You can't deceive a miner, the story tells. Those who work in the dark see everything. Chernobyl would be instrumental in collapsing the myth of communism from within. I was 12 years old, and we were told not to go out into the rain for a while. Toxic clouds might be forming above. Still, it fell, and our own drenched fates persisted. Besides, it's always raining in the mountains of the valley's minds. Now soldiers were returning to march over those contaminated grounds. Occupying what should be unoccupiable. Colonising their own fallout, which previously reminded us just how fragile borders really were to the merciless winds of change. Yet who or what was the source of the real contamination was difficult to tell. Maybe it's just the violence?

A deeper perspective was sought. Exploding towers simply reminded it's just more of the same. Besides, growing up in the valleys makes you more attuned to the subtle effects of wars of attrition. Buildings can fall in so many different ways. But does it really make a sound if nobody witnesses it? Slow violence, in the end, proves far more devastating as it takes a lasting toll on a peoples' ability to recover. Kazimir Malevich's *Black Square* reappeared in my thoughts. I was back in the black. Back in the darkness of an empty space. Back in the space of humanism's shadowed doubts. Malevich's radical 1915 work, painted at the time the Russian Revolution was still being planned, provides the ultimate testimony, the final witnessing. It's all about the blackness of the void. Nothing is objective here. It's all about depth. Looking upon it, knowing the history, what I could see was a perfect crime, the destruction of humanity and the very idea of a freely expressing artistic sensibility that might just have saved us. But this is also a reflection of what was to come. A Malevichean mirror of absence foretold. Not just a black screen. How we have learned to all desire a shiny surfaced existence, removed from the ability to touch one another in ways those in power never understood. Malevich's black vision is cracked like a wounded earth. Scorched and devastated. Its depth reveals the endpoint of all destruction, nothingness complete. Maybe it is the pupil that centres the tormented delusion of the tyrant's eye? Maybe it's a valley? Or maybe it's the final cataclysm too often reflected back upon the disposable of history? Yet despite the destruction now instantaneously mediated by global forces who are now tasked with managing the truths of war, the call to militarism continues apace. A new chapter continues to be written. Everything begins anew, even if it all feels so tragically familiar, so predictably business-as-usual as far as the violence is concerned. No idea how it will end. Nobody does. What is known is boys from the valleys will be continually asked to replenish the military machine, until such time as they are no longer needed.

ABERFAN

The town lay silently at the threshold of the passing storm. In one direction the dark clouds were continuing on their unrelenting journey, soaking the helpless lands below. In the other direction, the sky radiated the deepest of reds that even made the sun envious, ceremoniously accompanied by a perfectly symmetrical marriage of two jubilant rainbows. The air was an unsettling mix of heat and damp, which was further compounded by the immensity of the contrasts. A few family members joined us on the roof, wanting to observe the awesome power of nature in its most unmediated form. Several hand-held phone cameras appeared as everybody wanted to capture this moment. But what were they really attracted to? The beauty or the sublime terror? As I take a step backwards, I look upon the multiple screens, which held high in unformed procession multiplied the appearance of the coloured arcs across this beckoning horizon of hope and rebirth. It was a sight to behold, but it also deeply unsettled me as I am haunted by the symbolism. I suddenly felt the true weight of an unbearable sadness as I am returned to a land over 5,000 miles away. And as the sadness washed over me, all I could imagine was the colour being drained from these iridescent curves to leave before us a parade of white arches that have become so iconic to the story of the valleys. How does nature become the source of such unending lament?

It was 27 October and we had spent the earlier part of the day buying flowers for the family *Ofrenda*, or offering, as part of the Day of the Dead celebrations that were to begin in the coming days. The first day in this Mexican town is set to commemorate in particular those whose lives were tragically cut short in accidents or other violent acts. I find myself struck by the significance of this festivity; from the way it brings colour to death and the way it creates a healthy discussion on memorialisation. But the sadness doesn't leave me, for I know on this exact day just over half a century ago a funeral was held in a far-away village, which has shadowed the life of the peoples of the Welsh valleys ever since. Some tragedies are so exceptional that the place in which they occurred will be forever marked by the unhealable wounds they leave on the still weeping earth. In Wales the place where that wound is most visible goes by the simple pronounceable name, Aberfan. Maybe I was still being haunted by the previous night's "entertainment", having watched the dedicated episode from the Netflix series *The Crown*, which curiously brought me closer to the tragedy than anytime I could remember. It's strange how we sometimes need distance in order to have a deeper and more intimate connection. I had been trying in vain to convey what life was like in the place of my birth to my Mexican in-laws, then realising this episode at least conveyed the look of my childhood. Despite the glaring inaccuracies in the narrative and the setting, it was the familiarity to it all that brought this little town in Wales back into my migrated heart. I went to school in a Victorian building that looked exactly the same, I ran home through the same rain-sodden streets, I lived in the same terraced stone houses, I looked through similar windows that only mirrored others who lived exactly the same, and I too lived with a permanent reminder of one of those towering manmade mountains, which defined the scorched hillsides and would leave a lasting melancholic trace.

But it wasn't just the cultural memory of Aberfan and the poignancy of the date that was the real source of my troubles. For the first time in my life, I was experiencing what was commonly termed "writer's block". A metaphorical wall arrived as I faced the reality of a cascading blackness that emptied so much from our communities. The time had come to start writing about this tragedy, and I had never before felt such a weight marked by an absence that still appeared unresolved. I wanted to say something meaningful, humane, something that might resonate. But I also knew I didn't want to be parasitic to this tragedy. Heaven knows the people of Aberfan have suffered enough from those kinds of extractions. My wife tried to offer comfort and asked a straightforward question, which had more resonance than she could ever have imagined at the time: "Why do you need to include it in the book?" We need such questions to allow us to put everything into perspective. Still, she kept asking the same "Why?" There were after all numerous authoritative books written on the tragedy from both survivors and academics from outside the valleys who have meticulously documented the failures and done a great service to those communities in the process. I didn't want to repeat these efforts, nor try to appropriate the experience of others. That was my dilemma, for I also knew it was impossible to write a history of the valleys without Aberfan. Yet how could I possibly do justice to an event, which really does expose through the arrival of a tragedy so devastating and so difficult to comprehend at a basic human level the limits of all words, the futility of language? Nevertheless, I knew it had to be written, for the haunting was too great to ignore. The tale of those poor innocent children would become us all as we lived in the shadows of their absence. The loss of a child is the loss of a future. The loss of so many, the loss of a collective vision of promise stopped dead in its wake.

While the English were still hungover from celebrating that Wembley victory, on the morning of 21 October 1966 the residents of the Merthyr Tydfil area awoke to see the place covered in a thick grey fog. This was the start of another eerily familiar day. At around 7:30am in the nearby small village of Aberfan, above-ground workers started to arrive at Tip No. 7. They noticed something wasn't right but had no means for communicating as the telephone cable had been stolen. In the centre of the village, directly below, young children were making their way to Pant Glas (Green Hollow) Junior School. They would no doubt have been excited. It was a Friday, and the school holidays were about to begin. Some probably even hurried to school, knowing it would be over as the midday bell struck and its church-like sounds echoed across the valley. But just after 9am, the lights in the school began to flicker and a loud rumbling noise could be heard in the distance. Some villagers thought it was an earthquake. Others thought it was a tremendous storm. The mountain began to tremble and as if some infernal force could no longer be contained, it started cascading into the fog of the valley. But this was just the start. Moving earth broke water main supplies, only adding to the intensity as the slag heaps above rained down with catastrophic force. Approximately 105,000 cubic meters of discarded coal waste slid into the community and engulfed the school and houses below. Terrified little voices cried out. But everything was black. There were few signs of light. And soon everything fell silent. Children could no longer be heard. Nature stopped its violent scream. The birds stayed muted. 116 children and 28 adults were killed. Half the town's child population gone. In a small village of 4,000, everybody knew the children who would no longer be seen playing in the streets. Their blackened bodies dug up for identification, only to be reburied on the nearby hillside. The local Bethania chapel, which was once so central to local life, became a mortuary on that day. Like most things, it would fall into disrepair and close its doors as yet another symbol of abandoned hope. Volunteers took to the mountains and built a sandbag wall, hoping to stem the continued tide. Death certificates were handed out at the local chip shop. A mass burial took place on 27 October as an entire village, except the remaining children who were kept away, marched through its streets. Arm in arm, their silence broken only with cries. They wore their finest black suits reserved for weddings and funerals. The grieving families were flanked on the pavements to the cemetery by the police, ambulance services, firemen, Salvation Army volunteers and many others also dressed in black. Curtains were drawn as a symbol of personal loss. The procession walked slowly up the hill, also a unique feature of mining in these valleys, wrapped in a blanket of dignified exhaustion. Arriving at the expanse where their children were laid to rest, they looked upon the two symmetrical graves lined with little white coffins. Were they trenches? Or mirroring the layout of the terraced streets below, which invaded by a darkness still presented togetherness? A black bird flying over looked down upon the giant cross of wreaths, which were donated by people from all over the world, appearing like a distress call to the heavens arriving too late. Or maybe it was a demand for an answer from above? Why did the mountain slide exactly when the children were sat in their classrooms? Why not one hour before? Why couldn't it have waited until three hours later? Why not in the dead of night? A school made of flowers sits besides, a reminder of the fragility of it all. Thousands of mourners gathered in the cold as the light touch of rain continued to remind there would likely be more of the same. As they gathered, the shadows of the remaining Tips that had stolen their children were visible in the near distance. Charles Wesley's "Jesu, Lover of My Soul" was mournfully sung to the tune of "Aberystwyth". The latter composed by the same John Parry who wrote "Myfanwy" and who was born in the neighbouring Merthyr Tydfil. The first chorus was tearfully requited to a still silent God:

Jesu, lover of my soul,
Let me to Thy bosom fly,
While the nearer waters roll,
While the tempest still is high:
Hide me, O my Savior, hide,
Till the storm of life is past;
Safe into the haven guide;
O receive my soul at last!

The memorial service for the children of Aberfan lasted 13 minutes. What else could be said, when the pain was eternally suspended in the unforgiving air? Besides, how could one possibly mourn what was such an incomprehensible absence, which despite the appearance of representatives from every religion and political stripe, nothing any of them would say could bring their little spirits back to life? The valley now had a tragedy everybody could connect to with broken dreams and damaged hearts. The dirty black waters that flooded the village after the slide would soon be coursing through the veins of its people. Aberfan was not a place any of us needed to visit. The community which lost its children wasn't simply a location on a map, even though we knew it was just over the mountain from us. Aberfan was a tragedy we all learned to share in classrooms built just like those upon which discarded black rocks of no value fell upon disposable children with such indiscriminate abandon. Aberfan still haunts the collective memory of the valleys, its history, its suffering, its fascination with the reality of death, its political neglect. If the disaster had people questioning what God could ever oversee such a killing of innocence, in many ways, it would also define the secular life of the valleys and even the wider landscape of industrial Britain. Yet some are still on the surface, in danger of forgetting perhaps what happened in a few seconds as a catastrophe which was building momentum for decades washed everything away and whose name is still pained by the momentous loss.

Aberfan was the unbearable that resided in the unreachable depths of the blackness. Survivors would speak of its reckoning as coming face-to-face with a darkened abyss. What is a tip, after all, if not the bowels of the earth, the pit below, ripped out from where it belongs, and its very naming turned inside out? As one tip worker recalled,

> I was standing on the edge of the depression, sir. I was looking down into it, and what I saw I couldn't believe my eyes... It started to rise up slowly at first, sir. I still did not believe it, I thought I was seeing things. Then it rose up after pretty fast, sir, at a tremendous speed. Then it sort of came out of the depression and turned itself into a wave, that is the only way I can describe it, down toward the mountain... towards Aberfan village... I was looking down the

crevice, sir, down at the drop, and it seemed to me like as if the bottom shot out.

Aberfan was a testimony to colour. Black within black, depth upon depth, dust layering over dust, as the world sank beneath. The streets of Aberfan rose that day as the tormenting hill continued to breathe from within. Into the night, the smoke billowed from the ground as the black carried on creeping into the town. But what made that blackness so terrifying was its movement. Mining communities had lived in the shadow of the black for as long as they could remember. It was respected. Yet often, as with death, when the blackness was feared it was because they were heading in its direction. That gave them a semblance of control, or at least a belief that the dark matter could be tamed. Aberfan was different. The abyss itself was moving towards. And once it was unleashed, it showed no mercy for the innocent or the town in which they dwelled. That which was meant to be static and fixed into place, showed how it could move at tremendous speeds, like a black bolt of lightning striking across darkened skies to leave mortality in its pass. Death is not meant to run that fast.

Aberfan was buried underneath what the *South Wales Echo* at the time called a "black glacier", and the BBC later described as a "glistening black avalanche" of liquefied coal waste, the lingering memory of the colour is what dominates the encounter. "It was suddenly growing darker", Hettie Taylor, one of the child survivors, recalls, "and we couldn't understand it". Other child survivors like Bernard Thomas remembers the "wall of black", Gareth Groves "a black wave of muck", Gaynor Madgwick "turning my head seeing this black mass and trying to get up and run for the door... Then it was blackout", Phil Thomas of a "rumbling noise" followed "then by quiet and black", and Alan Thomas who, also speaking about the "black mass", added, "Every time we opened a classroom or took windows out, there was nothing there — it was just a black canvass from ceiling to the door". In all the recollections, the colour is the same.

Everything returns to the black valley. As another survivor Susan Robertson explained, "My abiding memory of that day is blackness and dark. I was buried by a horrible slurry, and I am afraid of the dark to this day." A fear that also stayed with Gerald Kirwan, who admitted "since that day I don't like the dark". Aberfan was a trauma that took its toll upon the survivors from within for decades. How terrifying must it have looked to see that black avalanche emerging through the deep white mist that hid its reckoning, until it arrived. But the black remained ever-present, and its infinite absence was revealed to be a force that contained all, for the peril it consumed remained inseparable to the way of life in these towns. And it would also carry over as the community laid its children to rest. "We just couldn't picture anything else", one of the bereaved parents Marylyn Brown explained. "The one thing I remember was all the people walking on the streets, obviously all dressed in black, walking along the main road to the cemetery. It was one mass of black."

Some lost more than most people could ever comprehend. Others lost everything. John Collins had his entire family wiped out as the family home was washed away with his wife and children inside. "It was as if life never existed", Collins told, "There's nothing left". The first rescuers on the scene were the town's women and older children. In a state of bewilderment, they were left to frantically scour the mass with their own bare hands. Most of the men were either sleeping or down in the mine as the day shift and night shift changeover had already taken place. The speedy arrival of the men from the pits with headlights still on was a welcome relief, for they more than any other knew how to dig the earth. They would soon be joined by the Mines Rescue Service, who were often tasked with dealing with explosions and fatalities below. The miners worked in teams and divided the ground as they would normally when cutting the seams. Aberfan was an ecology of suffering, which had turned this world upside down. The tragedy also symbolised a historical conjuncture where both religion and industrialisation had to reckon with their own histories, the false claims of their binding myths, from which neither has recovered. We might also say the contemporary fascination with the labours of man and its destructive impact on the environment, which geologists now term the Anthropocene in relation to the untold devastation humans have brought to the planet, could be literally traced to this catastrophic moment. If we needed to come face-to-face with the realisation most "natural disasters" were the fault of human excessiveness and not simply a smiting phenomenon from a testing God or a freak pattern of nature, surely Aberfan sets the tragic scene? This would bring to light two remarkable developments, which we tend to so often take for granted today. The remarkable power of televised humanitarianism, along with the inevitable problems such media spectacles can create despite all their best intentions. Aberfan was, in the words of the New York-based photojournalist Chuck Rapoport, "the first major disaster of its kind that was televised". He arrived for *Life* magazine to document what he called "The Town Without Children". Rapoport was not alone. Over 2,000 volunteers and reporters would eventually arrive, though it was already too late to help the children. No child was brought out alive after 11am. There were less than 100 minutes to save the poorly beloved of Aberfan. Those who were brought out after were taken to the chapel, their lifeless bodies laid on the pews and covered in blankets for the parents to go and identify. That place held a different kind of silence.

Black is the colour of the night. And as the night descended upon Aberfan, so a different kind of illumination set in. Silhouetted pictures of miners were set among a ruin of the present, which because of the atmospheric presence of the smoke from the burning fires below looked more and more like a scene from the Somme. As *Life* magazine's London bureau chief Jim Hicks told: "No one who endured this night would ever forget it — the phantasmagoria of coal dust and smoke". Other images that focused on the homes looked like a chaotic film set, as the miners and professional rescuers were now trying to manage the presence of well-intentioned volunteers who frequently got in the way. Nightfall was also backlit so that a world could be witness to every second of a tragedy unfolding. Such desire for witnessing carried over into the days ahead. We cannot underestimate how important some of this was in terms of how we remember Aberfan today, even if locals soon became very weary of outsiders. Rapoport is notable here. Having arrived in the village on 29 October (the same day as Queen Elizabeth), Rapoport found the village a "hostile ground: sad, angry, wet and cold, half of it still covered in grime from the tip's fallen slurry". By the time he arrived attitudes to journalists were already strained. Rapoport tells of a notable incident in the pub where he was staying when he came across the "toughest man in the valley", Dai George, who allegedly had a great dislike for journalists. He recalled how he convinced George he wasn't a writer but a "poet with a camera" quoting back to him Dylan Thomas as he won over the locals' affection. Rapoport would end up staying in the village until Christmas Day of that year. Of the many striking and black-and-white photographs he produced depicting the aftermath, the one that's stayed with me is of a single child in a playground weighing down upon the air as they are propped up by a merry-go-round. His gaze is fixated on the ground before him. His body suspended in the fall. The world may be spinning, but this boy in this park is lonely, isolated and frozen. What is going on in this child's mind as his chest is pressed against those cold steel bars, on apparatus which only gives merriment in the company of others who gift you their energies as they push the passenger into a delirium that sends the head spinning with the delight of friendship? Like so many of Rapoport's intimate photographs, this image tells so much through its sorrows, solitudes and silences. And as his moving photographic essay also told, everything for the months that followed, the continued rain and the falling snow, the laughter and cries, marriages and divorces, births and deaths, happened within the shadow of the tips.

Many of the journalists who visited Aberfan behaved with integrity. Deeply troubled witnesses to something that was startlingly horrific, they also tried to make sense of the devastation and pain encountered. We might recall the infamous words of the television presenter Cliff Michelmore, who reported on the evening of the disaster and was visibly affected:

Never in my life have I seen anything like this. I hope I shall never see anything like it again. For years of course the miners have been used to disaster. Today for the first time in history the roll call was called into the street. It was the miners' children.

Michelmore's account was touching because it was genuine and felt. He wasn't following a formula or telling viewers how they should feel, which is so common in disaster coverage today. Moreover, as Aberfan also showed, from the very inception of disaster coverage, when a catastrophe becomes a media spectacle, what matters most is the image of its occurrence. As one rescue worker recalled, "I was helping to dig the children out when I heard one photographer tell a little kiddie to cry for her dead friends, so that he could get a good picture — that taught me silence". There was a story to be told, stories to be sold, and so the town was overtaken by outsiders who wanted to tell it. Aberfan became a spectacle of a catastrophe consumed by the spectacle's own ambition. Just as the Americans and Russians were setting out to place their satellites into the orbital skies, so the idea that what was local would become global was already being played out through daily broadcasts. But there needed to be a filter to this news of the world. And when it concerned nowhere people, that filter was most often refracted through the lens of a rupture of epic proportions. Moreover, with answers already set, too often the narrative was presented to merely confirm preconceived ideas about the people swallowed up, not to mention the desire to sensationalise the disaster in order to sell copy. A situation that would be later fictionalised in Louise Walsh's *Black River,* which was partly inspired by residents' testimonies. Stereotyped narratives concerning residents of Aberfan would become more apparent once they ended up embroiled in legal disputes over compensation, along with fractious discussions with the National Coal Board and politicians concerning who was actually to pay to take away the unstable and psychologically wounding tips, which hovered over the village like mountains of death. The veteran Welsh reporter Vincent Kane, who has spoken at length about the failure of the media in supporting the communities in their times of need, wrote of these deadly mounds that encircled the village, six of which it should be added were already pensioned, as being the "seven pillars of sombre unwisdom".

Aberfan was a thunderous cry which still echoes across our shared landscapes of lament. It began with an unsettling sound. Then a torturous silence. A calamitous scream from the black earth matched by the inaudible voices of the drowned. But soon that cry turned to derision, the disbelief doubled by a catastrophe of an entirely political kind. Those in power sought a different kind of silence. A silencing of the truth. Nobody was to blame, it was insisted. Part of this was driven by the agenda of Lord Robens who, as Chairman of the National Coal Board, continually presented himself as a defender of the coal. In truth, not only would he invoke conditions of precarity to maximise profits, but he would also oversee widespread colliery closures and speed up the industry's decline. During his decade-long stewardship, the number of collieries in the United Kingdom fell from 698 to 292. In Wales, the situation was particularly acute, with the mining industry facing daily pressures to be either more profitable or close, which in practice meant doing everything to present the industry in a favourable light. The BBC documentary series *The Long Street,* hosted by Kane and narrating the history of coal in the Rhondda, was released in the spring prior to the disaster. Telling of the proud history of the miners' lives, it also captures this sense of unease. Having taken a few days to arrive at the scene, because he was being sworn in as Vice Chancellor of Sussex University, Robens' original denial of the known presence of a water spring upon which the tip was dangerously formed set the basis for so much acrimony. Yet while the disaster Tribunal was clear in its damning verdict of the National Coal Board, nobody was ultimately held responsible. The nine named individuals were largely absolved. None lost their jobs, and indeed many went on to work at higher pay grades. One of the most difficult things to comprehend was how Aberfan was an abdication of responsibility from those who were meant to represent those people the most. As John Collins stated, "I was tormented by the fact that the people I was seeking justice from were my people — a Labour government, a Labour council, a Labour nationalised coal board". A situation later felt as the communities were badly betrayed by the Cardiff MP George Thomas, or Lord Tonypandy, who was a miner's son. Then Minister of State for Wales, Thomas was one of the first politicians to arrive at the scene of the catastrophe. There he publicly lamented to the press how "A generation of children in Aberfan has been wiped out. There is an abundance of tips of this sort in Wales, and we shall be looking for the possibilities that it could happen again." Despite his early protestations, Thomas's offices were later occupied by grieving mothers who emptied upon its floor and desks bags of black sludge from the mountains the authorities were refusing to take. He would later be part of a political pact that orchestrated pressure on the community to pay for its removal. Thomas himself later moved to the right of the political spectrum, showing admiration for Thatcher and also being invited to speak at the wedding of Prince Charles and Lady Diana. Royalty might be pardoned for not feeling connected to the tragedy. The Mall was after all a million miles away from Moy Road, which was obvious to anybody who observed Queen Elizabeth's eventual visit eight days after the tragedy first struck, regardless of how much it was subsequently reasoned and the deepest of regrets stated. Her arrival also came a day after the last child's body was recovered from the earth.

Moy Road was situated directly opposite Pant Glas school. It also felt the neglectful weight of history bearing down. Today the street starts at Number 11, as the houses numbering 1–10, which were in the path of the storm, were destroyed. I recall another photograph, which is also difficult to forget. Three men are pictured outside a home, its exterior wall has been painted in a coating of the black. It wasn't uncommon to see valley terraces dusted in charcoal, but this was more than the slow build-up of black particles that were weathered upon the sides of homesteads. As one elderly man appears to be shovelling the debris, another looks resigned to the scale of the task. A third is bent over, just perhaps as a reminder of the visible reckoning of the furies and the fates. What on earth seems an unspoken feeling, precisely the earth is the devastating reply. You have the sense of something terrible, but what exactly is difficult to tell. Did the earth arrive to this dwelling or was it summoned up from within? The rooms are full, and yet the barren emptiness of the land's spatial inversion is so apparent. And what would happen if its pennant sandstone structure, less a castle but still often a tested barricade against the sweeping elements, was removed? Would we be left with a mausoleum, or a ghost made of the mountain, all negative and compact? Would its interior be petrified, catastrophically concentrating the blackness in a manifesting void of a home? Might everything within be embalmed, until it too was eventually returned to dust? A pandemoneous chamber of an impression casting the vanished, solidifying a shadow of a valley through which nobody shall walk? Or might the mountain feel regretful at the shape of its own disaster, having to look upon what it became and what it displaced? Maybe that is why it always feels like it is raining in this valley. For those houses in this world became so full of mourning, through its broken-out windows we observed there only to be an incommensurable blackness within.

Aberfan's tragedy was that it had all been prophesised. There had already been tip slides in the town in 1944 and 1963. Yet even though it was clear to locals, who continued to raise alarms about the ongoing flooding the village was experiencing and trying to insist to local authorities that the slide in 1963 was dangerous, not a single inspector was sent from Cardiff to survey the fallout. It was, as Kane observed, a mere "dress rehearsal", all fitted in the darkest of worn garments. More neglectful still was the failure to observe the recommendations of the Powell Memorandum dedicated to preventing *The Sliding of Colliery Rubbish Tips*, which was authored in 1939 following a major slide a short distance from Aberfan that led to a change in the actual route taken by the ancient River Taff, and later reissued in 1965 following an alarming incident at Ty Mawr Colliery in the Rhondda. Still, for the children, the tips were such a source of wonderment. In the summer prior to the disaster they would bathe in the spring waters that they dammed to create ponds, like their own natural hot springs. And like so many children from the valleys, they looked upon those tips as places of mysticism, adventure and discovery. Aerial photographs of the tips show just how monumental they were over the small town. As one of the children Alan Thomas observed of number 7 with also a tragic foreboding:

> The only way I can explain the tallest one is — Mount Everest. It was a big top peak. And whether it was the material, or the sun from the summer, this rock used to get very hot, so we never knew for sure whether it was on fire inside, like a volcano, because when it drizzled in Aberfan or rained, that tip, the tallest of them all, would always steam. It would always look as if it was a volcano with smoke coming off it. So quite possibly it was on fire inside — we don't know.

Aberfan was the price of coal, now counted in an unquantifiable loss buried beneath the weight. As versed in the poem by Charles Mayo:

> And the price of coal was the soul of these tales...
> For never before was the price paid in children.

What value should be attributed to the loss of so many so tender in age? £50 was the initial offer. Four years later the insurers settled upon £500. Yet as the families reminded, no life can be measured that way. As one resident, Francis Smith, put it, "Everything lost its value in comparison with those children". Often when children die, they stay that age in our thoughts. For generations born in the valleys after Aberfan, those lost children were never our elders. We become the same age as them for a while, then invariably leave them behind. And as generations pass, it's easy to see why the memory fades, even if something of that day still remains and its traces are still subconsciously felt. We feel the trace alone, for they belong to a time that's no longer lived. Hence, to do justice to the children of Aberfan, we need to walk with them in the present and let their tragedy be our continued guide as we try to make sense of what followed in the aftermath of their absence. Words of the survivors must also be heeded as we try to make sense of the psychic life to a catastrophe, which cannot be measured in how much it costs financially to remove what is dangerous from the plains of sight. Despite all the talk of systems of power and neglect, too often we can lose perspective of the taken. While some newspapers decided to print the names of the victims, the community has preferred not to speak of them individually precisely because they wanted to keep them as one. We might see this decision in contrast to tragedies such as Hillsborough where the public naming of the 97 have become an integral part of memorialisation in the face of forgetting. Neither is right nor wrong, but maybe the difference is location. Hillsborough wasn't Liverpool. Aberfan was Aberfan. They died at home. Their oneness in death was never in question in terms of where the injustice that took their lives occurred. Maybe the name is also more difficult to utter when the child has yet to grow into its potential? And who could read all of those appellations without breaking down when sensitised to a force that also sought to erase what that name would come to embody? What I do know is that for anybody from the valleys who looks upon the names of the deceased as they are written on the memorial cross adjacent to the graves, they will read all too familiar.

The legacy of Aberfan presented so many challenges in how a society was to deal with such collective trauma. What could psychology offer when survivors like Jeff Edwards felt they walked around with "death on my shoulder," in refence to the young girl whose head rested upon him in the dark? As Sue Elliott, Steve Humphries and Bevan Jones wrote:

> The treatment of people who'd suffered major trauma where death is close at hand was underdeveloped in 1966. What little was known came from the experience of "shell-shocked" soldiers after the First World War and the impact of military conflicts on men's minds. Aberfan was something new and terrible in peacetime Britain — a disaster involving whole families and large numbers of young children.

Many didn't want to give themselves over to treatment, because the culture of the victim wasn't something to be entertained. But even the psychology when required was used against the community, as survivors' compensation was subjected to the degrading practices of means-tested grief. The valleys had a proud history of fighting means-tested handouts, but it became part of the survivors' tale. Moreover, the tests carried out on a number of the children really pushed the boundaries of acceptable ethical standards and have even been open to claims of abuse. "That film *Frankenstein* is exactly what happened to us", Madgwick claimed, as she describes being taken to a psychiatric hospital and having all manner of tests conducted upon her, which she defined as a form of "torture". An experience backed up by Edwards, who described being placed into a chair and having a headset applied with electrodes and flashing lights in procedures that are more often associated with serious mental illness. "Are you afraid of the dark?", the children would be asked. "What do you think?", was an unspoken reply. These tests were authorised by the Aberfan Disaster Fund after legal guidance from their solicitors. This was in response to the Fund's intention to pay a small increase to the suffering families, especially to help with the trauma of Christmas. This followed the Charity Commission advice, which instructed, "before any payment was made, each case should be reviewed to ascertain whether the parents had been close to their children and were thus likely to be suffering mentally". How can we even begin to account for such a lack of basic humanism from an organisation tasked with upholding the charitable spirit, wherein both parents and children are tested in terms of how much they suffered before qualifying for meagre increases in support from donations that were given in good faith?

The sense of guilt was palpable. Fathers, uncles and other townsfolk carried a load, haunted by the thought that the labours of their toil were at least partly to blame for the torment. Many found solace in alcohol and silence. As one survivor explained, it wasn't that people "don't want to speak about them, it's because they can't". Mothers felt guilty for simply having sent their children to school that morning, for not saying the right goodbye. One mother was pictured staring out of her doorway, waiting in anticipation for her dead child who would never return home. Another took her own life, clutching a photo of her child in her hands. Rescuers felt guilty that they didn't bring out more children alive. They too became an often neglected part of this emotional economy of life-changing trauma. But the most tragic of all were the child survivors who also felt guilty. Guilty that they were alive, while their friends perished. Was it just sheer luck of having been sat at a particular desk? Why them? Why them? Living children thus became part of the haunting, as their joyful presence confirmed the absence of others and was more than some could take. "It took all the roses and left the thorns behind", one survivor was told, as the mother of another found her appearance too difficult to bear. So they also commissioned their own disappearance, staying out of sight, staying inside. Still the triggers continued, tormented by crashing sounds, uncontrollably crying at the sound of groups of other children, haunted by the familiarity of the earthly smell, though never in a predictable way. I think of the way triggering today is so easily deployed in a world where everybody feels like a victim, and I feel ashamed by the comparison. The only persons who didn't feel guilt or remorse were the National Coal Board, indifferent politicians and efficacious bureaucrats, along with a number of unscrupulous journalists. But how can a people move on when the town is the trauma? When survival can't be survived? After the disaster, the pit kept tipping and those black mountains were not just nightmares of the mind only reappearing when nightfall set. A number of survivors spoke about how the evenings were difficult, especially when the rains were falling and the familiar streams returned. They had become watchers of the hills. Oversensitive to the slightest movement. But that was the point. The mountains were still there, and the debris continued to slide. Time and again, the village would continue to be flooded by the black waters from those towering mounds. No compensation was ever paid. It never is for such communities, who living on the edges of time are classed as uninsurable. The fear throughout the valleys was also contagious. Schools would be shut down at the slightest suggestion of a potential rift. Too many others wore the marks of sleepless nights. And while elsewhere children were being drilled to sit under desks in preparation for a nuclear attack, the children of the valleys had the memory of when the drill was real, and the enemy was not imagined for its flight path permanently shadowed over their lives. The skies did fall that day in a town whose name is more than just a name. Aberfan — a town, a mountain, a tragedy, a memory, a child, a people, a crime.

Two decades later, Jeff Edwards, who managed to somehow get his life on track and escape the village, found himself back in the valley as a witness. He was devastated to find the same post-traumatic afflictions that were present in the adults of the town he thought he had left behind, were now being repeated by generations of the young and disinherited who were born after the devastation. "When I came home from London", Edwards explained,

> there was quite a lot of animosity in the community, people were hanging around the community and getting involved in drugs. When I was speaking to them, they told me traditionally they would have gone into the mining industry, but the collieries were closing, and they didn't have those opportunities and they turned to crime and alcohol and drugs to alleviate the boredom and despair in their lives. Many struggled with their mental health, which sometimes manifested as suicide.

Edwards, for his part, did what so many who leave the valleys can't bring themselves to do. He returned. I feel a person from the valleys' relationship to those towns is like the natural pull of a magnet, which one of the poles wishes to break. You see yourself as the positive and the valley as the negative. You feel opposed to all its stands for, and yet still it pulls you back, pulls you into its invisible orbit. Often what you see has you clamouring for a repulsion, but still it pulls you back into its fields of lament. Edwards would become a highly respected local politician and community advocate who channelled what he noted to be his life-long "survivor's guilt" into combating the new collective conditions of local depression. A striking blonde-haired child whose photographed rescue was also poignant, as he was the last to be pulled alive from the disaster, Edwards has campaigned tirelessly for the people of his town.

Aberfan was a lasting injustice that rained down upon a people for whom catastrophe became the norm. Beyond the tragedy, certainly the most contentious of all the subsequent battles was the removal of the tips. In just over a month, the Aberfan Disaster Fund had reached the unprecedented sum of £1 million (approximately £38 million today) from near 90,000 contributions. This would prove to be a great benefit to those in need, but also a curse. The media in particular took an avid interest in the management of the fund, and so did the politicians who were keen on using the fund to strengthen their own political capital. Everything was drawn out as a community was denied the ability to move on. As the poet and novelist Laurie Lee wrote on his visit to the town:

> Across from the school, and facing up the mountains stands a row of abandoned houses… Something has been done to clear them, but not very much. They stand like broken and blackened teeth. Doors sag, windows gape, revealing the devastation within — a crushed piano, some half-smothered furniture. You can step in from the street and walk around the forsaken rooms which still emit an aura of suffocation and panic — floors scattered with letters, coat hangers on the stairs, a jar of pickles on the kitchen table. The sense of catastrophe and desertion, resembling the choked ruins of Pompeii, hangs in the air like volcanic dust.

It took several months before work started on removing the ruins of the school. A new facility was then built and would open lower down in the valley in the year of my birth. In the same year the memorial garden on the site of the old school was opened by Queen Elizabeth and Prince Philip. It would take nearly two years of constant community pressure before Tip No. 7 was finally removed. And this was only done after the villagers agreed to pay £150,000 from the Disaster Fund to clear it, which amounted to some 10% of its overall proceeds. We can recall the words of Dylan Thomas:

> The hand that signed the paper felled a city
> Five sovereign fingers taxed the breath.

This extorted money would later be returned many years later with some kind of apology. Still, the tragic tends to find ways of returning in these towns. Much of the tip waste was subsequently relocated to a natural floodplain at the bottom of the village. It would raise the level by over ten feet. Part of the idea was to flatten the past and create a playfield for children, including a football pitch whose sinking tendencies I recall from elsewhere in this vale. Yet the longer-term effects of this proved disastrous as it ended up being the cause of widespread flooding of nearby streets. Residents on estates such as Pantglas Fawr would now be pictured rescued on boats as muddy waters entered their homes. It happened in 1979 and again in 1998. Similarly, it was decided that, while the cause was undeniable, nobody was liable, accountable or financially blamed. Faced with this history, it's hard not to stigmatise as tragic a town whose stigmata are so visible to all. Yes, there's a greening, but there remains the blackness, seeping out of memory and into the fields that have their own ways to remind us of it all. So what we can say is the recovery is endless and the fight unending. But that's not just for this town, it is for the valleys complete.

Aberfan was the valleys. It was the shadow of us all. And for those reasons, it also showed in a very concentrated moment of horror to be á place full of humanism, dignity and pride. Tragedy often brings out the best of people. It shows their compassion, their care, their willingness to help, their shared frustrations and tears, their nakedness as the inhibitions and daily trivialities that so often preoccupy our thoughts and govern our lives temporarily dissipate. On that fateful morning, the miners had never toiled the earth so hard. And alongside helping with the dig, the wives and relatives shared what they did to provide for their families each and every day, but now for the entire community complete. The exhausted were fed, watered and kept warm, despite the continued heavy rains. And still the miners kept digging, even though it was clear that no further children would be brought out alive. How could they stop when there were bodies to be recovered from the depths of the black mountain? While its ambitions had succeeded in fulfilling its horrifying plan, something needed to be rescued out of the abyss and brought back into the light of the next day. I still can't get out of my mind the image of that schoolteacher David "Dai" Beynon, who was found pressed against the wall of a classroom with his arms spread wide trying to protect the children who were stood behind him. Five suffocated children were held in his arms. A giant of a man, Beynon may not have been able to defeat the demon of the black mountain, but still he managed in that single act to show unimaginable humanism in death. He would later be eulogised in a poem by the Merthyr-born Leslie Norris. Some things deserve to be remembered, just as some tragedies refuse to be forgotten.

So what of that memory today? Can it say something to a world that would barely recognise those black-hilled towns? Could children today from any town in the valleys connect to that blackened time? They say that time is a healer. That may be true if the healing has a chance. But across generations, time is also forgetful. It can permit us to forget so that history repeats. Yet, observers to the events that surrounded the fiftieth anniversary of the disaster were notably struck by how its memory seemed more resonant than ever. Aberfan should never be forgotten, nor its place in history denied. There is no history of the valleys without Aberfan. It concentrates most its enduring blackness. There is no history of Wales without Aberfan. It has become an integral part of our national story. There is no history of coal without Aberfan. That which enriched the few and gave meagre sustenance to life, showed through the mist of the day its utter indifference to the plight. There is no history of socialism without Aberfan. A few miles down the road from where the red flag was first flown, how the vanguard failed when the collective most needed it. There is no history of ecology without Aberfan. What happens when the earth is unnaturally torn inside out, becomes a tale that makes Gaia continually sorrowful in these parts. There is no history of injustice without Aberfan. Time and again, those in power show most evidently here how they can provision alibis so that even the irrefutable appearance of truth can always be denied. And there is no history of the future without Aberfan. For it is in the presence of so many futures denied where we might just learn to appreciate the living.

Without question then, we have a duty to remember Aberfan. But it's not just what we remember, it's how we remember too. The coal that killed is no longer there. That has been reduced to a half-sunken wheel. Many of the bereaved parents have now died and been laid to rest with their children in Bryntaf cemetery, while those who still remain are no doubt still torn about keeping the memory alive. This is nothing new. A *New York Times* article from 1976 noted how Aberfan was already "Trying to Forget the Day Children Died". This was understandable. Memorialisation is after all a conflicted circumstance, fractiously torn between the desire to move on and the hope things may always be remembered. Memory and forgetting are twinned in this town. Thankfully there is no desire to return down below. There is too much madness in there. On the morning of the disaster, children and villagers noted how the coming earthly storm sounded like an earthquake. In many ways it was, though perhaps less defined by "aftershocks" than "afterflows", that like its catastrophic build-up, slowly seeped into the wider fabric of a now faithless bloodied shroud that was also stained with the faces of innocence. One of the most brilliant and kind intellectuals I ever had the privilege to meet and get to know was Zygmunt Bauman. A dignified man who fled persecution in the Soviet Union and later the Nazis, nobody could better read the historical moment. A central theory of Bauman's was how the collapse of industrialisation meant societies shifted from living within a time marked by solidity towards what he called our "liquid" modern times. In such times, we learn, nothing is fixed, no bonds secure, and nothing lasts. While such reasoning would evidently find its voice in the liquidity of the currency speculators that redefined the entire logic of global capitalism during the Thatcher years, I would begin to date its appearance on the day the children of Aberfan stopped breathing. For what they encountered was precisely a Liquid Terror that no fixed object could contain. And what would follow would be the washing away of everything the industrial world felt was permanent, lasting and undeniably true.

After that black river engulfed the town, many of its people believed less and less in those who served them. Aberfan showed the deep mistrust impoverished communities feel towards the Oxbridge-educated political classes, and even those who come from and yet forget the needs of the valleys. In fact, the response to catastrophe opened a rupture, after which the Labour Party's monopoly over the valleys would never be the same. Moreover, there was a realisation that if there was to be any kind of recovery, it was the community that needed to try and pull itself together. Yes, there were conflicts and yes there were divisions. There always are after a major disaster. Still, the survivors tried despite the denial. Women organised their own Young Wives Club and the men formed a choir to help vocalise what could never be said. The very first verse sang by the men would be Parry's "Myfanwy". They would practice in the Ynysowen School when it opened in 1974. Such responses are instructive. Along with simply finding reasons to believe in each other, which was a necessary step if they were to ever start finding reasons to believe in the world, perhaps the answer to a recovery was already there in affection shown to the poets of truth. As the locals understood all too well, it is the poet who speaks a shared ancestral language, for it is the poet who speaks the language of tragedy. They can also paint, photograph and perform the memory of suffering to touch something deeply human within us all. What's more, poets are not corrupted by the politics of the righteous, nor do they share a bed with those consumed by power and who come to such places from outside in order to save. They know life is complex, existence is fraught and full of imperfections. We see this in the Aberfan artist Ron Jones' work "Unspent Youth", in which the strident ride of the miner is still clouded over in a blue that's not of summer, but a deeper melancholic hold. Jones was born in 1926 and witnessed first-hand how the depression of the valleys took different forms, culminating in that disaster 40 years later. Yet, as Jones (who was also notably inspired by the history of the Spanish Civil War and seeing men marching down the valley en route to Barcelona in the 1930s to fight the fascists) and others testify, it is the poetic spirit which keeps us alive in the darkest of times. Is it any coincidence the valleys men returned to the power of verse and song? As the fiftieth anniversary dawned, the poet and writer Owen Sheers brought his own creativity to the cause by telling chapters of the story of Aberfan with renewed force. Featuring a captivating cast, *The Green Hollow* brought together the personal with the poetic to recast words that read so familiar, yet still manage through a new visual composition to evoke something timeless in the human. One verse in particular stands out as an evocative testimony, with Sheers retelling the tragedy from the eyes of a journalist visiting a catastrophe that destroyed a town:

> I couldn't help seeing
> one specific sight —
> The curtains of a house in a short terraced street
> I'd passed earlier that day.
> They were closed, which in Wales
> Not at night, means only one thing —
> a house where the seeds of death
> have been sown.
> I walked on, but as I did
> I looked down the rest of that row,
> which is when I saw —
> the curtains, they were drawn
> in every window
> Behind drawn curtains, 116 children's beds lie empty.

In the long night of Aberfan, it is undeniable how music is able to return something of the human within us. Songs of the valleys may be sorrowful. But they have depth all the same, which is where its imagination and the memory of its future resides. The poetic verse is the timeless testimony to the valleys' struggles and part of its ongoing fight against the omnipresent shadow of oblivion. So, in bringing a close to this chapter on the black-fated life of the valleys of South Wales, there are times when as authors we need to appreciate the limits of the written word and encourage readers to look to other sources for guidance. There are times when words need to be spoken and there are times when the music needs to lift so at least we can find ourselves briefly floating above the vortex of an abyss that continues to spin. To honour the people of Aberfan then, I would urge pause, allow the air that fills our thoughts the chance to breathe once again, and let the music guide a more poetic reflection. It is not just about lamenting, if it touches something deeper within, for in the moment we reach those depths is when real change begins as the fire in the earth is reignited.

I imagine the book as a doorway. As the reader turns the next page, they look upon an opening into another world. Another time. Stepping through, they find themselves transported onto a mountainside. They look down upon the quaint little village in the distance. The sun is shining, but these are empty streets. There is silence all around. Quietly a song starts to travel up the valley. "Cantata Memoria: For the Children" greets them on the hill. It begins with the beautiful and delicate chaos of the pitter-patter of invisible feet. "All Things Bright and Beautiful" rings out in the sound of joyful children's voices. This was a song that was so often jubilantly exhalated by so many in the morning assemblies. But as if from nowhere the sound changes. A new chaos descends. Or is it more the order of society now revealing its truer nature? Industrial. Progressive. Massified. Determined. A baritone voice cries out to the nothing. In the black silence it searches. Nothing again. But something is there. A growing darkness. Dead and still growing, growing within. In this moment, "Myfanwy" can be heard, but her tragedy also keeps growing. And the children's names are spoken at last. Maybe it took children to sing out the names of those fallen, dignified together, for they know nothing of appropriation and can still speak so loudly for those who have been suffocated away? As the visitor to the still tranquil lands feels the sorrow of the naming, another voice tells of who is to blame. "Buried by the National Coal Board" is reissued over and over. A forceful reminder of responsibility and neglect. But what does this mean as the music starts to fall silent? And what shall be wept when the shadow dies? Conducted by Karl Jenkins and written by Mererid Hopwood, "Cantata Memoria" is a lament for the valley. But it is also a poem sharing the same spirit of journey followed by Dante, as it moves us from the depths of suffering into the hope for a future in which the glimmer returns. To that end, it is a dream for a valley whose wounds are still so desperate to heal, and whose future will be forever defined as a land of the song.

DERELICT GODS

I arrived at the midpoint in the journey of my life. A scene of tragedy backdropped the sobering moment. If the mountain was a child, it was still crying a cascading river of black tears. Would they ever really stop? As I made my way through a thorny clearing in the brambled woods, I came across the ravine dividing this shattered world. The bridge across was forged from the most durable iron, in symbolic memory perhaps of a largely forgotten past that once branded these particular towns. Yet it stands now as a foreboding testament to the dangers that lay ahead. Its imposing structure cut the river, which today was rapidly flowing, its stormy rage still all too apparent. It was February in the valleys, and an uncomfortable rumbling filled the remembering air. Whatever the elements, they all conspire and take their annual toll as sure as the recurring seasons of mourning and death. A major mountain fire a few years back that threatened the nearby village of Troedyrhiw was now but a simmering memory, and the blackened mountainside once again covered in heather and windswept time. Upon reaching the entranceway to the bridge, the pass is policed by a murder of those now familiar silhouettes, which are completely indifferent to my standing. A number of charred footprints are visible on the ground. They pay no attention as I cross over, for their task in this place belonged to a greater mystery. Looking upon their oily feathers, I have since learned to recognise the regal esteem these dearthly messengers carry, which only adds to the magisterial terror their murderous appearance is able to convey.

I am back in the village of Merthyr Vale. I can feel the presence of Aberfan cemetery in the near distance. Just six decades ago those tips would have likely been visible from these streets. I am walking through the vacant homes at Crescent and Taff Street. Crescent was precisely that. And the Taff already scripted. The winds are howling up the empty arc of this abandoned area. I am slightly on edge as I cannot see beyond the bend. Empty streets are always more troubling than ones filled with even the most suspicious characters. The storm is passing, but there will be another in the months ahead that will force everybody to vacate all streets in these towns. I recall the *Sun* newspaper headline, which earlier in the year referred to this area as "Apocalyptic". They specifically focused upon graffiti, which emblazoned on a wall read, "Keep Out of Hell". What remained today were 100 or so abandoned terraced houses. Following a compulsory purchase order, the villagers were forced to move. Many would be rehoused in the neighbouring village of Aberfan. The reason for the enforced relocation was due to the constant flooding of the streets, which were situated on the bank of the River Taff. Global warming it was said was only going to make things worse for the inhabitants here, which again had no defence against the forces of nature. There is a consistent story being told, over and over, in these precarious towns populated by precarious people living through a constantly precarious time. As I walk deeper into the seclusion, an open doorway beckons onto an unwelcoming darkness within. I have seen the reported photos of the discarded possessions some hastily left behind. I dare not enter its premise. Not out of trepidation for something, but in fear of the nothing I will probably find. I turn the corner at the bottom of Crescent Street and walk onto Taff. In contrast to the former, it's probably the straightest road ever built in the valleys of south Wales. Fittingly it leads to a dead-end. At the bottom I look upon an abandoned playground. There are two sets of empty swings rocking back and forth in the wind that's spiriting away.

Narratives of hell are ever-present in this valley. Nineteenth-century Merthyr Tydfil was frequently described as the closest one would come to living in an infernal abyss. Some of the worst descriptions of economic misery and destitution in Victorian Britain are associated with this town. Built around the Cyfarthfa and Dowlais iron works, early paintings depict an industrial setting where the Hadean world is brought to the surface of the earth. A notable example is George Childs' *Dowlais Ironworks* (1840), which shows the toil of men and women backdropped by a fiery landscape, which burning endlessly is indifferent to their lauded over plight. The fire also appears like the severed arteries of the earth bleeding into the skies. We might compare this to J. M. W. Turner's *Dolbadern Castle* (1800) in Snowdonia, which, painted a few decades earlier, mythologises the beautiful landscape of rural Wales. Despite the gloominess of life and its relationship to the Welsh Prince Owain Goch ap Gruffydd, who was imprisoned at the castle, Turner's artwork still speaks directly to the sublime qualities of place that is evidently connected to heavenly majesty. Literary visitors who came upon Merthyr were struck by its apocalyptic imaginary. The billowing smoke created a suffocated world that only added to the pervading sense of the abysmal. As one John George Wood wrote, Merthyr appeared "like the smoking ruins of some vast city, a prey to the devouring element". Another witness added:

> Hardly anything can be conceived more awfully grand than the descent on a dark night into the Vale of Merthyr, from any of the surrounding hills. On a sudden the traveller beholds numerous volcanos breathing out their undulating pillars of flame and smoke, while the furnaces below emit through every aperture a vivid light; the whole country seems in a blaze.

Such harrowingly contrasting images were further described by George Borrow, who observed:

> The mountain of dross which had startled me on the preceding night with its terrific glare, and which stands to the north-west of the town, looked now nothing more than an immense dark heap of

cinders. It is only when the shades of night have settled down that the fire within manifests itself, making the hill appear an immense glowing mass. All the hills around the town, some of which are very high, have a scorched and blackened look.

The noise only added to the drama as the fires continued to rage and the furnaces perpetually roared out like Dante earlier imagined Satan devouring sinful flesh in the deepest recesses of the underworld. As Edwin Roberts described of his initial walk in the town in 1853,

> ... with a half-stupefied sense of the mighty energies of men and fire combined, such as we might feel in the neighbourhood of some occult monster, with horrent form and myriad antennae — my ears and pulses throbbing with the rush of ceaseless and sounding machinery... ten or fifteen minutes' walk brings you in front of "Penydaran" iron-works, and you stand outside the wall gazing on a scene that seems like a vision [of] Hades in its milder form. Just now it does not seem as if Acheron was belching forth fire and flame; and that the horrible noises described by the poets as appertaining to the infernal regions, were, for some reason or other, subdued.

And yet, for writers such as Roberts, this hellish terror was still horrifyingly alluring. "Terrible as is the aspect of the blast-furnaces", the writer added, "I doubt not if the puddling furnace does not realize a more perfect and Dantean 'hell of fire' than even they do. One looks into the troubled molten sea with something very like awe". Sublimity was part of the attraction as the iron and coal were brought into an infernal union whose marriage was irresistible to behold. But as history often shows, these brimstone marriages of spectacle and seduction prove to be deadly beneath it all. I recall the final words to the Chilean writer Baldomero Lillo's short story "The Devil's Tunnel", published in the 1904 collection *Sub Terra*. Having heard of her son's death in a mining disaster, Lillo narrates, a mother who has become so overwhelmed with grief, having already lost her husband and two other sons in similar ways, commits suicide by throwing herself into the blackness:

> The body was lifted by the shoulders and feet and was laboriously placed in the waiting stretcher. María de los Angeles, upon seeing that ruddy face and that hair which now seemed drenched in blood, made a superhuman effort to throw herself on the body of her son. But pressed up against the barrier she could only move her arms as an inarticulate soundless cry burst from her throat. Then her muscles relaxed, her arms fell to her side, and she stood motionless as if hit by a lightning bolt. The group parted and many faces turned toward the woman who, with her head on her chest, deep in an absolute trance, seemed absorbed in contemplating the abyss open at her feet. No one ever understood how she managed to jump over the barrier or the retaining cables. But many saw her for an instant as her bare legs dangled over empty space and she disappeared, without a sound, into the abyss. A few seconds later, a low and distant sound, almost imperceptible, erupted from the hungry mouth of the pit along with a few puffs of thin vapor: it was the breath of the monster gorged with blood in the depths of his lair.

One area in particular of Victorian Merthyr developed a notorious reputation. The district of Pontystorehouse, or "China" as it was called in what some believe was in reference to the Opium Wars raging between Britain and China at the time (which also fed the insatiable demand for iron), was home to all kinds of criminal and illicit activities. We might also mention here the important role played by the ironmaster Sir John Bowring, who established a large ironworks in the nearby Maesteg during these years. A number of historians have laid the cause for the start of the second Opium War directly at the door of this noble Englishman, whose industry was inseparable to the "white devil's" profits from violence. Alongside the China description, locals also referred to this area as "Little Hell" in reference to its punishing living conditions. Little Hell became associated with a criminal underworld, whose leaders reputedly had the titles of "emperor" and "empress". Prostitution was rife, as were child pickpockets. They often worked together in collaboration with local thugs. It was a quintessential no-go area, populated by drunkards, thieves and rogue characters who preyed upon new arrivals and also themselves. In large part, the establishment of the Glamorgan police constabulary in 1841 was in direct response to the endemic problems blighting this town. Merthyr was a giant slum. Entire families lived in tiny stone huts, which had no toilets nor sanitation. The very poorest would be forced to live in cellar dwellings. Narrow streets were overcrowded, while children would play in the open sewers in the company of dogs, rats and other vermin. The streets of Merthyr were a petri-dish for all manner of pestilence, whose ever-present deathly callings and disfigurements only added further to the hellish vision. Such conditions were the principal cause of the 1849 outbreak of cholera in the hot and dry summer months. In July, as the infectious disease started to spread, 539 people died in the town. A month later 36 people a day were being killed by the disease. It was only the onset of winter that brought an end to the epidemic. When it was over, Merthyr recorded the second highest death toll in the country. 1,682 of its population died as the devil's spies thrived. Indeed, the lords of these flies looked on from a comfortable distance as the town's crucibles of fire continued to burn. By the mid-nineteenth century there were 200 furnaces blackening the air, which produced over one million tons of iron each year. More than 40,000 people lived in these wretched conditions, where diseases such as typhoid continued to spread throughout the community like a biblical plague. Everybody was vulnerable to facing a premature end, with the average age for recorded deaths in 1852 being 17.5 years young. Less than a half of Merthyr's destitute children lived to see in their fifth birthday.

It's in this abysmal, violent and debauched industrial setting that the Nonconformist movement and its chapel architectures start to take a hold over community life in the valleys of South Wales. While it's tempting to view the history of Nonconformism as a form of resistance to the Church of England, which has been inseparable to the British system of rule, in reality it was a deeply conservative institution that preached piety, servitude and temperance. Indeed, one of its most significant achievements was the Welsh Sunday Closing Act in 1881, which banned the sale of alcohol on the Sabbath. This was the first Act of Parliament applied only to Wales since its annexation, which although finally affording a certain independent status, was nevertheless informed by prejudicial attitudes to the drunkenness of a people who were thrown into the belly of industrialisation faster than anybody and without anything to protect them from being devoured. Although this law on drinking was far from strictly adhered to, as the valleys saw the emergence of a number of illegal drinking holes that would be a common feature a few decades later during Prohibition in the United States, for near a century the chapel still largely defined cultural life in the valleys. We might also say that within the chapels is where the idea of Wales being a "land of song" was properly birthed. But chapel culture was more than choral practice. It was politics, and it was life. They were the place where people met and most ideas concerning behaviour and action were discussed. A frequently cited figure tells of one chapel being built every eight days in Wales during the nineteenth century. The result being that by 1905 there were 151 chapels that seated a congregation of 85,000 in the Rhondda valleys alone. This constituted some 75% of the population, who the chapels were able to call upon as part of its membership. Invariably, this reach afforded the elected ministers significant local influence over many aspects of social life. Such power would be fully evidenced upon the eve of World War I, as many ministers followed a wider Christian tendency to openly call for the poor to sign up to fight in the "Just War," as they resurrected old Augustinian ideas in a battle now being presented as between the forces of good and evil. "*Gwell Angau Na Chywilydd*" ("Death Rather than Dishonour") was frequently called out from behind the ministerial lectern to the impressionable masses who were being shamed into slaughter. The impact was telling, as within eight weeks of the war being declared 2,000 miners from the Rhondda had enlisted in the military. Only four years after troops were deployed on streets of Tonypandy, now the local vicar closest to the pit at the centre of the dispute was joining a chorus to effectively create a Welsh Miners' Brigade with battalions of thousands who were willing to die for those who previously sought to destroy their rights. Pacification and war are not always strategically opposed. These sermonised recruitment drives, however, proved to be a monumental error, as tens of thousands of young men never came home by Christmas and instead died in the mud on God-forsaken fields. The pastoral bind that was once unquestionably granted to the chapel was broken as people slowly looked for solace, comfort and protection in a new, caring God of a more material and human kind.

Despite the piety of this religious setting, we shouldn't overlook some of the more colourful characters associated with spiritual movements in these times. A notable personality was William Price of Llantrisant. A qualified surgeon, druid, chartist and Nonconformist, when he wasn't amusing and scandalising locals by parading through the town stark naked, Dr Price provoked in more lasting ways. Price was part of the failed 1839 Chartist uprising and an associated party to the Newport riots, which resulted in him fleeting to Paris for a while. He made his escape dressed as a woman. Upon returning to Wales, he set about reviving ancient Celtic ideas and became more fascinated in the ancestral histories of his fellow countrymen. He promoted vegetarianism, advocated free love, taught that orthodox religion enslaved people, refused to wear socks, wore eccentric clothing including a trademark fox skin headdress, continued to appear on occasions naked in the streets and grew his beard long down his chest. Born in Caerphilly in 1800, Price settled back in the valley town of Llantrisant in 1866. A number of years later he married a local farming girl who was 21 years old. Price was 81. The well-attended ceremony in Pontypridd held at the spiritual "Rocking Stone" site was a predicably eccentric affair full of colour and flamboyance, and even featured as part of the marriage ritual three women dressed as the three graces. Two years later, Price fathered a son who he named Iesu Grist (Jesus Christ). Tragically, the baby only lived for five months and died from unknown causes. Now an avid druid, Price didn't want to bury the body as he felt it would contaminate the earth. He therefore took the dead child to the mountainside and began the ritual of burning the corpse on a coal and wood-fired pyre. The law-breaking and blasphemous ceremony was however disrupted by the local constabulary and an angry mob who rushed up the mountain and took the child's body out of the flames. With a post-mortem removing the suspicions of foul play and infanticide, Price was instead charged in Cardiff with the illegal disposal of a body. Price defended himself and managed to convince the judge the act of cremation was neither illegal or inhumane. The judge agreed. This verdict proved to be a pivotal moment in galvanising a movement that successfully brought about the later Crematorium Act of 1902. It made Price something of a Victorian celebrity in the process, notably delivering many public talks. On his deathbed, it is alleged his final words were "Bring me a glass of champagne", which he drank and then passed away. His body was taken to the hillside in Llantrisant and burned on a two-tonne coal pyre. It is said that over 20,000 people attended the ritual.

It had been raining constantly for over a week. Black streams were running down the hills and the blocked drains from the debris only added to the accumulation of dark water painting the streets. It was difficult to tell on that evening whether the blackout was causing the anxiety or a trepidation of what might happen in the unseen echoes of the night. As the lights went out without any apparent cause, residents frantically knocked on each other's doors asking to borrow candles, which they had thought were consigned to the previous decade. Was it the storm which caused the electricity to fail? Or was it something more harrowing, which was slowly creeping out of the void? The men in the street conducted an audit of the torches, then a gathering of workable batteries taken in negotiation from children's toys, which saw many doubting infants scream out in anger and confusion. Still, the residents needed to know what was happening in the unseeable expanse behind their homes. The fear was genuine. Images of a cascading darkness were still all too vivid. Within the black, it was now understood, resided a more menacing blackness. Aberfan was only 17 years in the distance. And while the people in these towns still couldn't make sense of it, they felt its presence every day as they looked upon those volcanic mounds blotting the lands. Maybe they were overreacting? Maybe the battles to prise the children's batteries weren't helping? What they did know was their worries of it happening again, happening to them, were not unfounded. What they also knew was they could only rely upon themselves to offer guidance and protection. Outsiders only tended to arrive when the unstoppable force of an earthshattering disaster had already passed. A number of the men decided to go up to the mountain and check to see if it had been moving. No doubting it, enough proof of its ambition was already in the streets. But it wasn't really about whether the giant black tips behind the home, which, stacked upon one another, doubled a mountainous landscape twinned in the enormity of its potential, were moving towards the dwarfed streets nestled beneath their shadows. It was by how much. They had no means of telling. Still the nerves told them it was enough. A lengthy discussion proceeded in the torrential torchlit rain to ascertain whether an evacuation would be necessary. Nobody really knew. Besides, where would they go? Several families stood in the streets for a while, until it became clear the children would probably perish more from the wetness and cold as the mountains now stood watch over these trembling bodies. The kids were more eager to stay, making sure they got their energy sources back, knowing full well it would take several months before they could be affordably replaced. The men agreed to take it in turns, patrolling the night and listening to the faint rumbling of the stones, waiting in anticipation for the light to return. They only lasted about an hour until the batteries died, and the rain soaked their determination. The black mountain stood silent as morning broke.

I know that was a Saturday because the following day we headed to the Boys Club down the street, also situated beneath a towering heap, which was probably the highest and steepest of all the spoils in this town. Whenever it snowed, this was the first place we headed. Convinced of our learned geological engineering expertise (years of discovery had us reason that nobody knew the layout, contours and faults of those mountains better than us), we surveyed the base of its structure and still asked ourselves how the hell a mountain can actually move. Naturally we knew it would slide under foot every time we set out to reach its summit. That's what made the ascent more of an unpredictable adventure, especially when racing to the top. But we had no idea how they came into formation. They were simply part of the landscape. While it was decided the Boys Club would remain closed for another two weeks, despite the fact the all-season precipitation was a permanent fixture, it was also decided our game that Sunday morning would go ahead as planned. The rains were still torrential. So 13 sodden souls jumped into a minibus and set off to the village of Clydach. The pitch was built on a flattened area at the base of where the Cambrian Colliery was once situated. The disaster there in 1905 was pivotal in the nearby Tonypandy riots a few years later. On that occasion 33 miners were killed, which would have been much higher had the blast not occurred during the change-over between day and night workers. 66 horses were also killed. Luck is also measured by tragedy in the valley towns. Another explosion happened in the same pit in the year before the Aberfan disaster as firedamp killed 31 miners. It was caused by poor ventilation. This would be the last major accident to take the lives of miners in the South Wales coalfield. We ended up losing 9–0. As a centre-forward I spent most of the game stood on the halfway line in the freezing cold. Not so much a tale of singing but crying in the rain. I have no idea whether the trauma of the previous evening crept into my consciousness as I stood weeping in that circle marking my location upon this losing pitch in time. Maybe it was the humiliating scoreline? Maybe it was because the pitch was more accurately described as a lake, and I feared my cheap boots were done for? Or maybe I believed the rains would simply hide my tears?

Looking back, I now see Aberfan was more than just another unfortunate tragedy, which reveals the fallibilities and failures of man. It truly affected the psychological life of the valleys and its belief in itself and the world that only seemed to be weathering a people as sure as the storms. On the seventieth day of the Aberfan disaster tribunal, Desmond Ackner QC, who was representing the people, completed his closing argument concerning the "horror of this disaster" by citing the Nobel Prize-winning author Bernard Shaw: "The worst sin toward our fellows is not to hate them, but to be indifferent to them: for that is the essence of inhumanity". We know there is no distinct separation between religion and secularism. Every secular idea we know is a reworking of older theological claims, which still seep into the proof-demanding minds of even the most logical, rational and scientifically certain of all human beings. At the very moment industrialisation found itself on trial, it was no coincidence then to see a return to religious language, for the two were never really separated to begin with. Even as the three great monotheistic religions of Christianity, Judaism and Islam were replaced by the equally universalising claims of Capitalism, Socialism and Fascism, so the naked appeal to a power greater than any single individual could comprehend fully was reimagined for a secular age. Invoking Shaw in the way Ackner did was not then a departure from the monstrous mechanised nature of the crime, which saw the tribunal labour over the lines of communication, the technical procedures, the who said and did what in the daily processes of material extraction. If there was a devil, it was in the detail. And it was in the detail of indifference that the catastrophe was revealed as being something far greater in its meaning than any act of mere recklessness.

The first reporter to arrive on the scene following the Aberfan disaster was John Humphrys from the BBC. He described what he encountered as a "scene from hell". The same language was used by Alix Palmer, who at 27 years old was sent by the *Daily Express*. It was her very first assignment. In a letter to her mother she wrote, "You probably noticed that I was in Aberfan this weekend. But you will have no possible idea of what hell it was. No newspaper could ever paint a picture terrible enough." In her report for the *Sunday Express* the day after the tragedy, she reported, "Sunday was dreadful too because the full realisation of what had happened had begun to hit home. The church services were not beautiful. They were terrible. But the bravery of those people was incredible. I came home on Monday night having learned a great deal about life and death and finding it difficult to believe in anything at all". One description called the mountain "the evil black tongue". Aberfan represented more than just a dark ecology. It was belief-shattering. In the biblical tradition, the Apocalypse appears as a cataclysmic moment of judgement in which everything is put on the line. This is said to begin as the trumpets from the heavens ring out with fire-burning rocks falling form the skies, filled with the blood of humanity. Metaphorical or not, fire-burning rocks fell upon Aberfan on that mist-covered morning as the children walked through a blinding light, until the darkness descended upon them. Truer to its original meaning, the apocalypse is said to be a moment of unveiling through which the state of the world is fully uncovered. Apocalypse brings everything into the open, including the belief structures upon which the society was founded. Implicit within this must be the idea that an apocalyptic moment can only occur if belief itself was put into jeopardy. And that is where its earthly meaning is tied to the notion of the falling skies. Crucially, what we have found in modern times is the more apocalyptic moments rain down, the more our answers fail. This invariably leads to the disavowal of every myth held dear. Witnessing each of the members of many religious denominations walking to the burial site as the Aberfan children were laid to rest, was a clear indication they knew each faith was also finally being buried alongside. The power of their orthodox Gods and the prevalent Nonconformist gospels were already fading in these towns. While there were six chapels of worship still operating in the village at the time of the disaster, attendance had been falling sharply since World War I. But this was different. Indeed there was a catastrophe behind the catastrophe, in which belief itself found it impossible to breathe as the stench of the mountain laid everything bare, including the deepest anxieties that trouble the mind. Echoing a verse from Grahame Davies' "The Graves at Aberfan":

The hearts of every woman, every man
— for distance is no hindrance to dismay —
go to the rows of graves at Aberfan.

The prayers of every capel, every llan,
bring to the village where no children play
the hearts of every woman, every man.

Those who can find no God and those who can,
saints who despair and apostates who pray
go to the rows of graves at Aberfan.

The separation that no sense can span
will break forever, one October day,
the hearts of every woman, every man.

You who believe that God must have a plan
— tell it to those whose memories today
go to the rows of graves at Aberfan.

All that we fear the most since fear began,
the tide of black no love can keep at bay.
The hearts of every woman, every man
go to the rows of graves at Aberfan.

Those black tides that brought to the surface the most primordial of fears not only led believers to question the truth of Christianity. As that song of sorrow was carried from Merthyr Vale over the tops of each and every town that constitutes the valleys of South Wales, so another belief system was also facing its own judgement. No God dies instantly. They are slowly replaced. For this to happen several Gods can exist at once in the minds of followers. Yet what was happening here was so tremendous, every God that made a claim was being asked to justify why and how it could allow something like this to happen. Just as Nonconformism was being questioned, so people were further questioning an ideological kind of faith manifest in mechanised dreams. State-led socialism also abandoned them in their hour of need. Aberfan's sorrow then was a passing moment for us all. It concentrated our attentions. It deepened the focus, into the nothingness that offered nothing back. It also mirrored back to us another kind of dereliction which, born of human failure, resulted in a dereliction of the heart. The valleys of South Wales were the heartland of industrialisation. And not just in terms of raw productive effort. Whatever the conditions, the beating hearts of the valleys were full of passion and pride. But the hearts stopped in Aberfan on that October morn, and slowly with them the veins that led out into the network of lives that could no longer find strength in the ground. If terror has us fleeing as those children tried to do when the blackness came tumbling down, the horror of its witnessing which followed (as invoked by Ackner during his closing summation) created a cataclysmic statis in which nobody was able to move. It is telling that one of the children survivors referred to the initial stages of the tragedy as "pandemonium". A word with origins in Greek mythology, it would later be translated in Christian theology to mean a place inhabited by demons. Indeed, while Milton had us imagine the pandemonium as literally being a mountainous palace in hell, the artist John Martin pictures a fiery river that is unstoppable in its destructive intent. "Pandemonium then," as the child survivor Bernard Thomas tells,

> children rushing around and screaming. When it hit there was a tremendous crashing and next, I felt being lifted up, desk, everything was pushed on top of the tidal wave. I didn't realise what was happening, it was all black. I thought it was the end.

Such a sense of horror persisted, which is why the desire to run away has for my generation always been more than merely economical. We too were in search of a different meaning, something more to life than merely this, hoping to find it in the future, without knowing that what we really needed was to dig further into the ancestral black earth.

Finding a deeper meaning requires moving beyond looking at the dereliction of the valleys in terms of its location. Yes — the trauma belongs to these towns. But space means nothing without a richer appreciation of time. We need to attend to the time of the valley, which reveals its own fragmented wounding. Aberfan represented a blackening of time, where a community was thrown into a purgatory as real as the recovered clock from the school that stopped the moment the blackness arrived. 9:13. The time the valley stood still. Upon this face, for a few brief seconds a gateway opened into a veritable void. The outstretched arms appear so reminiscent of images of crucified hands, where the welcoming embrace is turned into the ultimate test of faith. Such hands were not simply about a momentary cessation in the unending rotations of an overdetermined time, which had become so normalised in industrial settings where every second was marked by a tick. They pointed to a different temporality. As one hand pointed to the east in nostalgia for an industrial past that sustained life, another pointed westward to a tragic present where the edict "every second counts" truly took on a more fateful meaning. So while observers will be right to note how Aberfan served as a reminder of the ecological dangers present in the valleys of South Wales, the river ran much deeper. What Aberfan has demanded is that we don't just see such disasters as a moment of realisation where untold devastation reveals itself in the form of some sublime and unstoppable force on an epic scale, however world-changing those tragedies may be. In the moments of its deliverance, Aberfan presented to us something requiring a more intimate understanding of a slow violence that eventually matures, which also forces us to look deeper into the lasting blackness into which life descends. A vision of the disaster, in other words, that's equally marked by the absences and disappearances of its lasting effects as it is by the visible terror of an unimaginable suffering.

I was conceived in a time of darkness. Throughout 1973, much of the United Kingdom was living under blackout conditions. Following the demands from miners to redress decades of wage stagnation, negotiations in the previous year with the Conservative government had broken down, resulting in the first major strike to be called by the National Union of Mineworkers since the 1920s. Without coal, the country was literally plunged into darkness and a state of emergency was declared. People were forced to live by candlelight. While some temporary progress was made, as a result of the economic shutdown inflation soared and so the miners' brief gains were wiped out. They now refused to work overtime, having a major impact on useable coal stocks. The government introduced a number of energy-saving measures, most notably the introduction of the three-day week, which commenced on New Year's Eve in 1973. With electricity severely rationed, the entire country was living through blackout conditions and many in poorer communities like the valleys without any warmth during the wintery months. Heating was officially limited to one room and people returned to bathing by heating water in a kettle or on a stove. Panic-buying also set in, as there was a familiar run on items like candles, tinned foods and toilet paper. It seemed the only way out of the impasse was a general election, which was called in February 1974 and returned the Labour government of Harold Wilson to the helm. One of his first acts was to offer the miners a 35% wage increase. The restrictions were lifted on 7 March, five days after I was born. This would be the miners' last real political victory. Meanwhile, on the other side of the world, new fires were raging that would steam up into the atmosphere and very swiftly push the ideological winds covering these lands in the opposite direction. Following on from the US-led coup in Uruguay that June, the violent overthrow and murder of elected President Salvador Allende in Chile on 11 September 1973 would have monumental significance for the international order. While the likes of Che Guevara had been assassinated a number of years prior, this was the first time US Operation Condor sanctioned the killing of the first democratically-elected Marxist president. Not only did this show the violence Western societies were willing to authorise against ideological foes, it also created a space where the free-market ideas of Hayek could be properly tested. Augusto Pinochet soon became a darling of the new capitalists the world over, including very shortly after Reagan and Thatcher. Tragically, 12 days after the Chilean coup, one of the greatest poets to have ever lived, the Chilean-born Pablo Neruda, died. Whether he died of cancer or state poisoning is very much open to question. We might recall how Neruda was elected to the Chilean Senate in 1944 as a communist member. He only decided to stand for office having been convinced by the nitrate miners of Antofagasta, with whom he forged a close friendship. Following the outlawing of the party four years later, Neruda was forced into hiding and the miners protected him for several months until he managed to escape into Argentina. That country would be subject to a similar coup two years later. During his clandestine flight,

Neruda worked on *Canto General*, which was partly inspired by the tales of the miners and how they connected to the history of colonisation. The language of poetry became his resistance. Yet as Neruda anticipated, and as the South Wales valleys would soon learn, the free-market God that was willing to do what was needed to kill its ideological challenger had little care or concern for its more disposable congregations. Such communities were merely asked once again to learn to suffer in life, to accept the piety of being poor, and to open themselves up to an invisible force, which would test more than it would treat, lacerate more than it would love. So, as the invisible hand reached across the mountains of South Wales, its extending fingers created a new depression in the skies that would leave the believers lost in a familiar wilderness of doubt, in which once welcoming streets would become more alienated and broken.

I leave the family home and decide to talk a walk in the rain. Sometimes the damp familiarity is comforting. I walk past the boarded-up Bethesda chapel and look upon a few attached amateur portraits that indicate some attempted restoration. There is one of Paul Robeson. I do wonder why nobody has turned the entire complex into large art studios and resurrected its still grand chapel room for concerts and public talks. Surely the lofty space alone would be an attraction for many creatives to come and work in the valleys for a while? Maybe that's what happens when a place loses its belief. It feels like nobody wants to listen, nobody wants to make the journey. I walk out of the village and into the neighbouring town of Pentre. These streets show more signs of dereliction than most. Walking up the hill I gaze across to where the black doubled mountains behind our previous home used to reside. They were bookended by two other monumental structures either side, which dominated the village. I remember when I first saw they had been flattened and the debris more evenly spread across the ridge. I strangely felt a deep sadness, slightly traumatised by what was no longer there. Those black mountains were an integral part of my childhood. They gave me a sense of bearing every time I needed to find my way into the past. I still miss them. I still search for photographs to remind me of how things were. I carry on walking and look upon the open expanse to my right, where the black mountain slid into the streets over a century ago. There are no signs of that history, besides we now look upon the slide of a more economic kind. The hill used to be teaming with local stores and vendors, butchers and bric-a-bracs, including two high street banks and an Italian coffee place. They have all closed. At the top of the hill stands Ton and Pentre Labour and Progressive Club, which was one of the longest-running working men's establishments in the Rhondda. Unionists and activists frequently met here. That too is boarded-up and the memories of its past secreted in plain sight. There is something truly symbolic about the dilapidation of a place whose name alone testifies to everything this valley once stood for. There is no labour anymore and the only thing progressing is the bad weather. Still, a familiar landmark beckons before me as I look upon the only bank residing in this town. It's a local nightclub, which changed its name during the early 1990s as the banking revolution was complete. The venue dates back to 1913 and was previously a 600-seat cinema called The Kings Hall, which began running silent movies. Given the raucous nature of the place, it would undoubtedly benefit from its own temperance. This was the place where we mostly ended up on weekend evenings when our journey into inebriation began. Saturday nights were certainly alright for fighting, and it wasn't lost on us that the only banks in town were more like Wild West Saloons. What we deposited was immediately consumed so at least we might forget our troubles, until another fractious kind of trouble inevitably arrived later in the night. During Thatcherism the focus for capitalism was no longer about extracting wealth from hard labour. That belonged to a more primitive and laborious time. Empowering the bankers, she was part of a monetary revolution whose purpose was to make money from other people's money. But what happens when there is no money to put to work? In this economy, the people of the valleys were effectively two steps removed from the concerns of those powering the new financial order of things. Like a disinterested God, the Tories merely precipitated further the slow demise of these streets. Further down the road stands in ruins the once familiar Polikoff's social club, which is where many an evening was spent between male miners and female workers of the same named factory. It's where my grandparents often met as they learned ballroom dancing. Directly opposite is where the Salvation Army is located. It was where my grandfather stood as a child in wait, and where a new precarious congregation now stand. Destitution and love are so often lived in such close proximity in the valleys of South Wales.

The rain is now falling at a heavier rate, and I look upon the long line of families patiently waiting. As it was nearly 100 years ago, heating and food poverty still affects so many in these towns, who feel the weight of history pressing them down. Indeed, if Britain in the past decade has fast become a Food Bank Nation, one of its capital outposts is the Rhondda. With many local services all but decimated and starved of funds, feeding the disbelieving poor is once again placed into the charitable hands of organised religion. Situated on the exact same site where a chapel once stood that was the centre point for the soup kitchens during the Great Depression, the Salvation Army, working with the Trussell Trust, in the village of Pentre continue to be tasked with providing food relief to the hungry. According to the Trust, for the past few years the Rhondda district has accounted for more than 10% of all handouts in Wales (these numbers would be far higher if we included other former mining valley areas, such as Merthyr, Blaenau Gwent and Caerphilly). Between April 2020 and March 2021 alone, of the 91,611 parcels provided in Wales, 10,064 were given to families of this valley, with more than half provided to children. The City of Cardiff was allocated during the same period 9,033 parcels, which is still a desperately high number from one single source of surrogate welfare provision. While these numbers are nearly double what they were only half a decade previously, they only really provide a snapshot of a much wider and deeply felt social malaise. And that was before the start of the energy crisis that threw these exact same people further into the depths of hardship. With inflation soaring, increased demand was being brought into sharp relief by a fall in donated supply. Media reports indicated that during the winter of 2022, the demand for food bank provisions tripled what they were the previous year. The charity and the Salvation Army also requested that donated foods required little or no warming or else they would be of no use to people here. Fuel poverty is more acutely felt in these valleys than anywhere in the United Kingdom. So once again as the people of the Rhondda were being thrown into the cold and dark, what the history of the valleys shows is that, for a century, the very idea of living in a zone of crisis has always been a close-to-home reality and never just a televised spectacle. Some kinds of misery only really grab the attention if they can be turned into entertainment, while others are fodder for some to intellectualise suffering upon new digital playgrounds, which is home to pitiful forms of performativity a world away from the people who stand on these streets and who simply wished the weather would have been kinder. Can this dereliction ever be lifted? Can these people find reasons to believe in anything?

In 2021, the results of a census were released that asked people of their sense of nationality and religious affiliations. For the first time, less than half the Welsh population considered themselves Christian. The responses marked as "non-religious" were recorded the highest in the valleys, with areas of Caerphilly, Blaenau Gwent, the Rhondda and Merthyr all suggesting a majority of non-believers. The figures recorded here were higher than anywhere in England. We could surmise the same figures would be repeated should the same populations be asked about ideological affiliations today as well, which has also markedly declined over the years as any vestiges of socialist belonging have become as hollowed as the Labour clubs. The non-working men now largely drink at home and while away their troubles in isolation and loneliness. They don't speak to any God, because they know none are listening and even if they were, they didn't care. One of the concerns with mechanisation was how it gradually alienated the worker from the productive process. Miners especially felt this as their skill and craft was slowly taken over by machines that turned them into mere operators that could speed up the extraction, speed up their demise. While alienation however may lead to a sense of isolation within the workplace, it is different from loneliness. The lonely feel like they are truly alone in the world. And they do not enjoy the richness of contemplative solitude, the authored demand of being alone with one's thoughts provides. The lonely cannot think because their thoughts are consumed by absence. They cannot act because they have no belief in bringing something into the world. What they become is easy prey for those who seek to politicise their anguish and replace their desires to simply be part of something with hate-filled belonging. Loneliness and totalitarianism are inseparable. The latter can only exist when the former endures. Loneliness is a closure, for the mind, for the heart and for the spirit. It condemns. But like people the world over, we are entering into a new realm of loneliness today, which masquerades as connection. For poor people especially, the digital revolution has only brought more anxiety, more precarity, more insecurity, more separation, more loneliness. We have become alienated from ourselves and the world that used to give meaning and purpose. Children of the valleys feel this most acutely, as the proliferation of digitalised syndromes cannot be separated from the sense of fatalism and despair about the future. Loneliness belongs to the future. It is marked by an incessant colouration of blackness, which is not a beautiful void of creative possibility, but a suffocating wall of nothing. That points to a dereliction of the self, which no community-focused "app" can possibly seek to restore.

Like a dying God, dereliction doesn't happen overnight. It's generational. Its violent affliction is cut by a slower temporality. Until it's there. Witnessing the dereliction so evident in every town in the valleys today, I am forced to think about the children that remain and what promise of a future they hold. Children are dreamers. What matters is the myths we pass onto them. To my estimation, part of the story we need to retell concerns a rediscovery of adventure, where they can learn to appreciate the complexity of the world and the comedy of existence. It's a bit of a cliché to say we spent most of our childhoods playing in the streets. In truth, when we weren't galivanting across the mountains like the most ill-equipped intrepid explorers, defying all scientific explanations as we proved immune to the onset of windswept pneumonia, we could be found experiencing the full boredom of freedom in the backstreet alleys or what locals called "the gullies". Aside from the precariously framed glass panes that were too often the victim of an overeager footballing incident and whose damages were seldom paid, the problem with the streets was that youth were always exposed to the prying eyes of 100 potential reprimands from shadowy figures just waiting to reveal themselves from the darkness of the inner sanctum. Each house was fronted with just as much fragile window as weathered stone, which meant nothing occurred without the entire street knowing about it. This was social media of a more human kind, webbed together by the fraying curtains that were the only mediating concerns for us. The backstreets, however, were beyond the watching gaze of those who wished to suck the fun out of every possible occasion. Garden walls were high enough to avoid detection, which meant these spaces could be properly called our own. As such, it was in the gullies where many of my more mischievous formative developments occurred. It was in the backstreets of the valleys where I had my first fight, resulting in a loss that could only (as always) be accounted for by a "lucky punch" and which gave me a lesson in the shameful bruising of an ego; where I kissed my first serious girlfriend who was visiting her grandmother from afar and who I ended up spending two weeks with huddled in the freezing rain without barely saying a word as the drops fell between our frostbitten noses; where I saw a friend repeatedly kicked in the head by a gang membered assailant whose yellow trainers turned red as the blood flowed, and as he lay on the ground was subsequently beaten with his own skateboard until he lay semi-conscious and gasping for air; where a pre-pubescent group of us discovered the sodden pages of our first nude magazine that had us looking in disgust then throwing the offending object into a nearby allotment at the sight of a hairy member from the opposite sex, which would have had lesser reaction were a rabid broken-toothed rodent to have jumped from the page; where we spent hours teasing the giant spider with the grassy promise of food in that black hole in the wall which appeared to have a depth defying its outside structural appearance, yet for whom we had nothing but a respect born of a real curious fright and whose eventual absence we surely mourned; where I smoked my first cigarette, which was swiftly followed by my face turning yellow and a severe bout of vomiting that to this day had me vowing to never put my body through that again; where a few of us upon learning of the death of a local troublemaker who would terrorise the area from time to time and had succumbed to a bag of glue which suffocated his lungs from within, stupidly celebrated by trying to get high on muscle antifreeze, immediately resulting in the most excruciating collective headache possibly ever shared; and where I first got blind drunk consuming a bottle of Mad Dog 20/20, which did nothing for the vision except turn you into gutter-crawling beasts of a different kind, also swiftly followed by the vomiting and the mother of all headaches, which produced a congregation of kneeled prayer-givers wishing to be taken from the vein-popping terrestrial hell of it all there and then.

Headachingly normal recollections aside, there is a qualification that does need to be emphasised here. It is clear to any inhabitant or visitor that the valleys are not the same as they were near half a century ago. Due to various grants and schemes, most of the houses are now furnished with double-glazed windows, and many of the frontages cleaned and painted in a way that truly marks respect for the homestead. The dignity and pride, in fact, have always been there, despite the smiting winds of history. There have been notable relative improvements; indeed, I know that a generation on from mine may not even recognise some of the images of the valleys I have painted. The blackness has largely been blanketed over in a more comforting coniferous hue. The streets are now filled with cars, which do provide some means for temporary escape. The air does feel lighter, even if the rains persist and the dark clouds continue to form. Children are seldom seen walking the streets in broken shoes and rotted jeans, benefitting from the importation of cheap clothing from overseas that was part of a logic which led to the widespread closures in these towns. But like a glossy magazine, the frontsteads and the affordable throwaway attire often mask a deeper vulnerability. The abandoned buildings are still there in every town, marking a century of notable dereliction. And the hopelessness remains behind the filtered faces of the manipulated social media smiles. Indeed, the children are seldom seen walking the streets at all, having less been abducted by imaginary ghouls we frightened ourselves about, and more by devices that abduct the imagination and steal the playful soul of youths. You'd understand properly what I meant by walking around the new sites of absence which have become defining to the valleys of South Wales: the abandoned backstreets. These zones in which we naively and yet learnedly flirted with risk are no longer teeming with the young, who are nowhere to be seen. Yet as I return and walk around these empty spaces, I still see how they reveal in the lost decay the unmediated reality of the valleys that is hidden in plain sight and yet something only the elder generations who lived the past can properly see and recall.

They say the past is a different place. Stood here in the backstreet of my life, I feel that unending sense of purgatory return, which as Dante noted needs some kind of reckoning for a new journey to begin. Yet as I gaze upon this worn and decrepit green door, I am lifted by the honesty it possesses. Why this door has captivated me, I still don't know. Maybe I am still subconsciously taken by the South Walean reincarnation of Elvis Presley, who is the son of a coalminer and former communist who goes by the name of Shakin' Stevens, and whose rockabilly cover that I could be singing in this moment was the very first piece of vinyl I owned. The years of moisture have taken their toll, as the cracks in the paint reveal deeper cracks in the wooden structure behind. A sharp, perturbing nail reveals a certain defiance, which promises to both guard and wound like a misplaced love who doesn't quite know the savagery of the thorn. The moss build-up that is home to a veritable micro-ecology of bugs and mites shows that human hands haven't touched this for as long as the memory of these backstreets are able to recall. Rusty hinges only add to the sense of widespread corrosiveness, as the greens and reds combine in a vibrant colour formation to which I have surreally become so accustomed. But it is the knotted eyes that draw me into a conversation with this abandoned relic. She seems to be standing there, nakedly worn and yet unashamed by the passing of old weathered time. How she must have secretly looked upon generations of the young, all telling in her stowaway presence their own dreams of escape and wishes to simply open her doorway into another place, another life. I imagine the imprint of long-lost children, all shadows and bone, who sat with their chilled backs to her risen torso, laughing with each other with a more joyful abandon as they sought to conspire with the elements they had long made peace with. We certainly learned the hard way about the importance of picking your fights. I can't help feel that the children of these towns would learn so much more about their history, about themselves, if they once again walked around these forgotten corridors and observed the life they inhabited, instead of being seduced by the distracting simulacrum of a digital world that's merely selling them illusions of an existence that is literally and metaphorically out of reach. But maybe they would be forced to confront a reality that's too intolerable to bear? After all, the doorways to our desolation have tended to reopen the moment we feel history bring the source of our shared forced abandonment to a close. Then again, maybe the real dereliction belongs to the graveyard of the forgetting mind?

A BOY FROM NOWHERE

I was born in 1974. Domestic terrorism appeared in this year of my arrival, as the IRA began its bombing campaign on mainland Britain. This was another reminder of the legacy of colonisation that would continue to have a profound impact on the political landscape. President Nixon resigned in disgrace, lying like the best of them, while Muhammad Ali defied all the odds and showed how a sportsman can truly transcend any sport by defeating George Foreman in that Rumble in the Jungle. The socialite Patty Hearst was kidnapped by the Symbionese Liberation Army in Berkeley, California. She would later join the movement and appear on film robbing a bank. Manchester United were relegated from the English First Division thanks in part to a goal from their former legend Dennis Law, who now played for their City rivals. Not far away, Bill Shankly stunned Liverpool Football Club by resigning and would be replaced by the relatively unknown Bob Paisley. They would become my childhood team and Paisley would lead the club to unprecedented European success. In the year the World Trade Organisation would be established, von Hayek won the Nobel Prize in Economics, validating the revolution that was soon to follow. The jazz musician and composer Duke Ellington passed away, as the Black Panther Angela Davis published her autobiography. An unknown Hungarian professor named Erno invented the Rubik's Cube, while the first *Good Beer Guide* was published in the United Kingdom. The scarf-wearing Tom Baker was revealed as the most flamboyant and eccentric of all the *Doctor Who* space-time travellers. He would later become the voice of *Little Britain*. A 67-strong Native American Tribe called the Kootenai declared a peaceful war on the United States government. Their settlement would be 12.5 acres of land. The Seventh Earl of Lucan Richard John Bingham, or Lord Lucan as he was commonly known, disappeared without a trace following the murder of his children's nanny. He has never been found. A rather forgettable World Cup was held in West Germany and won by West Germany. The tournament signalled the end for the gold-plated Jules Rimet trophy, which was replaced by the Italian sculptor Silvio Gazzaniga's more ostentatious solid gold design. I first came to know of these sacred objects through prized replica models which were bought to accompany my Subbuteo 1986 World Cup edition, whose teams included the Argentinians and the Germans. As Patti Smith released her cover of "Hey Joe" that was adapted for the gun-toting Hearst, Carl Douglas had dancefloors "Kung-Fu Fighting", while Bob Marley invariably sang out the slow ending to many evenings with "No Woman, No Cry". Stephen King and his wife stayed in room 217 as the only guests at the Stanley Hotel in Estes Park, Colorado before it closed for the winter. That night he dreamt his three-year-old son was being chased through its long corridors, which became the inspiration for his psychological masterpiece *The Shining*. While closer to home, the Mid Glamorgan County Council's education director wrote bluntly to the Secretary of State for Wales about the living conditions of the former mining communities. He simply declared, "The valleys are dying".

I was born into this moment. A moment of monumental significance and monumental insignificance without any discernible contradiction. The world was violently and creatively ablaze. Yet elsewhere it simply deepened the stasis as the wheels of progress slowly ground to a halt. I was born into towns which once stood for something and were populated by people with meaning and purpose. I was born into a nowhere land, full of nowhere people, ghosted by the past, discarded by the rest. I was born, like all of us here, within, absent of an open history, denied being part of a world in the making, without the promise of a future in a time that the land forgot. I was born into a wound as deep as the valley itself, into a collapsing void, which every God that visited refused to heal. I was born with nothing else but this reminder of dereliction and hopelessness, with nowhere to run, everything to hide. For as long as I can remember, it was drummed into us that to be a somebody, there was a need to leave these dying towns that were slowly decaying before our eyes. There were only two roads one could take out of such perdition. A military march or educated flight. My fates had now thrown me into the invisible hands of the latter. And yet I couldn't help feeling the disinterested hands throwing those dice were still loading. Were we not already defined by our deficits? Were we not reminded constantly of being nobodies, who needed to prove themselves to simply "amount to something"? And what did that entail? To think as if one already belonged elsewhere? To shed the skin of poverty and the black dust of its misery that covered us each day beneath these melancholic clouds? To embrace the credence of individuality and the newfound gospel of material happiness? To deny everything of my past, my parents, my forebears, my town, my valley, my life? I soon discovered that, to overcome this life, it was necessary to educate myself *out of the valleys*. It wasn't just about physically leaving. I needed to psychologically inhabit the elsewhere. That was the haunting script that lay before us, which I now see contains a far greater depth of delusion and madness than the darkest Shakespearean recesses of any Hamlet's mind. Yet to think, feel and act like valleys people do would be the surest way to guarantee my failure in life, as there would be no means for outliving the post-industrial corpse. Tom Jones later sang about the conditions faced by men for whom history already determines their place in his rendition of "A Boy from Nowhere", curiously for a musical about an Andalusian matador, whose production was put to a halt due to the first Gulf War. Then again, perhaps Marvin Lee Aday, who knew far too much about mental states of anguish and depression, cried it out with a more applicable resonance. We were after all in the middle of nowhere. Stood somewhere near the end of the line.

Knowing there was a border to somewhere waiting. With the only thing possessed being a tankful of misspent time.

I'm nearly half a century into this all too fleeting existence and I find myself walking around the abandoned rubble of my former school. I feel like I am back again in a nowhere place, neither somewhere nor anywhere, at least with any meaningful coordinates which might allow me to navigate that place we call the past. As I walk over broken bricks that once disciplined ambition and taught us to believe that escape was the only viable way to recover any measure of hope, what I do know is that a deep well of trauma lies beneath these ruins of education. Yet what I see before me today are nothing but collapsed memories, mostly discarded, and lost in time beneath the scattered stone debris. Its vacated classrooms pulled to the ground and as overgrown as the mountain's forests reclaim the hillside. Some of the frames from the windows I would often gaze out into the dense woodlands now lay broken and rotted amongst the overgrowth. Everything returns, it seems. Only the familiar red bricks provide any indication of its former identity and purpose. As I walked around the site of the former Pentre Upper School, I couldn't help thinking about the fates of children who were taught to know one's place or to be psychologically prepared to face the future by learning how to flee from this impoverished life. Once a former Victorian grammar school for the select, it was later converted into a self-contained facility to house first-year comprehensive students. It was meant to be a gentle introduction to the secondary system before making your way over to the school proper in Treorchy, whose modernist blue structures could be seen on the daunting horizon. We would often stand by the playground fence looking at the senior premises in the distance, listening to stories of how children who ventured into the toilets would have their heads flushed down lavatories or simply beaten up for no good reason. I'd like to say the stories were exaggerated, but sadly that wasn't the case. Beside the school, through the trees, stood a rather impressive house, by valley standards, which still there today was the home for a while of William Abraham. Pentre Secondary, or "Sec" as it was affectionally called, was an imposing three-storey structure perched on the eastern side of the upper valley. Rumour has it the school was built the wrong way around, so its front faced onto the concealed, densely forested mountainside, symbolically limiting any natural chance for enlightenment. It was situated above the rectangular façade of St Peters Church, locally known as the Cathedral of the Rhondda, which offered a poignant reminder to say a little prayer before heading up for the day's "education". While it had many similar features to other schools in the valleys, its high walls, which featured brutal steel fencing, made it feel more like an asylum or correction facility. Both had an element of truth. The school was in a dire state of disrepair and was set for imminent closure. Our year would be the last cohort of students to walk through its intimidating disciplinary gates. The doors would permanently shut in the summer of 1986 and reduced to its current abandoned state a few years later.

The school had an eerie and sinister presence, which often made you feel rather unsettled and on edge, especially if you happened to find yourself alone walking through its corridors or up one of its unlit staircases situated at either end of the building. There were some traces of its former grammar school grandeur, with a number of the classrooms and the headmaster's office featuring ornate wooden facades and panelling, though these had also seen better days. Once I was sent out of a music lesson for being too disruptive and showing no interest in learning how to play something by Peer Gynt on the torturous plastic recorder. The music room was situated in the depths of the school, adjacent to the wood and metal workshop, which often featured students who really had nothing better to do than grind away the shards of time. My triumph was a metal key tab that took weeks to file into its far from oval shape. As I was stood out in the corridor, the noise of the screeching machines echoed down the lonely windswept corridors, while the double-hinged doors moved open and shut without a badly adjusted tie-wearing wretched soul in sight. The experience had far greater disciplinary effect than anything the teacher threatened. The school and its grounds were said to be haunted. In 1962 a fire broke out in a chemistry laboratory, causing one of the school masters to suffer a heart attack and die on the premises. Fire damage could still be seen in a blackened and sealed-off room some 20 years after the tragic incident. His ghost was said to walk around the school corridors and woodland behind. In the summer after leaving a few of us decided to break into the now abandoned and boarded-up building to prove our manhood and show who was the bravest. Having entered through the side door as the sun was starting to set and armed with a few pocket torches, we only managed to make it up one flight of stairs before hearing a noise on the floorboards above. We scarpered and never spoke to each other of the incident again.

The school was marked by its segregations. While the boy's entrance took you up a winding road where the delivery vans also travelled, the girl's entrance had steep stairs covered in trees and bushes which at least gave it some floral appeal. Teachers also used this more dignified walkway, as I would later find out with painful consequences. The playground was split, deliberately separating the boys from the girls. It was forbidden to enter into the others' territory, which often meant if your football went over the dividing fence, a young lady had to be identified who would be willing to return it without suffering the public humiliation of rejection or, worse still, being outright ignored. Students were separated in class according to aptitudes, the As, the Bs, and the remedials, or the "rems" as they were cruelly called, often featuring the troublesome, the neglected and the disabled. The best teachers focused on the As, while the worst disciplinarians with their intimidating methods were tasked with keeping the others in line and minimising the disruption so that the school could at least present a semblance of order. I was in form 1 AD, not so much *Anno Domini* (though at times it felt like that), but named after the initials of the form teacher, which at least gave us some recognition. Diners were held in the lower primary school as the upper had no catering facilities. Every Monday I needed to do the walk of shame and wait in line to collect my free diner tickets, which were given to the most destitute families of poor children. We also benefitted from discounted school uniforms which, made of cheap and irritable polyester, also marked your allegiance to the locally impoverished. Such public displays at least made the others appear relatively more enriched. Today the same dynamics which make a spectacle out of the shame of being poor are repackaged into mainstream entertainment. Calling out the destitute, like I was during this weekly ritual, standing up and standing out as member of a burdensome group in front of the entire class, the "benefits" of poverty are turned into a form of pornography to make others feel better at your expense. This was also my first introduction to black market economies, as some students would sell their tickets for a reduced rate at the dining hall entrance, while a few of the more entrepreneurial would get themselves into trouble with the headmaster so they could gain access into his room where the tickets were stored. They worked in packs of three. When the first was summoned into the room for the dressing down, the two outside would start a fight with each other knowing the head would come charging outside in a fit of rage. This commotion would leave the abandoned child inside free to steal a roll. The school eventually caught on and so introduced date stamps and required you to write your name on the backs. There were random spot checks enforced at the tills.

Punishments by teachers were routinely administered upon the recalcitrant with varying degrees of severity and would often involve various teaching implements now put to a more gravitational use. The most frequently used would be wooden rulers that would be lashed down across the palm of the open hand, with the reactive closure of the fingers strictly forbidden. This spectacle also took place at the front of the classroom with the rest of the students watching on, with the lashes ranging on the whipping scale from one to three for being persistently annoying, onto ten for the most disobedient of talkbacks. More spontaneous would be the aerial use of the blackboard duster, which for the assailant was assisted in the accuracy of its unsuspecting flight by their solid wooden backs. In geography one afternoon a particularly impressive event occurred as the duster connected with the back of a boy's head from a notably accurate teacher who was a good 15 yards away on the other side of the classroom. The student's back was turned, while he continued to talk away unaware his lack of attention and disruptive behaviour was being observed and each sentence merely adding more tension to the soon to be released velocity of the erasing projectile. The impact resulted in a halo like plume of white particles emitting from behind his bruised cranium. I tried to adopt the same principles one wintery day having spent quite some time constructing in my frozen hands the most perfectly round snowball, which was primed for action. As it left my hand enroute to the unsuspecting and exposed legs of a delicate girl in the near distance, I watched in slow motion horror as it whizzed past while in the same moment the headmaster's upper torso started to appear from behind the hedge, which concealed the steps to the girl's walkway behind. The accuracy with which it hit that unsuspecting and already stern moving face was quite something to behold. To my greater horror, as he furiously turned around, I was the only boy in close enough distance, and torn between wonderment and guilt found myself frozen to the spot. I was duly marched up three flights of stairs, my feet only partially on the ground while lifted in the air by the hairs on the side of my head aside my left ear. By the time I reached the top a small trickle of blood was running down the side of my face. I was made to sit outside his office all afternoon as he walked in and out ignoring my presence. Nothing further happened, though I lived every terrifying punishment in my thoughts in what was one of the longest afternoons of my childhood. Corporal punishment ended in 1986 within state schools in the United Kingdom, the same year I attended this institution. Looking back, it seemed

---

a number of the teachers knew the end was coming and, like an unapologetic empire knowing it's about to fall, took every opportunity they could to administer its last rites.

Children would also be the perpetrators of their own masochistic punishments and rituals, which you came to expect, especially from trusted friends and close acquaintances. There were elaborate rules and practices set for administering affectionate pain to others. While the placing of drawing pins on seats was a daily hazard that required constant checking and vigilance, it was the presence of those solid brass compasses, the type that allowed you to draw with notable precision circular lines for no good reason other than to prove celestial ingenuity and circumnavigation so denied to so many in these parts, which put you in a permanent state of heightened emergency. Armed with a sharp, pointed end that was more ferocious in design than any surgical needle, the chances of being stabbed fully in the leg at least once a month while walking down a crowded corridor was as certain as Liverpool FC winning the league at the time. To say its insertion into the unexpecting thigh was painful in the extreme, leading to a deadened and bruised leg for the day, was an understatement. Though since you always knew the perpetrator, it seldom led to anything more than a grimace and holding back of the tears while giving the limb a stiff rubbing. Only a fool reacted immediately. The pleasure was always in the surprise, requiring just enough time to elapse and the memory of the wounding to fade from immediate concerns. How we learned revenge was best served in the unexpected coldness. This was physics self-taught through practice, which proofed the irrefutable law stating that for each and every action there would be an equal and opposite reaction. Our grading system was measured in deep piercings into the bodies of prepubescent boys. Its graduates all marked by the indiscriminate nature of collective punishment, which in one way or another gave you just enough room to laugh in the face of our collective tragedy. This is why working-class comedians have always been able to convey the desperation far better than any middle-class social scientist or hyper-moral leftist anointed with some elaborate questionnaire or theorem that grants privileged insight into neglect. No unlived theory can possibly capture the meaning of a child's laughter, which echoes a courageous refusal even when they really want to scream against the world. Our poverty was never a concept, its violence never an object to be studied. Within these walls, we became learned students in the art of a dark comedy. Laughter became our language of survival as we continued to dance like paupers on blighted hills. And how we laughed, each and every day, taking delight in the small mischievous gestures of classroom compatriots or in the more rehearsed school renditions, which on one occasion featured a class of 20 kids slapping their reddened cheeks to the Lone Rangers theme tune with each one of us slowly breaking into complete hysterics.

We may have been nobodies in a nowhere place, but at least we had each other in those early years. Of course, I can look back now and see the hardship, the poverty and the suffering. But we learned how to survive, as nobodies together laughing in concert at the tragedy of it all. Then again, maybe the idea of being a nobody itself was just a social construct? And that beneath the shallow fog that covers over so-called nowhere places lies a deeper well of knowledge, which brings us much closer to what it means to simply be human, all too human. What can appear in the eyes of power to be a nowhere place, can be everywhere to some. Yet we shouldn't romanticise either, nor should we deny the gravity of hardship. Nowhereness is real, as much as its psychological impacts are deeply engrained. We were acutely aware that we lived in some backwater land, isolated and forgotten. Children and even adults often joked about the possible encounter with cavemen and dinosaurs the further you went into the valley, which revealed something within the comedy of how the locals imagined the place. Nowhereness was an imagined force for truth, internally felt and often embraced by those who had long made peace with their tragic fate. Nowhere is this more apparent than in the desire to educate oneself out of a place of named misery. Such desires are not simply about ambition. They reveal the innermost truth about nowhere lands and nowhere peoples. The more my education continued, the more I was taught of the need to break the collective chains tying me to the past. We were being held down, not just by the weight of neglect, but by time itself. The emblem for the senior school was a phoenix rising from the ashes, or should we say rising from the blackness. Invariably, this was always an optimistic ambition, which had very little resonance to most of the dejected souls who often couldn't wait to leave the comprehensive system. So many had no idea what lay after, but who really has any viable conception of the future at 16 years old, especially when the future is seldom talked about in any positive way? If the past is a place that takes great courage to venture into, the future is a place that can be read like the most terrifying landscape that is full of unknown dangers and yet certain all the same. Back to Stephen King, the first book I ever read of my own volition was *Salem's Lot*. It resonated deeply. I quickly saw how this wasn't just a book about monsters. It was a book about isolation. About a small town which literally has the blood and soul sucked out of it. A town that has lost its belief. Where only the few could venture beyond and seldom few ventured within. A town in which the children are stolen and appear like haunting apparitions at the window. It was also the book which taught me that words on pages are simply a point of entry into the more enriching and sometimes more terrifying life of the mind.

Unlike King's ending, in these towns the vampires had won. And their real strength was that nobody could ever see them. Maybe it wasn't a phoenix on that school badge after all? What I do know is that nothing can simply be eviscerated unless it is met by an even greater force, which turns the fragments of memory into a black dust. Yet, to deny any plausibility, such a force must appear as natural as the wind. That was the terrifying brilliance of Hayek, whose speech on that stage in Sweden a few months after I was born and these valleys already declared morbid would help unleash a force upon industrial communities the world over as righteous as it was unforgiving. And who could resist? Intellectually, materially or just with raw brute violence? The natural force of carbon would be swiftly displaced by the natural force of the free market. The state would be presented as an impediment to prosperity; indeed, it was the reason why horrors such as Aberfan could have occurred in the first place. There was some truth to this, even if the idea of the "free market" has been proven to be a misnomer. Hayek showed how the state was inherently inefficient, corrupting and could even result in the arrival of the worst kinds of tyranny and economic serfdom. Along with Milton Friedman, what was suggested was an entirely new theory of radical freedom, which celebrated the rights of individuality to the point of positively welcoming inequality. What mattered instead was the individual, freed from the ideological chains that bound us to the collective and the mass hysteria of its thinking. Society, truly, he maintained, was an impediment to economic growth, which in turn required opening up its veins to allow the divine flow of money to circulate uninhibited. But what of those towns, these towns, which had nothing left to extract? And what of those lives who were so dependent on the state that to live without it would prove catastrophic? Well, the collateral damage was simply just like any other natural accident. There was no blame attributable this time, even if entire communities were rendered disposable. Besides, nature has a way of readjusting herself. It may take time. And it may cause hardships in the short-run. Still, the sacrifice of the social at the altar of individual freedom will be worth it. So, you see, the vampires were not daemonic at all. They revealed the better angels of our nature. King's haunting version, however, was far more convincing.

At the height of the mining boom, one of the most influential community organisations in the South Wales coalfield was the Miners Institute and its network of libraries. These would become increasingly important as the power of the chapels began to wane and the miners' leaders were intent on educating the poor through the written words of socialist authors and the like. Numbering over 100, the Institute libraries would also become a place where children could be introduced to literature and the community showed its own willingness to invest in the education of its own children, so often neglected by the state. So many miners wanted a better future for their offspring, and as far back as the Tonypandy riots it was increasingly apparent the alternative to the pit was a learned escape. This was duly noted by Aneurin Bevan, who in respect to the Tredegar Institute in 1926 observed:

> There is no colliery town in South Wales which could hold the candle to Tredegar for its library and institute; more money is spent on books here than in any institution of its size in Wales. But two institutions have grown up in the train of the industrialisation of the valleys which are more responsible for moulding the character of the miners than anything else and these were the Sunday Schools which cultivated the gift of expression and the Workmen's Institutes which (had) provided the reading facilities.

At its peak, this Institute's library alone boasted containing over 100,000 books that were available for the public to borrow. It was the miners who led to the creation of such Institutes and paid for their upkeep through compensatory payments from their salaries. While the founding impetus for this can be traced back to the 1890s, the Institutes grew more in stature from 1914 as war broke out in Europe. Part of this was driven by an emerging conflict between the chapel and the socialists, many of the latter being notably against the war effort and also tasking themselves with becoming the dominant influence over an increasingly secularising local population. If the chapel spoke of allegiance to God and faith in the afterlife, the Institutes were part of a new language of congregation that spoke of allegiance to socialism and the improvement of life in the here and now. This would be reflected in the changing stocks of books held, which research shows slowly moved away from

Nonconformist literatures to texts with a more notable political and economic focus. The impact was profound. By the 1920s most of the libraries in the valleys were distinctly managed in accordance with a proletarian ethos. The libraries in the mid-Rhondda stood out here in terms of their commitment to radical literatures, with the Institute's administration led by notable political activists. In the space of a decade, these Institutes replaced the chapels to become places where the miners met, and their ideas and social concerns discussed as part of open public forums. Some of the halls were so grand, they were home to the aforementioned cinemas, and lent themselves to concerts, theatrical performances and sporting activity. In the prominent "Little Moscow" Institute, for example, the local Mardy communist football team trained in its halls during the times of the Great Depression. Others held boxing matches and welcomed prominent speakers from elsewhere. In the post-war years, the financial and political power of the Institutes grew, which was in turn put back into education. Whilst fiercely "independent" in their educational provision, some Institutes even provided scholarships for promising students to attend university. Such Institutions were completely unique to the South Wales valleys. We might even argue they took the need to bind radicalism with a pedagogical revolution, which was both materially visible and accessible, more seriously than anywhere else in the socialist-inspired world.

Yet, as the mines declined, so did the Institutions that provided the surrogate means for educating the working-class masses. Much of this was instigated by external forces, from the 1944 Education Act which, moulded on the idea of "One Nation Conservatism" for educating children after the war, for the first time provided free secondary education in the valleys towns, to the continued closure of pits and their declining financial power, which also cut the funding support the miners provisioned. Without the contributions from the miners' earnings, there were no Institutes. Partly subverting local militancy, local authorities also set up their own competing libraries, which were less concerned with stocking Marx & Engels than Mills & Boon. They would, however, eventually fall the same way, as their money streams were savagely cut away. Across the valleys, most towns now feature boarded-up ruins of former Institution grandeur, which still occupy a prominent place on the main streets that so many walk past without knowing of their vibrant past. Many of them are covered in a moss and weathered residue also revealing of the fact that not every reclaiming by nature and processes of greening are beneficial to communities. They have become mausoleums to past thought, standing impervious to the elements yet completely fragile to the winds of ideological change. Nearly all their books have vanished, the most valuable plundered by outsider bookdealers, and many others simply destroyed. It is estimated that within the two decades after World War II, near ¾ million volumes disappeared. The same was the case for many of the Institute library records that would have testified to the more intimate life of the miners' families' reading habits and their literary and cultural interests. There was no interest at the time, it seemed, in preserving the heritage and memory of the intellectual life of people in these towns so often labelled as "uneducated". Traces of their lives have been erased like so much that is associated with the disposable of history. How many of those books simply found their ways onto burning pyres? And what would the people of the valleys give today for the return of such an archive?

Decades after the closure of the Institutes that were already a derelict mystery in my mind, I would arrive at university and begin the task proper of reinventing myself. This in reality meant re-curating my past. Nobody at university likes to admit they came from abject poverty. Nobody wants to be a nobody in a place where being somebody is part of the default narrative. But at least I arrived before the age of social media, which did allow for a complete fabrication of one's past without any evidence that might prove otherwise. Kids from poverty today are denied that one and only advantage, which they once silently mastered from a young age. Surviving in the university as a poor student would require a number of falsifications, including where you were actually from, even if, as I eventually learned, nobody knew where the hell the Rhondda valleys were anyhow. It was like a place that was once marked as central to Empire and its industrial machine, was simply wiped off the map. In order for me to arrive, the place where I was from had to be somewhere to be seen. So, I ended up lying about not being from a nowhere place which nobody had any knowledge about in the first place! Such a false, broken-mirrored illusion. Yet perhaps there was some benefit in the realisation that the privately educated are so often oblivious to those who live in lasting conditions of oblivion. Still, having made my escape, the last thing I needed reminding of was the past. I needed to leave the memories of that landscape behind. For I knew its shadows were following me. Its mountains part of the cartography of my mind. So, it's true, the imposter syndrome was real, even if you know that behind the facades of confidence, the wealthy and truly privileged struggled when anything remotely disrupting to their vision of the world came their way and upset their fragile, entitled sensibilities. You live a lie, because nobody wants to come out as the nobody who's somehow smuggled their way in, the boy from the valleys who will learn to think, speak and act with all the politeness of an educated and cultured social commentary, which at every turn denies the poor boy within the simple ability to be themselves without being marked by pity or prejudice. Or as John Lennon once said, "There's room at the top they're telling you still, but first you must learn how to smile as you kill, if you want to be like the folks on the hill".

It was a typically inclement day on this Thursday morning. It is 9 November and the 15-year-old child was stood against the fence in the playground. The clouds above looked ominous, but the break in the weather meant that it was possible for the children to venture outside for their mid-afternoon respite. The child cuts a solitary figure, seemingly staring into the middle distance, partly focused on the mountainside, yet in his mind he could be anywhere but here. He had fallen out with a group of friends, though he didn't really miss their company. Most of them were talking about leaving school and gaining their freedom, whatever that meant. Some had already fallen into drugs, the others into some delusion of adulthood, which at least meant they were able to drink copious amounts of alcohol on a mid-week afternoon while playing pool in a local bar known for being liberal with age restrictions. The child had largely been alone since the beginning of term, distancing himself from everything around. He had no real sense of what troubled him so much; he just knew something wasn't right and was unsure if he was destined to live another life. Had he been born at the wrong time, into the wrong body, thrown out in a merciless game of chance into a place, which somebody who wrote the rules would eventually discover to have made a tremendous mistake. Maybe he would wake up and realise he was Ian Rush after all, and that child's existence was just a bad dream? Still, every day seemed the same, felt like a tragic version of the eternal return. His hands gripped onto the cold steel rail and the child felt a small tremor. There was an earthquake elsewhere on that day in 1989, whose aftershock continues to rumble. Without any meaningful friends, the child finds comfort in the flight of a solitary bird flying in the distance and landing on a tree. The bell rings, which breaks his attention as the hordes of children rush out of the gloom. Looking back into the direction of the mountain, he notices the bird has vanished. Has it finally escaped?, the child thinks to himself. It probably collapsed and died, he reasoned. After all, all the roots around here are as toxic as the weeping lands into which they are submerged. Is there any surprise the desire to rip up all such binds has such an appeal here? Later the child would learn of the significance of that day. The importance of those solitary moments. The contingency of that separation from those boys who would have a marked bearing on his desire to give flight from these nowhere lands. He was already planning in his mind on leaving. He had in fact already left.

I am sure that some psychologist, armed with the latest anthropocentric thinking and who so wished to make a name for themselves, could devise a theory of collective trauma that's particularly acute to the valleys of South Wales. Synthesising a number of well-established theorems in the fields of psychology and ecology, in lieu of a more citable study, let's just call it the "Ecosis of Trauma that's derived from the Black Mountains of a Melancholic Mind". A trauma so deeply rooted in the toxic soil, it would take a mass neurological migration to even begin to think about any sense of personal and social recovery in the life of the collective mind. A trauma that literally comes from nowhere and dwells inside its emptiness. The strange and curious thing about being born in the valleys of South Wales is that you publicly live a state of inherent contradiction and denial which defines each and every relationship. What is most often associated on television as being Welsh is the dialect of the valleys, even if the people of the valleys are looked down upon and discriminated against even from other people within Wales itself. If you think of the sound of Wales, it's the choirs of the Rhondda, yet the people of this place are the ones whose voices have most often been silenced. If you think of Wales's proud industrial past, it's rooted in the efforts of those men and women of the coal-facing communities, even if that industrious past has given rise to decades-old assumptions concerning idleness and welfarism. And if you think of welcoming and resistive communities in the face of historical oppression, the people of the valleys stand tall and defiant, yet today appear to be the face of intolerance, social ignorance and embodying the worse of segregating intellectual nativism. No peoples could live through such contradictions and not emerge scarred, especially if you know from a young age that such contradictions are externally applied. Just as no people could live through a century of depression and not carry within their souls the memory of a collective trauma, whose pain runs so deep it wells up into the imagination to replace the dreams of a better life with a neurosis of absence that not only internalises one's sense of inferiority, but also underwrites a further demand for psychological intervention based on the assumed personal failures and deficiencies of those who simply cannot cope any more with conditions that nobody could possibly deal with, as nobody should.

All of this takes its toll and for those who want to leave; there is a different kind of trauma that awaits. Subconsciously you slowly start to lose your accent, for you know this is the surest way the violence you are said to embody will be detected. Tones will soften and words will vanish. Locals will ask you, "What happened to your accent?", as if you suffered a terrible accident, though they also detect the shame you are fighting. Others are less forgiving, listening to the voice of a traitor, the one who left and speaks as if they are better than us all. It is curious today how little racism scholars talk about the prejudice of dialects, then again, given the selective colonial denials, perhaps it's not so surprising for what it reveals about its framing. Soon you learn to despise the land you walked upon, blaming its streets for your misery, looking back upon memories with a new sensibility that turns rootedness into unbelonging. I don't belong here, you cry. I never did, erase me from these towns. Remove me from your photos. Carry on as if I were never here, it's better that way. But there is no clear roadmap out of it. I don't want to be from this nowhere place. I don't want to be a boy from the valleys. Yet where does this end? Soon you don't feel like you belong to the nation. You have nothing in common, you convince yourself, with those who choose to remain. And soon you feel like you don't belong anywhere at all. This makes you realise you have no past to speak of. Still, as they promised, there is a glorious future that awaits. But what happens when you realise this is the trauma? That without the past your life means nothing at all? That the nowhere place held a greater meaning? And to be uprooted from your language, culture, and history meant you truly dwelled in a no place for all? So you look for meaning in idols and fantasies, fetishizing objects as a substitute for the loss. Though still you convince yourself that this is happiness, and besides, there's more expensive wine to soften the palate and detached houses to testify how you won a true civilised call.

The murder of boys could be seen frantically running down the steep hill and into the grounds of the church below. Something had scared them half to death in these twilight hours as nightfall returned to the valleys. On occasions, the way the evening announced itself was a sight to behold. As the sun set in the westerly distance, it was as if the darkness was rising out of the ground and summoned back into the beckoning skies. The old school yard was now empty as the raven stood quietly, gazing at the lonely child who stayed behind after his compatriots had fled. None of them noticed that one still remained. They gaze at one another for a while with a curious suspicion and respect. Eventually the boy sits beside the bird, stroking its crimson feathers, while communicating with his hands about his desire to fly up into the darkness and beyond the territory of the night. A whispering wind echoes out of the open door at the side of the abandoned old school. The bird gives flight and enters into its open pass, and swiftly ascends up the spiral of stairs, its silhouette visible through the small broken collage of windowpanes. Without hesitation, the boy follows this messenger into the entrance and up the first flight where he stops. Gazing down the hallway he sees the corridor strewn with pages of discarded books, which he never had the opportunity to read. He reaches down to pick up a volume that features Rodin's version of Dante on the cover before he is startled by a noise from the floor above. It echoes the same tune which caused his friends to run for their existence. The raven is calling, so the boy continues up to the highest, entering into the hall where so many children once gathered and announced. Yet something feels different as the boy grabs his thoughts. The walls have partially fallen and some of the roof is exposed. The boy turns back to the stage where the black bird was sitting, but the raven has now been replaced by a grey-haired man who speaks with confidence and pride. He talks of his journey, his escape, and his adventures. And he looks at the boy and promises him more of the same. He talks and talks, about life, the world, the wonder of it all. But the boy doesn't respond as the wise old man intended. Indeed, the more he remains silent the more the building around starts to fall. The man's voice slowly begins to quieten, and his posture cowers as he lowers to the floor. As the roof rips apart, the man pleads with the boy to say something, but the child simply watches as the heavens are revealed. The man now seems desperate as the walls begin to crumble, so he turns to the boy and asks, "What is it that you want?" The boy sits down to consider the question, as the bird reappears, and the presence of the man fades away. "Just don't kill me", the boy tells the raven, at which moment the school collapses and the bird flies away.

I often think what it would mean to write a survival guide for working-class kids on how to navigate the university. The truth is that you never stop feeling like you don't belong there. You always feel that your past will eventually be found out, that you will be outed and the real boy from nowhere laid bare on a stage in front of an audience, which will find nothing of meaning as it looks upon his nakedness. The raw realities of poverty are not a pretty sight to look upon, which is why so many prefer to simply look away or hide behind their own comforting theories of self-awareness concerning privilege, entitlement or whatever becomes the next profitable concept of the month. But I don't need to tell working-class kids this, even if the vocabulary helps. They know the raw realities of power more intimately than any social scientist. And that is what gives them an advantage, even if those who will eventually teach them will try to convince them that they know its intricate workings better. If the measure of poverty were to be found in a book, it would often be the one or two volumes the poor child possesses, reads over and over, and cherishes because they appreciate what privilege really looks like and knows with every limited page the real meaning of scarcity. I was always struck by the way the libraries of the wealthy looked so pristine. Then again, as I have learned, the image of intellectualism can be as much a spectacle as anything else, especially when displays of knowledge are put on show without a single grubby mark made by impoverished hands visible on any of the pages. It is not some elaborate theory, even if the problems of the world are indeed complex. It begins with the reality. Everything else is just filtering some preconceived bias. So, this survival guide would begin by reminding them that their passion and experience is their greatest weapon. That they should be prepared for a world of deference that often masquerades as opportunity. That their language will often be received as hostile and aggressive by those who feel threatened by their very presence. That they should be wary of those who cannot see their problems, but just as wary of those who seem to be allies, yet who constantly speak about the world in moralising and highly judgmental ways that makes them indiscernible from preachers. But most importantly, I would write about what it takes to recognise there is nothing "lacking" within, nor are they some intellectual problem needing to be solved. They are perfectly fine, just as they are. It's a complete cliché today to ask what advice you'd like to give to your teenage self. Yet maybe we got this all wrong? For I can't help wondering what advice that teenage boy from nowhere might impart back to me. Would they be proud of my achievements? Or ashamed of what I buried in the black earth? Would they see the trauma of severance, and would they think it was all worth it? Would they delight at my returning to the valleys to say things I already knew back then, but desired to forget so that I could become a force as natural as the free market wind? And what of this knowledge I possess? Is it not as fragile as that ruined school? Or might that child lead me back to the source of the ancestral stone, whose location I can no longer remember?

From where I stand in the "privileged position" that I occupy today (a position that's held by every single academic without exception), two pictures of the valleys appear before me. There is a valley contained. Its identity was lived in sweetshops, butchers, bread makers, boys clubs, girl scout halls, and played out on the rugged and imperious remnants of a fading past.

This is a valley that was home, yet a valley that was defined by its limits and policed our categorised lives accordingly. Then there is also a valley marked by a split, which is both topological and also deeply bound to a psychological severance whose cut never seems to heal. The Rhondda in particular is interesting for its inhabitants know they live within a valley that's doubled. We are twinned with ourselves, mirrored from within. Children of the valleys know what it's like to make peace with the schizophrenic nature of existence. We embody the double, speaking to ourselves as we try to outrun our shadows. We have even managed to turn the world inside out as the sense of claustrophobia that once defined conditions deep within the earth moved onto the lands above. Our mountains are always closing in, making us doubters of their intentions and even turning conifers into cages. I have seen this doubling played out so many times in the reflecting eyes of my childhood friends. I have known the quietest and gentlest of boys reveal the greatest of rages, whose passion was so pent up the explosive anger was more than any individual could contain. And I have seen joyful spirits descend into the most desperate of silences, no longer having the words to speak out and lift themselves from the sorrows. I too still carry that doubling, always questioning and doubting myself, always feeling that belonging belongs to others, always feeling that behind reality is another reality waiting to reveal its ambition and remind you that the shadow of the valleys will ultimately reign supreme. This is what nowhere properly means to me. A nowhere that is so engrained you are always searching for somewhere, but even when you make it, it's never quite what you imagined and always shadowed by a past that threatens to seep into the most colourful of dreams. Anybody who is born into a psychosis of nowhereness never finds the somewhere. For what they are searching for can never be really found, as it's buried deep in the sands of time.

None of this is easy to retell. Not just in terms of memory, but when confronting the need to do it with justice. The thing about educating oneself out of a place is that it is far more difficult to find your way back in. It's rather easy to culturally move across the social divides. It doesn't take too much fortitude to master the codes of civility, to spot what is necessary to thrive in a bourgeois setting, to recognise a mile off the faux radicalism, to be at one with the performativity of it all. Of course, from time to time, despite your best intentions, that boy from the valleys will reappear, which will often cause those with power to look upon you both aghast and with curiosity. Sometimes they cannot hide their revulsion, especially when you challenge their conceit. But the entitled have always been fascinated by the lives of the poor. This is part reassurance, though part of a deeper anxiety that they suspect the impoverished truly know how to live without any of the masks of appearance, which everybody who enters those circles needs to wear. The bourgeois fascination with resilience is the latest manifestation of this, as are the attempts by those from financially privileged backgrounds to claim they are the true emotional victims of history. It would be far easier to train somebody from the valleys to speak the language of privilege, than it would to take somebody from privilege and have them truly feel at home in a community without any of its securities and comforts. Maybe if I have had any success in this life, it's precisely because I provoked that curiosity? Though I like to feel I simply see things just as they are. That is why the entry back proves so difficult. For you need to leave all the airs and graces at the welcoming doors of neglect. The cities you've lived and the possessions you've required, none of that means anything to people who are more interested in fighting for an existence. So, a return to nowhere demands far more investment than any visit to a palatial hall. It also demands more honesty and respect, for those without cannot be so easily persuaded. And who could possibly deny them the right to be suspicious of do-good intentions, especially by those whose agenda is to profit from neglected histories?

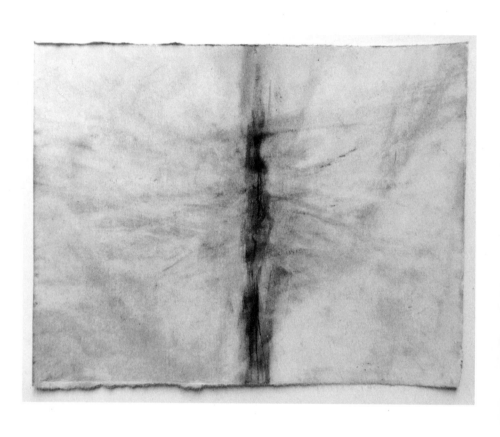

PRIDE & PREJUDICE

The passing of age has afforded to me more appreciation for the brilliance of Charlie Chaplin. Maybe it's because I recognise how his life, in so many ways, maps onto the conditions my generation had purposefully left behind. Part of this is informed by nostalgia for an image of the valley I read so much about but never properly knew, as it belonged to another place in time. That was a valley populated by a welcoming people, who although desperately poor, still knew their place in history. But part of it is also inspired by the lived knowledge of power, how it operates to silence the loudest of screams, and what it takes to even begin to get one's ideas recognised when the markers of poverty still remain so defining. Like the valleys, Chaplin's demise in both standing and importance was a direct result of a mediated society that literally found its voice. His silent toils and labour were undone by the power of the spoken word, which focused the attention away from those who had learned to master the silence and learned how to make their presence felt in other ways. The black and the white would also be overcome by a world that revelled in the glaring colour of the spectacle and the desire to turn on those artificial filtered lights. This would only accelerate in the post-war moment, as the power of the media shifted the centre of gravity of the world's attention away from the producers towards those who were able to create an illusion of production, whose spectacle was divorced from reality. The result being that nowhere people would increasingly be lost within the screen, except when the occasion of a tragedy afforded a return. There was, however, one notable exception.

At the dawn of the television age, it was a boy from the valleys who arose to become one of its most celebrated and iconic figures. A son of a miner from the village of Pontrhydyfen in the Aber valley, the twelfth of thirteen children, Richard Burton would become the most famous man in the world for a while. His home town of Pontrhydyfen was built around the local colliery, and there was even a pub in the village called the Miners' Arms. Another prominent landmark in the town is the Y Bont Fawr bridge, built exactly 100 years before Burton's birth in 1925. The bridge was formerly an aqueduct, which supplied water to the Cwmavon blast furnaces. Both the pub and the bridge would later be memorialised in photographs featuring Burton and his aging father. Aside from his commanding on-screen persona, what set Burton apart was a voice that seemed to be summoned from the depths of the pits below. It was as recognisable as his hardened and cratered face. However, it was his passionate and tumultuous relationship with the equally famous actress Elizabeth Taylor that took his stardom to unseen levels. They become the very first global celebrity couple, which in life became a tabloid epic as watched and fated as the story of Cleopatra that brought them together. Burton and Taylor lived for a while in the Mexican town of Puerto Vallarta, which would later become a celebrity Mecca. Born during the Great Depression, Burton embodied the hardship and toughness, but also the passion and sense of local pride that defined the valleys of South Wales. He also had an acute sense of history and his place in it. As Burton declared in an article published in the *New York Times* in 1974, "To play Churchill is to hate him." This was in recognition of the role Burton was set to play in a film titled *The Gathering Storm*, to which he added: "I realized afresh that I hate Churchill and all his kind. I hate them virulently." Burton's comments were directly challenging the leader's own place in history, and especially the insanity of violence he authorised against German and Japanese people during World War II. When growing up, I never met a single person from the valleys who spoke about the actor with anything but affection.

This probably had everything to do with the fact that Burton never lost sight of who he was or where he came from. As Burton recalled on the legendary *Dick Cavett Show* in 1980:

> It was during the depression, my father was a miner and all my brothers except my youngest brother were miners and they all got out of the mines except the very oldest one who loved the mines so much I couldn't bribe him out. There was no way I could get him out. And he stayed in until the bitter end so that he died — he died last year. And you can imagine how tough the constitution of the family is, that with his lungs full of dust he lived until he was 79 and he was very angry because he didn't make 80.

This interview, more than any other, reveals the pride he felt in being a miner's son, which he claimed possessed a different kind of nobility:

> There is a great seam which I believe is called the great Atlantic fault and it starts in northern Spain in the Basque country, and it goes under the bay of Biscay and it comes up in South Wales and goes under the Atlantic and comes up in Pennsylvania, so that if you took a Basque miner and a Welsh Miner or a Pennsylvania miner, and if you could blindfold and transport them they would know the coalface the minute they saw it... My father used to talk about it as some men used to talk about women. Talk about the beauty of this coalface... When you perhaps think of me as being born with a silver spoon and so on, miners believe themselves or believed themselves anyway to be the aristocrats of the working class... They were skilled workers, that coalface was a magical creature... Every little boy's ambition in my valley was to become a miner because there was the arrogant strut of the lords of the coalface.

We cannot speak of Burton without acknowledging a notable contemporary of his from the valleys, Stanley Baker. Another miner's son who was born in Ferndale in the Rhondda, Baker was an accomplished actor and producer. Arguably his finest moment came as he produced and played the lead role in the 1964 film *Zulu*, which told of the Battle of Rorke's Drift. The film was narrated by Burton, who was a good friend of Baker. It also starred Ivor Emmanuel, another miner's son born in Pontrhydyfen, but a stone's throw from Burton's home. Emmanuel was orphaned during World War II when a wayward German bomb hit the village in August 1940, killing his father, mother, grandfather and sister. Following in the footsteps of his grandfather and father, he then started to work down the mines, until Burton gave his aspiring acting career a lift by putting in a good word to a stage director in London's West End. A few years prior to the release of *Zulu*, Baker was offered the role of James Bond in the film *Doctor No*. He turned it down, not wanting to commit to three films. A previous co-star by the name of Sean Connery was recast in the role. Both Baker and Burton were avid socialists and were continually accepted as still being part of the working class, despite their fortunes and fame. They also continued to return to the call of the valleys throughout their lives. One of Baker's last roles was to play the father figure Gwilym Morgan in a 1975 BBC serialisation of *How Green Was My Valley*. A notable focus of this adaptation is the youngest boy Huw, whose academic ability allows him to consider a possible future away from the mines. That is, until a disaster arrives. Thankfully, on this occasion, the cast was largely made up of Welsh actors. Baker's stellar performance was said to be inspired by the struggles his own father endured, which was applauded by Burton. Baker also drew upon the lingering blackness of these towns. "I'll tell you how close people lived to death," he once explained,

We made a guy once for November 5th and carried it through Ferndale on an old bedstead, asking for pennies. We knocked at one house. A woman came to the door, took one look at the guy on the bed and fainted. We had to run and fetch the neighbour. You see, she thought it was her husband being brought back home dead from the pit.

Although, like Burton, Baker ended up dying from the excesses of his own life, in his final moments he declared no regrets. "From the beginning I have been surrounded by love", he told his wife. "I'm the son of a Welsh miner and I was born into love, married into love and spent my life in love".

While struggling with ill health, Burton's last role was nevertheless fittingly cast. Playing the role of O'Brien in Michael Radford's adaptation of George Orwell's *1984*, which was released in that year, Burton appeared before us like a new kind of Caesar whose power was far more difficult to dethrone. Although *1984* was written as a prophetic mediation of a dystopic future, when the year actually arrived many elements of its prose had become inseparable from reality. As Umberto Eco noted, "at least three-quarters of what Orwell narrates is not negative utopia, but history". Yet, while we often associate Orwell's classic with the advent of Big Brother, Radford's film properly emphasised how its prose is more than a critique of surveillance societies. It is about total power, the monitoring of life, the idea that thought can be controlled through indoctrination, that humans can be manipulated like some giant experiment, that resistance is futile, love is superfluous, poetry is abject, the workers irrelevant, and that humans can be broken. It was a film then which equally was resonant with Thatcher's Britain as it was an Orwellian fantasy. It was after all released in the same year the miners' strike began as working-class communities were torn apart from outside. Burton was cast after Connery turned down the role. This was after some deliberation and concerns about his alcoholism. Understated, what's striking about this adaptation, and Burton's performance, is the utter bleakness it manages to convey in a way that leaves little room for optimism. It is also a film that's unbounded from traditional ideological moorings. Burton in fact could be a powerbroker working at the heart of any modern political project that disregards the masses in the name of progress. The film was released in October 1984, a few months after Burton was found dead. Co-star John Hurt, who had been staying at the family home in Switzerland and was one of the last people to see him alive, left Burton on the final evening alone as he read a book of poetry. How compelling to imagine him once again reciting in his defiantly rageful tone Dylan Thomas's "Do Not Go Gently into That Good Night", as that wise man too knew as he reached the end, only the darkness was right. A *New York Times* obituary described Burton as a "self-destructive" and "troubled spirit", who, they added, "was the most nominated actor who never won an Oscar and the most famous British actor who was never knighted". Despite these truths, they also reminded how the prodigal son of the valleys showed no personal regrets: "When he reached the age of 50, after a five-year career slump, he called his own life the best role he had ever played: 'I rather like my reputation, actually, that of a spoiled genius from the Welsh gutter, a drunk, a womanizer; it's rather an attractive image'".

Back in 1984, the walls of my bedroom had their own distinct dystopian look. I had managed to acquire an official movie poster to John Carpenter's cult classic *Escape from New York*, which had a rerun in the local cinema. We would venture there from time to time to see if they had any free giveaways. The film was beyond my years, but it was the first time I looked upon the face of liberty, broken and laying in the streets. It seemed like everybody was trying to run, everybody hoping for some kind of escape. I recall the poster's description, "breaking out is impossible, breaking in is insane". Maybe those mountains were imprisoning after all? Our bodies were certainly policed the moment valley trains arrived in Cardiff on the weekends. The film captured the bleakness and increasing violence that started to consume so many parts of the world in the mid-to-late 1970s. It is a film about ruination. But it is also a dark comedy about the expressive nature of tensions defining the age. As I think back to the ridiculous wrestling scene in the movie, another more bizarre icon from the valleys comes into focus who would be the source of much bemusement and delight for people of the valleys. At the same time the American film industry was increasingly bombarding audiences with the spectacle of violence for entertainment, the children of the valleys were re-enacting the pantomime moves of the likes of Big Daddy, Giant Haystacks, Rollerball Rocco and Kendo Nagasaki. The manoeuvres were largely harmless, at least that is until we became seduced by the more violent and sexualised show of the Americans, which had untrained youths trying to carry out headlocks, piledrivers and body slams to the cause of many a playground injury. Another son of a miner, the wrestler "Exotic" Adrian Street, left his unforgettable impression on the sport and in the minds of the valleys children who laughed at the outrageousness of it all. The BBC's *World of Sport Wrestling* that aired every Saturday afternoon was amongst the most viewed programs on the station. There was something alluring about seeing unhealthy bodies in spandex pants thrashing each other around in awkward ways for the masses. The appearance of Adrian Street in particular marked a watershed moment in this televised "sporting" arena. Born into a mining family in the valley town of Brynmawr, Street paraded his crossdressing gaiety with makeup to match, and even weaponised it with his trademark kiss. Street's persona was notably confrontational. As he would repeatedly call out: "I have so many ways to hurt you". But unlike Rocco (the American), who the public despised, Street won their affection. His gaiety and flamboyance weren't something that was any longer a source of cultural dismissal. Street would also later admit to having a certain physical altercation with the paedophile and rapist Jimmy Saville, who at the time was part of a cultured elite whose predatory behaviour was protected, even though it was the working classes who were so often presented as the violent.

While Street was a household name by the early 1980s, his crossdressing in the ring began more than a decade earlier. He was in many ways ahead of Bolan and Bowie, not to mention the later new romantics who started to normalise within British culture alternative sexual identities. In terms of the new romantics, while attention often focuses on the likes of Boy George, the valleys also have their own claim to this movement, which further challenges stereotyped notions about the people who are born in those isolated hills. When I was a teenager, if men were effeminate, they would often be referred to as being "a bit strange". Sometimes this was said as locals simply didn't have the vocabulary to describe what they didn't understand, other times to conceal undeniable prejudice harboured. We should not romanticise tolerance in the valleys, as much as we should condemn what's a complex social condition. We might turn our attentions here to Matthew Warchus's film *Pride*, which retells how gay and lesbian activists helped support the families of the striking miners in the Welsh valleys during the 1984 strike and in the process of showing solidarity became part of the struggle. Claims of strangeness were literally embodied in a new romantic pioneer Steve Strange, who was born in the Gwent valleys town of Newbridge. A notable extrovert and frontman for the band Visage, Strange felt the need to escape from the valleys in order to break away from the sense of isolation. He knew he didn't belong there. After watching the Sex Pistols at the notorious concert in the valleys town of Caerphilly, which happened two weeks after their infamous television appearance on *The Bill Grundy Show* that resulted in a spate of cancellations and protests, Strange became acquainted with the legendary Malcolm McLaren, with whom he worked designing artwork for the band. Shortly after he met Midge Ure, with whom he formed Visage. With Bob Geldof, Ure would co-write and produce the charity song "Do They Know It's Christmas", along with being the co-organiser of the Band Aid and Live Aid concerts. Visage's most popular electronic sound was "Fade to Grey," which speaks of isolation, coldness, blackness and the rain. Strange would later settle in Porthcawl, following his well-documented addictions and mental health problems, which were further exacerbated following the death of his friend and INXS frontman Michael Hutchence. The day after Hutchence's death, Strange's London home burned to the ground, destroying all his possessions.

He later died in 2015 aged 55. At his funeral in Porthcawl, the coffin was carried by Boy George and the brothers Gary and Martin Kemp from the band Spandau Ballet.

As the 1980s progressed, New York was still on my wall. But it was no longer a dystopian nightmare. It was the ultimate destination. America was the dream. It was however joined by a poster of the undisputable baddest man on the planet who came from those mean streets, Mike Tyson. I was 13 and even my bad luck years weren't taking me anywhere. Completely unaware of the different hair structures between the races, I went to the local hairdressers and asked for a "Tyson haircut". I ridiculously ended up looking like the Brazilian Ronaldo from that World Cup in 2002, which I watched in Mexico. It lasted for a day, until my mother ordered me to shave it all off. I now looked like some skinny-legged, pea-headed fascist and was even cheered by the fat-boy leader of a local gang of skins I bumped into as I was making my way on foot to the sport centre in a village in few miles away. My unfortunate haircut at least favoured me on that day. But the violence of these gangs and the local conditions in which we lived was real. On several occasions I would witness friends and others from the valleys being beaten to within an inch of their lives. I was also slashed with a Stanley knife on one occasion by a gang from another valley as I was set upon amongst the caravans in Porthcawl. I think they probably mistook me for a local, then again it probably wouldn't have mattered. While the violence was territorial and influenced by other dystopic gangland films such as *The Warriors* and *The Wanderers*, by the time the 1980s arrived the identity-based violence of the previous decades was slowly fading away. Born of the counter-culture revolutions, such violence was always destined to be, well, fashionable. And like all fashions, it soon exhausts itself. So, despite the fact some kids still liked to sport as little hair as possible as they terrorised other white kids, when the violence wasn't tribal it was either linked to football hooliganism that happened down in Cardiff or increasingly tied to the emerging drugs economy.

The latter in particular would become the most dominant kind of violence carried out by gangs who knew there was very little profit to be had by simply calling for the very few immigrants to leave. Yes, the violence was about local conditions. But locals wanted money above all else, not least since they were now being sold on the ideas of material enrichment. Drug violence has been a permanent feature of the valleys ever since, with frequent news reports telling of murders, kidnaps, large seizures of drugs and weapons, along with revealing the nature of the organisation that sees the valleys connected across the county lines into places like Liverpool, Birmingham and Manchester, which reach out more widely to the main centres for the global narcotics industry, notably Mexico and Afghanistan.

Bookended by the collapse of the Berlin Wall and the devastating attacks on the World Trade Centre in New York, which again seemed to show liberty crashing into the streets, the 1990s were in many ways a lost decade. As the left continued to conduct a great deal of soul-searching, while following its favourite pastime of ripping itself apart as it witch-hunted traitors within its ranks, so the real power of Thatcherism was realised through its effective normalisation. Her ideological revolution was a success and even resulted in a profound transformation in the Labour Party, which under the leadership of the aspiring Tony Blair in 1994 all but abandoned its own socialist pretensions. The zeitgeist of this moment was powerfully captured in Will Hutton's *The State We're In*, which became essential political reading. It was also matched by the writings and influence of Anthony Giddens, whose "Third Way" ideas resonated with the middle classes who wanted a more acceptable vision of social justice. You could have social justice, after all, it was claimed, without too much economic redistribution. And yet despite the triumphant claims of liberalism, how were societies still to account for the continued tensions, the endemic social problems that were causing so much concern in blighted post-industrial areas, along with the emergence of new kinds of violence that were inseparable from newly formed global shadow economies? The answer was not political, it was reasoned. The cause of all these problems was as a result of underdevelopment, which couldn't be separated from the decline of industry and too much reliance on the social state, whose inefficiencies in the end simply held people back. And yet there was still a positive story to spin. For while conditions in communities such as the valleys were economically deteriorating, the emerging information and communications revolutions made possible by the arrival of the Internet and digitalisation would contribute to a shattering of older hierarchical systems of power. There was no longer a need to focus so much on the material networks of the valleys, its cascading rivers and fattened arteries, its underground tunnels, its train lines, its roads connecting isolated communities, its movements of people, and the stemmed flows of its past ideas. All that could remain static so long as people started to embrace the new logic of globalisation, which increasingly meant that while they may no longer speak to the world, at least the world could arrive to them through commodities, culture and sadly criminality. Moreover, in this world of spectacle and delight, the very meaning of consciousness was being transformed — image consciousness had properly arrived for us all — which in turn meant that if politics was to mean anything, it must be paraded as a spectacle that also seduces.

By the mid-1990s, in the United Kingdom every kind of identity was being liberated as suddenly everything became cool. Even Britannia herself could be remarketed as a feminist icon, sexy and defiant. Culturally at least, it didn't seem to matter if you were Welsh, black, queer, or even from the valleys, there was now a newfound optimism in the televisual world. We even had a lad from the valleys called Steve Jones fronting primetime cultural shows and by all accounts dating Pamela Anderson and Halle Berry. Optimists might say that finally the old political and cultural order was breaking down as the marginalised were finding their voices. Cynics might suggest that the proliferation of this new kind of identity-based awakening had everything to do with a new chapter in the history of capitalist exploitation, which realised there were far greater profits to be made the more identities proliferated. This was the setting in which my entry into the experience of university was located. I had escaped. And I was proud to have done so. But what now? Just as Marx was being declared dead, that's when I started to take politics seriously. In truth, from the moment I arrived at university I was deeply suspicious of the sad militant cabals who had ready-made answers for every problem under the educated sun. And besides, while I knew first-hand the structural violence of Thatcherism, I also learned about the violence of communism through the words of Alexander Solzhenitsyn, which I knew couldn't be so easily dismissed. That was one of the reasons I found it hard to connect with the university socialists. Besides, the way they carried on was just all a bit too performative, predictable and posturing without setting the imagination on fire. Something else also perturbed me. Why were all these posh kids so keen to present themselves as down with the working classes? Whichever university you entered, they always had the same set-up. Stood in procession behind foldaway tables, you were sure to encounter one who dressed like a shop-floor worker, another who looked like they were about to set off for the wilds of Nicaragua, one who had read one book by Noam Chomsky and would relay at any given opportunity a volley of irrefutable facts about everything attributable to US imperialism, and a silent elder who having read Marx and Engels too many times looked as worn as his copy of *Capital*, which he knew nobody else on the team had bothered reading. I did the reading, both of the Marxists and the capitalists, the latter especially proving instructive in my critique. We should always read the people we find dangerous. That's the only way we can properly understand. Perhaps another reason I couldn't abide the middle-class Marxists was simply how they wore their politics with a saddened look that was also as uniform as it was dull. Taking my leave from Richard Burton, who always appeared immaculately dressed, I never had a problem with fashion, or should I say, when you grew up having to wear clothes designed to be functional instead of actually fitting, the last thing you want to do is join up with sermon-wielding life-choicers who, sloganizing the world, reminded you of just how consciously drab ideology can become. Or as Burton might counsel, just because you dress poorly doesn't make you a radical, as much as to say that dressing well or taking care of one's appearance doesn't make you a capitalist. Some might counter here and say this all represents a monumental contradiction from what I previously claimed about the power of the image in the age of the spectacle. It's impossible not to carry an image. As with politics, life is an aesthetic. The poor know the wear of this more than anybody. What matters is how it connects to styles for living and existence.

As I became more cultured into the intellectual fabric of the university setting, so theories, insights and vocabularies were sought that would allow me to try and point to the source of oppression. I would later learn there was no such source, except of course the blackness. What I did however quickly learn was the people I personally despised the most were the ones who often spoke the loudest in terms of their unfounded belief to be on the right side of history. Maybe that was why I found some kind of solace in the postmodernists for a while, which was rather inevitable as it provided a nice way to account for my sorrows without having to really confront the person I was or had become. If I was suffering, it was because of tradition and everything the political orthodoxy put on a bird-shit-covered plinth. And so, why would I want to celebrate my Welshness, my heritage, my forebears, if they hadn't just laid the foundations, but actually dug the holes deeper into which the children of the valleys fell? I now see much of this was a grave deception, revealing how I was guilty of being seduced by obfuscating theory because it made me feel more intellectual, and how it was inseparable from the way radicalism had been taken over by a new bourgeois set. I wanted to be radical, but I also wanted to belong. Maybe that was the real Third Way? It should be added, while such radicalism emerged out of a profound suspicion of every possible truth, it has since ended up fully collapsing truth into emotion and in the process has found new ways to demonise and castigate as inferior the poor and uneducated of the world. I can now see that we are all grounded in some traditions. And instead of rushing head-on into a future that leads to nowhere, what people need is a richer appreciation of their history, a stronger connection to the ancestral, which speaks to a more poetic future. The forces of the historical right have for far too long claimed a monopoly over tradition, which is further compounded today by those who speak of being on the side of humanity, while showing an utter contempt for the lived realities of so many living in a zone of post-industrial collapse by deploying a language that's arrogant and condescending.

It's now exactly a decade on from my disastrous Tyson haircut and I find myself living on top of another hill that is closely surrounded by a notorious housing estate. As a student, I was living in the white working-class area of Bramley in Leeds, dwelling in a cheap homestead that lacked any heating and basic homely comforts. My hair was now worn halfway down my back and often ponytailed. This wasn't a return to that rocker look that defined my teenage years, but an attempt to be a cool clubber with pretentions of glamour, even if my wardrobe was consistently black. Moody, it seemed, could also be stylish. With my money largely spent on clothing and alcohol, I was again largely living off baked beans on toast, or what as children we humoured ourselves by calling "skinheads on a raft". The poor often make a game of their food to distract from the monotony of consumption. We took great delight in destroying those flotillas. Not much had changed in the material conditions of my life, except the idea that the future was now an open destination. I was going somewhere, at least in my thoughts. It was the summer, so I was taking leave of my studies. When I wasn't working in a newly formed mobile phone call centre, which was as demeaning and soul-destroying as any work I had ever undertaken, I whiled away the days and evenings getting drunk and passively high from the cannabis clouds that filled most rooms in the house, which my ex-squaddie flatmate atmospherically induced. He taught me a great deal about military life and the challenges ex-soldiers face as they try to adapt back into the civilian world. It is the end of August, and I awoke around 4am in a semi-conscious state on the sofa. The television was on but didn't bring any clarity for it was also now an integral part of our higher state of sofa-dwelling consciousness. An older analogue set, there was a break in the tube, which meant everything appeared in softly focused hues of pinks and purples, only adding to the psychedelic feel of the house. As the news broke, at first, I thought I was part of a dream sequence as surreal as a previous night's chase, having caught a local heroin addict trying to break into the home. How different worlds can often collide in the slumber of the night. The fairytale had become a tragedy. The body of a princess broken and shattered in a Parisian tunnel for all the world to see. Princess Diana died on 31 August 1997. And yet as the news of that violent crash appeared through the damaged screen, my mind drifted and I was stood in line as the married couple's cavalcade travelled down another of those familiar terraced streets close to where I once lived. It was 1981 and Prince Charles and his new wife were on a three-day tour of Wales. We were now living on the valley floor, which we moved to a few months prior to their arrival. This was a potential improvement, though at the time our family of five were all confined to one bedroom (including living, cooking and sleeping) as my parents set about months of complete renovation. The destruction of the old wooden slat walls and chimney stacks meant the house was continuously full of black dust during those summer months. This terraced home was enough distance away from those black mountains, though the presence of the mines was still made evident to us. All the streets here had some kind of connection to the landed gentry. We lived on Augusta Street, which was so named after the daughter of the landowner Crawshay Bailey.

Surrounding us was Crawshay Street, Metaxa Street (named after his wife Elizabeth Selena Madeline Metaxa), with the Royal cortege invariably travelling down Bailey Street. Whilst their visit was largely welcomed, there were some incidents and security concerns. Apparently, a firebomb needed to be diffused in Pontypridd, which was attributed to an unknown group called the "Workers Army of the Welsh Republic". They were part of an emerging violent militancy that appeared in Wales in the mid-1970s, which also included groups such as Meibion Glyndŵr and the Free Wales Army. The children of the valleys had no such concern. There had already been a street party and even though we had no idea about what was being commemorated, we were easily bribed into supporting the entire show of the public's affection through the lure of jelly and custard. We waited in the rain for an eternity, and then they flashed by in a matter of seconds. For the rest of the day, people were consumed by the most potent of questions, "Did you see them?" Some were convinced they waved directly at them, and one apparently caught the princess's affections. That was the very first time I was exposed to the true spectacle of power. I would also later learn how it revealed the valleys' fraught and contested relationship to monarchy.

A week after the twenty-fifth anniversary of Diana's tragic death, my thoughts have taken me back to the Welsh valleys. Memories of death always lead there. The last time I visited was the funeral of my grandfather, who died towards the end of the lockdown. At least we could attend the service and bury him with dignity. He died 92 years young, the last of his generation from the top end of the valley. A handful of neighbours lined the streets as his coffin drove past. He wanted a horse and carriage, but alas, even in death some dreams elude the people in these towns. It's 10 October and some establishments throughout the valleys are once again full of commemorative bunting. But on this occasion a different funeral has come to the town. The Queen had died. While some paid it no consideration, tributes were being led in places like Aberfan. Led by the child survivor Jeff Edwards, some locals spoke with affection about Her Majesty and how she did provide a sense of constancy to a runaway world. I couldn't help feeling this was also part of a nostalgia trip for a world that was long since passed. What also struck me was how the critical voices had changed. If there was condemnation of the institution which she headed, it no longer had the weight of previous years. Indeed, in terms of wider critical appraisal, it seemed this hereditary bastion of symbolic power had undergone a profound transformation in the order of concern, from being situated at the apex of a class society to the apex of a racial one. Had people here simply become aware of this? And in paying their respects now also further revealed their guilty biases? To appreciate these attitudes, we need to recognise the history of these towns. While the people of South Wales have raged against the aristocracy throughout most of recorded history, their relationship to the Royal Family has always been more complicated. But the valleys are not unique in this regard. Such tensions were no different to those comically shown in Barry Hines & Ken Loach's *The Price of Coal*, which narrates the absurdity of a fictional visit by Charles to a coalmine in Yorkshire during in the bleak years of the late 1970s. On that occasion, the miners are tasked with improving the aesthetic look of the mine so that the Prince can gaze upon its cleanly charms and bring a certain prestige and pride to a largely ignored community of townsfolk, which was already there, albeit understood in far more common ways. Moreover, as this drama showed, for the working class, whether they are on the open moors of Yorkshire or the deep-set valleys of South Wales, for those who profess allegiance or at least acceptance of the Crown, their sentiments cannot be separated from a lasting sense of deference that is no different to what can be witnessed by other colonised non-white peoples the world over.

In the week the Queen died, the defining word that filled the air was "History". Yet trying to get some distanced perspective on the performative outpourings of loss and loathing that marked the spectacle of this event, I found myself watching once again Richard Attenborough's *Oh! What a Lovely War*. A 1969 stage play readaptation, it draws upon the songs sung by soldiers in the trenches of World War I. A war we should note that was ultimately caused by the fading nihilistic power of monarchical rule across Europe. Such cultural productions that use the power of comedy to ask searching questions of the human condition, should have a marked impact on how we view the Imperial history of Empire and the millions of young men who needlessly died in a moment that should never be forgotten on the fields of the Somme and Passchendaele. Poor white men, who come from communities some today called privileged, fighting in the mud and gas, most destined to die in some corner of a foreign battlefield, for something they still deferred to at a loss. But poor young men who still, as the film shows in its surreal and yet savagely comical way, found humour and laughter, comradeship and collective voice in the utter ridiculousness of it all. There was also much talk of "tradition" in the days that followed. Sat in the home I grew up in, I reflect more on what that word meant to us. Like working-class people across this nation, it was less about regalia than it was ruggedness, less about privilege than it was the rituals of poverty. In fact, our tradition looked more like Caroline Aherne's *Royle Family*, which is a tremendous historical document that captures better than anything I have witnessed the doldrums of working-class life, especially the laughter and the silent rage that fills the close-knit home. Scenes from that sitcom still have me roaring aloud, because the comedy there brings us closer to the poetic truth of poverty, revealing the dark humour that is woven into the fabric of everyday life. And I am sure just as many poor people wept at the death of the fictitious Norma as Elizabeth. Mindful of this, I appreciated more fully in that reflective moment how those who condemn the comedy, condemn the tragedy. And in doing so, they rob us of the tools to dig beneath the spectacle and symbolism by reminding ourselves of the ridiculousness of history. An element that has been so essential in the eventual fall of tyrants, which the cultural warriors of today would ask us to forget and leave behind in their concerns with how the confrontational and dark comedy of the poor is the insensitive vehicle through which actual forms of violence against minorities is most easily justified.

While the nature of the threat is overstated in places like the valleys, we should not however be totally blind to the problem of white terror today. Such prejudice is there, even if it concerns a relatively small group of people who have narrated their own politicised truth to the nature of their plight. Predatory groups have notably appropriated discourses on the War on Terror, which provided an opening into towns that once defiantly fought fascist ideologies. Attention could focus here on the case of a Breconshire-based soldier, who although not Welsh, was stationed in the area and was arrested under the terrorism act as he prepared for a coming "race war". Affiliated with the Nazi-saluting and Swastika-brandishing group National Action, who reportedly held meetings in Bridgend and elsewhere in the valleys, he tried radicalising other soldiers based in the camp. Equally troubling was the earlier appearance at the Abercynon "Valley Commandos Motorcycle Club" venue of Neo-Nazis wearing Klan hoods and staging a mock lynching. Such racial intolerance hasn't appeared overnight. Indeed, it continues to morph as these pages are written. During the 1980s a number of known persons in the upper Rhondda could be seen openly speaking of their membership of groups such as the National Front and Combat 18. They didn't hide their allegiances, indeed they wore the insignia as a badge of honour. Such displays were later apparent in a 1999 BBC Wales documentary, *A Welcome in the Hillside?*, which suggested racism in the valleys was now endemic. A claim many locals found deeply offensive. Still, the groups have persisted and continue to attract national media attention. Following Brexit and the valleys' overwhelming decision to vote Leave, concerns with intolerant localism were amplified. Knowledge of the Wales Defence League, which became influential over the later-established English Defence League, added to this worry as the potential for more organised forms of violence was suggested. The WDL directly rallied against what was more broadly presented to be the new existential threat. Namely an Islamic invasion of the United Kingdom. Some researchers claimed the WDL was first named by its valley members. This has led some to claim the valleys were becoming a "stronghold" for far-right groups, whose messages were slowly but surely appealing to the disillusioned. Despite evident abjection, the stronghold narrative doesn't however match the reality, though it is clear that hate crimes are increasing and more vigilance is demanded. As with the previous movements that have promoted fascist ideas in South Wales, the WDL was very much linked to football hooligan culture in Cardiff. The WDL would later disband, though the casual violence has since taken new forms. More recently, attention has also focused on other valley groups, which seem to be able to amplify beyond measure their rather insignificant relevance due to social media. One group was photographed trying to indoctrinate youths by taking them on fieldtrips to Porthcawl, which reports claimed to be linked to a revival of fascist interpretations of national socialism — albeit without the reading. They openly used the image of the killed soldier Lee Rigby to show how the militarism of the New Wars was again being mobilised in the valleys. While such groups can be easily dismissed in terms of their political appeal and their leaders' names shouldn't be mentioned for that gives them the notoriety they desperately crave, their presence does raise urgent questions about how the history of the ideology is taught in these towns.

Following the brutal assassination of George Floyd in the United States in 2020, the anger soon led to protests in many of the world's locked-down city streets, including in Cardiff and Swansea. It also didn't take long before the demand for racial justice was quickly appropriated by the online cultural warriors who turned their accusatory attentions to the realm of popular entertainment. In the United Kingdom, this began with a coordinated attack on the writers and actors of the trivial sitcom *Little Britain*. A TV show which ran between 2003 to 2007, it rode the identity politics wave with considerable mainstream success. It was a show in which every identity that had found its public voice in the previous decade could also now be parodied and the focus for ridicule, without exception. Despite however the broad sweep of its stereotyping reach, the focus homed in on the portrayal of a few distinct characters deemed to be culturally and racially insensitive. Let's be clear here. *Little Britain* wasn't the product of intolerance. It was a form of multicultural and cosmopolitan brutalism. Indeed, while some found offensive certain character portrayals, I detected no outcry about the representation of the disabled underclasses who feigned injury (in a wheelchair) while consuming copious amounts of alcohol. As somebody who grew up in a family with a disabled father who was unable to work, I know what it is like to be routinely taunted by such assumptions. But if we are offended by cheap comedy to garner even cheaper laughs, then surely our sensibility needs to be checked. I am not suggesting the offended should have more "sensitivity training" or "learn to take a joke" (though undoubtedly that would help). What I find more offensive is how British television was stripped of such artistic quality, how it ended up producing such cosmopolitan drivel, which showed how middle-class sensibilities ended up commissioning dumbed-down entertainment, which a new generation from the same class now wanted to correct because they apparently were more sensitive to the cause. All the while, the docile masses were blamed for laughing about it, for what else was there to laugh about, all along the way?

At its best, comedy, like all artforms, has the capacity to touch human life while knee-deep in the mire of existence. It is inseparable from the crooked timber of history. Nothing speaks of decadence and privilege more than when a society turns against the comedians. Yet this is precisely what is happening today, as the ability to laugh in the face of tragedy has become something a vocal intelligentsia simply cannot abide. Without being too reductive, when people live in the presence of tragedy, they often either find comfort in gods, therapy or laughter. It is perhaps no coincidence to see middle-class radicals especially take aim at comedy, for their world is deeply invested in both the therapeutic model of governance and also moral righteousness of their ideals. Yet, without comedy, I know the people of the valleys would have long since been crushed. Strangely, those who condemn the comic do so by appealing to a victimised humanity. But if humanity means anything, surely it's the ability to find reasons to believe in the human, especially when the dark clouds of existence seem inescapable and the weathered body still manages to humour and laugh as the storm continues to rage. I cannot think of a single working-class comedian who believes comedy should be censored. I could list too many bourgeois radicals, however, who repeatedly take offence on other people's behalf, for something said that speaks to a darker humour. This is not about revelling in the offensive just for the sake of defending some ideal of free speech. It is to recognise that the truth of humanity means nothing without the means to laugh at the absurd tragedy of it all. Besides, truth would never be true if it wasn't unsettling, like a bad taste joke, nor would it resonate if it didn't speak from the heart. But of course, this doesn't sit well with those who wish to push further the victim model of politics, for it ultimately underwrites their own ambitions to be the saviours of the wretched.

The valleys have produced a number of successful comics, most notably the Caerphilly-born fez-wearing Tommy Cooper, who in 1984 died on stage during a live television broadcast in front of millions. Tragically, or perhaps ultimately fitting, the crowd continued to laugh as Cooper fell to the ground, believing his collapse was still part of the act. Despite the heroics of Cooper and others like the proud martyr (the translated name for Merthyr) Owen Money and Ruth Jones of *Gavin & Stacey* fame who was born in Bridgend, the first comedian I properly observed to truly touch the hearts of people in the valleys was an outsider. While Adrian Street was experimenting with his androgynous aesthetic, Billy Connolly showed how such gaiety was compatible with a distinct and affirmative masculinity. Like the people in these towns, Connolly's early life was a tragedy. And yet through his stories about growing up in the notoriously tough area of Govan, onto the demands and hardships of working in the shipyards, he showed how comedy could humanise a tragic experience and break down all kinds of social boundaries. Referring to his comedy as a form of "beautiful cruelty", Connolly has noted how people learn to laugh at their misfortune and find humour in the madness. "The best way of dealing with the dark side of life," the comic has stated, "is to laugh right in its face. Everybody knows death is coming. They try all sorts of tricks, religion etc, to deal with it. But comedy can release you from your terror." This is something I would witness time and again with my father, for whom the ability to joke was essential if he wasn't to be crushed by the weight of his own misfortunes. It was far more important to his wellbeing than any visit to an emotionally sensitised shrink. Such understanding should also have us consider how the systematic production of vulnerability is very different from saying that vulnerability is somehow natural and defining. Too often today, critics of anything remotely masculine default to claims of "heterosexual white male fragility" when it comes to explaining the emotional outrages of men in communities like the valleys (which is hardly a community at all today) show in their behaviours. Leaving aside duplicitous arguments that white men should expose more about their feelings (but not "those" feelings that are politically disagreeable), the concept of fragility ultimately begins from the premise that life is inherently vulnerable. Fragility in these terms is all about overcoming the emotional protections heterosexual white males continue to maintain, which is nothing more than some over-coded normative standard that denies revealing the truer and more enlightened sensitivities as determined by the feminine order of things. Yet, just as queer politics has been mainstreamed for decades (just recall here the Welsh character Daffyd from *Little Britain* who incessantly demands their exclusivity as being "the only gay in the village"), so our understanding of subjectivity has long since collapsed into essentialised narratives of human vulnerability, which is precisely what the capitalist system demanded and now thrives upon the more and more the faux outrage persists. As a society, we have fully bought into the notion that the entire social order is fundamentally insecure by design, and so what's needed to bring about true liberation is to speak more openly about how we feel. None of this will help address the underlying conditions devastating the valleys of South Wales. But at least it may help some of the middle classes feel better and more emotionally superior to the affectively backward poor who cannot express what they really feel.

As the statue of Edward Colston was being thrown into the waters in Bristol, it was clear that a healthy public conversation on the legacy of colonisation and slave ownership was long overdue. We needed to refocus our attention on the likes of Colston and other slave owners such as Wales's own Thomas Picton, who although the most decorated soldier in the Napoleonic War was a brutal colonist who enslaved and authorised the torture of black people. We also need to extend this to people like Churchill, who as Burton already alluded to, was a racist, tyrant and guilty of leading many war crimes that demand our attention today. But as I argued in a previous chapter, what's really at stake is precisely how we conceptualize the very meaning of "the colony" along with how we deal with the vexed question of prejudice. In terms of prejudice, we know it takes many different forms. We also know that no people should be able to claim a monopoly over the figure of the victim. While the focus on racial violence in recent times has been important, in terms of prejudice I am left wondering about what happened to the discourse concerning white-on-white racism? Whether that was a racism against the Welsh, the racism against the Irish, or as the former world heavyweight boxing champion Tyson Fury (who has openly spoken of his fondness for the people of the Rhondda) pointed out, the racism against gypsies, such concerns have largely dissipated in a world where new kinds of essentialisations have been birthed. Would we deny Fury his claims to having experienced prejudice because he is a white heterosexual male who some believe harbours misogynistic and homophobic views? Welsh DNA is far more complex and interwoven such that the very idea of "whiteness" is always part of a much broader colouration. Indeed, what is often erased is precisely the visible markers of our interbred and culturally diverse past. The history of whiteness needs to be critiqued and its lasting effects openly challenged. This is especially the case in terms of white supremacy and its reimagined fascist mythologizations, which have gained some dangerous traction in these towns. But such a critique has to engage with the complexities of the story and competing visions of whiteness. I have no allegiance to whatever colour, even though the black shadows my life. In terms of the already widely decimated white communities left to decay within their own post-industrial carcass during Thatcher's Britain, the very idea of whiteness was far from seen as something that bestowed privilege or even inalienable rights. Indeed, while in the Welsh valleys amongst the most respected and wealthy persons were the local Pakistani doctors who by that time administered most of the medical practices, those who looked the whitest were often the poorest of the poor, malnourished and robbed of all forms of sunlight. Whiteness was the surest sign of belonging to a group in truly abject poverty. The relatively wealthier and healthier went to great lengths to tan their skins, from cancer-inducing holidays in Spain to daily visits to the melanoma-inducing tanning salons. Every Friday, the local bars would be full of strangely coloured "white" people, from dark mahogany to sun-kissed orange, long before Donald Trump arrived on the scene. A leader who would however tap into the growing sense of resentment in towns like these, which can be found dotted across much of the post-industrial world.

The opposite of pride is humiliation. There are many explanations and theories put forward as to why a person is drawn to extremist ideas, which end up legitimating in the mind violence and hatred. While there is no singular explanation, we cannot deny the importance of economic destitution and the way daily struggles lead to resentment. This becomes particularly acute when those struggles are politicised, and others become the scapegoats for conditions which they often have no hand in creating. But economics alone is never enough to explain the complexity of human behaviour. If it were, we would need to ask why more people are not so violent in the world. Some of the most welcoming people I have met have the least to offer in terms of financial wealth. Of all the theories, the one that still remains lesser explained yet seems to smack history continually in the face is humiliation. We know how humiliation in Germany after World War I led to fascism. And we also know how a sense of humiliation in Iraq gave rise to Islamo-fascist groups such as ISIS, against which the new wave of race warriors drew their particular calling. But humiliation too can also be complex and cannot simply be understood through single moments, like a boy on the street who is floored by a punch and taunted and teased in front of the town. Humiliation can slowly seep into a psychology of denied meaning, pushing down upon the soul a sense of worthlessness and having a person believe their life has no value or recognition. Humiliation is watching one's father lose their job, walking yourself into the job centre that has long since given up and will find no work for somebody marked by your deficits. It is seeing your friends and community live the same conditions, day after day, while society floods your dreams with every glittering prize that's meant to be a marker of success and the outcome of one's efforts. Humiliation is trying, over and over, but realising the train leads to nowhere. It is to live within a state of permanent precarity or dependency in which the forces that control one's life are completely out of your hands. It is to look upon oneself in the mirror as the hangover meets the bitter morn and see a broken reflection that's only breaking more with each fracturing day. It is also knowing that the factory that makes such mirrors is selling them cheaply to everyone in the valley below. There is no pride in such mirrors of denial, so is there any wonder that some will pull out a fragment of broken glass and cut away at the self or the body of others? We cannot excuse the violence. But we must do our best to understand the desperation. In these times, we must be attuned to the ways the language of pride has also been appropriated by those who seek out the hatred or claim only for a very specific grouping that's got culture on its side. And we must also address the question of alienation and ask whether our own language merely serves to humiliate further and push those who feel they have very little deeper into the will to nothing, which is where fascism truly resides.

Attitudes to European withdrawal refocused attention and critical concern upon the valleys of South Wales. How did they have the temerity to leave? Was it a lack of education? Was it because of some inherent prejudice or intolerance? Unscrupulous leaders no doubt played their part in that episode, notably politicising immigration by adopting a very familiar colonial strategy. Divide and rule was reworked as the local precarious were waged against the globally vulnerable. As low-paid workers and the unemployed in areas such as the Rhondda were encouraged to see those fleeing conflict in Syria and elsewhere as being the true source of their problems, so the masses ended up voting for even more containment. But what did that matter anyway? The middle-class entitlement of travel membership of the European Union bestowed was of little importance to populations in the valleys. We might also say the idea of containment too is of marginal concern for a people who mostly will live and die in these heartbroken towns. And yet, all of that, we might say, now belongs to history. What matters looking ahead is how the sources of local anger and resentment can be turned around, so the very idea of a community can be recovered from the ashes. Economic prospects for the valleys look pretty bleak. Despite the many problems associated with industrialisation, at least it was for a time driven by the desire to create full employment. And even if there was a notable and exploitative hierarchy to production, at least it was for a time underwritten by an appreciation that a person could and should take pride in their labour. Not only is so much of contemporary work patterns and their mechanisation demeaning and lacking in productive achievement, but it is also slowly declining as the labours of man are being replaced by organisational models of production in which the human is playing less and less of a productive role. If there is an existential threat today, it is not the question of race. The most profound challenge facing humanity is how to find dignity and pride in an emergent economy where the very source of meaning is being undone by automated systems. The future for the valleys is in peril. But it is not from migrant workers. It comes from the invasions of machines, from automation to artificial intelligence, no persons can any longer compete with, let alone those who are already exhausted and find themselves needing to run several years just to catch up to a spot that's vanishing into the digital air. Some might counter here and say people need to retrain so they have the new skillsets for this digital economy and its unlimited potential to mine new opportunities. Others might argue that we need to rethink the entire logic of material production, so that the people can recover a sense of pride and a true greening of their world. Unless this is acted upon, then the distractions of race will surely be amplified. And the white terror that is bittering the hearts of the few could become a more formidable problem in the future.

Countering the seeds of prejudice in the valleys demands an educated response, which is informed but also willing to listen to local concerns that are becoming more deeply entrenched. There is a need to reach out to persons believed to being holding intolerant views and try to work through issues in a manner that doesn't condemn from hyper-moralising digital pulpits by "better sensitised" people whose discourses are condescending and lack local appreciation. Children of the valleys need to be taught the rich history of these lands. They should learn about how they are all descendants of migrants, how the valleys have a proud past, how that pride was a catalyst for historical struggles against fascists, and how there was once a strident idea of welcoming outsiders, who like their forebearers wanted to make a home within these mountain passes. They should be introduced to the likes of Paul Robeson and have a broader appreciation of the history of colonisation, including Wales's fraught relationship within its divisive systems of rule. They should be taught the history of militarism and why not every war is the same. They should become students of ecology and appreciate how ecological conditions are key to creating thriving atmospheres which can colour the imagination. They need to learn of the coal, have a respect for the darkness below, while also appreciating how the blackness led to Aberfan. They should see how the fruits of past labour that fell from the trees were ultimately black rocks that toxified the earth. They need to understand these processes, but not to simply castigate the efforts of previous generations as destroyers of the world. Not everything from the past, children should be shown, needs to be burned away. And they should be taught more rigorously about the poetry of the valleys, its song and prose, its silences, its myths and its visions, not to simply create a new set of dreamers, but precisely to create a new set of dreamers who may just have the imagination to transform the lived conditions of this black earth. We know none of this can happen within the artificial confines of digital terrains, which has been disastrous for politics as it feeds divisions and makes us all less tolerant of different ideas. The valleys don't need to be sucked further into a digital revolution. It needs a dignified one. And it needs to tackle the underlying causes of humiliation, which no discourse on white privilege could possibly address, as it seeks to humiliate further a people who at the moment only have the bare threads of a once-imagined past to cling onto with the unworn clamour of redundant hands.

IN SICKNESS & IN DEATH

We owe ourselves to death. That much I have come to accept. Thinkers have long reasoned that philosophy is about learning how to die. Despite the compelling appeal of this proposition, such a claim however affords the thinker too much luxury and distance. In lands swept under the shadow of a black fatalism, death is forever an intimate companion. It is always there, frequently touching you on the shoulder, reminding you of its fate. In the valleys, the appearance of death is encountered from a very young age. It watched over us from the hillsides, it dressed us with a frequency, which marked it as one of the most defining characteristics of the place. The wear of the black was as common as the rain that filled the carved, gloomy expanse. And death further conspired to make us ever more doubtful of a more prosperous future, which would probably never arrive, at least not in our lifetimes. Yet for those who live in poverty, death is also a strange bedfellow who is rightfully respected. We don't just laugh in its face. We solemnly reach out to befriend the blackness. This is not a surrender. People still somehow need to find reasons to believe in a tragic world. Does that not command a humbler kind of transgression? Not to live, so that we may be put on a plinth for all to remember our naked ambitions, which are driven by the immortality complexes of those who want to be as eternal as gods that both create and ultimately seek to replace. But to have us look upon life in the company of death's constancy. To already crossover into the blackness of the impenetrable abyss and gaze back upon life. Perhaps then not fatalism at all? More a relationship to death that opens a more astute philosophy for life.

In many ways, the past is also dead to us. For what are memories if not apparitions of light, fragments of a lost time, hauntings of a passage that do not conform to the dictates of a chronological world? Like stowaway phantoms, memories come and go without any sense of origin or destination. Memories are ghosts. They also speak to us using different words and revealing different messages as time goes by. Yet memories are more real than anything those armed with reason and secular logics of truth have dared to conjure when thinking about the life of the mind. But what happens if our ghosts are plagued with a sickness? And what happens if death is also a haunting whose ailments never seem to heal? I am haunted by two early memories. Both of which feature my father. The first is overly sentimental. I feel the cool grass on my feet, which are able to trample over wildflowers without causing any damage. The land is green, and the conifers stand as if they were always just there. There is warmth in the air and my mother is relaxing in the soft, hue-filtered sun. We have been playing football and I challenge my father to a race. The memory rolls like a seamless series of stills from a Cine camera, which had its own comforting effects. I am caught in the eternal present of childhood. He gives me a head start, which I am sure I won't need as I was one of the fastest in the school. This had probably something to do with the fact that I was so slight, my body encountered zero wind resistance and if nature was indeed favourable, would push me on to Olympian speeds. For three quarters of the race, I am sure I am in the lead, having left my father for dead. Then out of the brightness he emerges, fast and assured, bursting with energy and life. I was probably around seven years old at the time. That was the last time I ever saw my father running. It was the last time I recall seeing him emerge and stride into a triumphant light. And it was the last time I recall feeling I was just a son to a man whose ailments I had yet to understand.

The oppressive weight of impoverished skies is yet again pushing down on the people of these towns. Hesitancy fills the void as I pull my father onward, encouraging him to move faster as the queue for the bus in the distance is nearing its end. It's almost as if he wants to watch it drive away, preferring to stand in the pouring rain. We are already sodden as we get onto the overcrowded bus. He is holding my hand tighter than normal as the transportation veers just as much sidewards as it does straight ahead as it makes its way around and down the valley bends. We breathed our own kinds of seasickness on these precarious roads, which no Roman would have surely built. I feel the pressure inside building as the moisture from so many damp bodies creates its own atmosphere that steams up all the windows. Even the driver seems to be struggling with the visibility. After a short while a number of elderly ladies leave in disgruntled unison just before the village of Treorchy, which creates a jostle for the vacated lots. With a stunted frame belittling my years (my nickname was now "titch" on account of the fact I could pass for somebody a number of years younger, which was often used as a cost-saving measure on public transport) I weaved my way through a pack of bodies to secure a place, though the wetness of the seat's cheap, dirty fabric is hardly appealing. At least it's better than being tossed around on the brown surface waters covering the aisle. I notice my father is irritated. Maybe it was just all the commotion? He never did like cramped spaces. And he often found the company of others a bit too claustrophobic. Sweat and rain now conspire in their perspiratory descent down the brow of my forehead. Like any child in this situation I proceeded to draw on the window faces of humans, some of which were inspired by the grotesque. For as long as I can remember, I had a fondness for drawing devils, demons and contorted stares. I hear a woman beside me shriek. Could my masterpiece have frightened her that much? As I turn, my father had vanished. Following the eyes of the women opposite, I look down upon the floor and see his body consumed by a frantic possession. His torso is thrown into a fit of spontaneous rage as his blood and glucose levels skyrocketed. The affliction of his diabetes had returned. A number of passengers simply look on in judgement, thinking he was yet another man who should have never fathered a child. I can forgive their impression. Alcoholism was now rife. Time fractures as my thoughts drift as my father also slips in and out of consciousness. Witnesses might also add watching a young child pulling out the insulin from the father's coat pocket, calmly measuring the load and administering the injection into his left arm. There was nothing heroic about this. I was a part-time child carer, well-practised in such procedures, which meant I was used to the breaking of the skin, the sight of blood, while ensuring not to sever a vein or break off the sharp spike in the patient's body. It's only a couple of years on from that idyllic day, yet this is a different life I now inhabit. My mind is a swirl as the blue flashing light is mixed with the pungent smell of street gasoline. I notice a rainbow in the waters, but I now see it has no mysticism and, even if it did, it could also evaporate as easily as I could wipe away the joy from a misty, glassed inscription. Drawn out faces appear before me in the window of the Italian cafe. Its kind-hearted owner brings me out an exotic nutty biscuit, reaffirming that foreign food really does taste better. Coffee has since been the most reassuring of smells. I now see his face covered in an oxygen mask as the door to the ambulance closes and it slowly drives away. I keep standing watch until it disappears, perhaps to be sure it's heading in the right direction. Sat in silence, I head back along the same route, just gazing into the impenetrable beyond, until I get home and cry out "East Glam, Mam, East Glam".

My father had suffered a hyperglycaemia attack that sent him into a diabetic coma. He would have several of these in the coming years. How can you regulate diet when food consumption wasn't based on heathy living choices but simply affordability? The state he lived was constantly veering between the "hyper" and the "hypo", the too much or the too little of what we all normally take for granted to simply be alive. He had been taken to the East Glamorgan hospital in Church Village, situated past Pontypridd. Prior to his illness, my mother had briefly worked as a trainee nurse in a nearby mental illness facility situated in the former Hensol Castle, which was built on an estate that dated back to 1419. Over the years it would be in the possession of a few notable aristocrats and renowned ironworks masters, including members of the Crawshay family that ruled over Merthyr. In July of 1930, it was opened as a "colony" for 100 men who were declared to be mentally deficient. Workers there often felt the place was haunted. The rumoured findings of flocks of dead blackbirds in the attic who managed to enter but couldn't leave only added to its foreboding. What does it say about a place when even the messengers of death are unable to perform their duty? It has since become a luxury wedding venue, stripped of its darker past. Having told my mother what had happened, her immediate task was to work out how to get the money together to first get me back up to the top of the valley to stay with my grandparents in what was becoming a tragic prequel to the dark-fated comedy *Groundhog Day*, before heading all the way down the length of the valley and on to the hospital in a trip of some 20 miles. Even the prospect of death in this place has a price that so many struggle to consider.

The chronic problems of sickness and ill-health in the valleys of South Wales began with its rapid industrialisation. Its effects stayed throughout the decline, which has remained depressingly constant. While we might recall here the misery of life during the Victorian era, it's no coincidence the later impetus for creating the National Health Service was birthed in the valley towns. Although it had been operating in some capacity for over a decade largely dealing with Royal Air Force casualties during World War II, East Glamorgan hospital was officially declared open as one of the founding NHS hospitals in 1948 by Aneurin Bevan. Bevan was the son of a miner. He knew the effects of the industry, having lost his father to pneumoconiosis. Bevan also worked for some time in the local Tredegar colliery having joined its underground ranks at the age of 13. He would be notably politicised during the upheaval of the Great Strike of 1926. Having already won a scholarship to the Central Labour College in London, funded by the South

Wales Miners' Federation, during the years between World War I and the Great Depression he fully rejected the Nonconformist ideas that were a defining part of his family upbringing as he embraced the writings of Marx and Engels, amongst others. Three years later he would be elected as the Labour Member of Parliament for Ebbw Vale, with locals noting how he would often be seen walking and speaking aloud to himself on the hillsides as he sought to overcome a speech impediment. Following the release of *The Beveridge Report* (1942) that provided a blueprint for a "cradle-to-grave" social policy based on taxation, the resounding victory for Labour three years later (despite Churchill's war victory) resulted in Bevan being appointed to the Ministry of Health. During the war years, Bevan was one of the most prominent and vilified critics of the coalition, notably chastising the government for the restrictions it imposed on the press, along with its powers of internment. He also repeatedly called for the nationalisation of coal, while indicating his desire for the British to concentrate more on building an alliance with the Russians on the Eastern Front and not seek favour or help from the United States military. Only a few years into his role, the NHS was founded on 5 July 1948, partly inspired by his own experiences with the Tredegar Workmen's Medical Aid Society, which was run by a miners' and ironworkers' federation to provide medical care by deducting four pennies a week from worker salaries. Integral to A. J. Cronin's influential *The Citadel*, which notably highlighted the problems of dust-related disease that would pave the way for an entire rethinking of the ethical code of social responsibility, it is estimated the system supported some 20,000 registered patients in the decade before the NHS's arrival. Prior to Bevan's intervention, miners were often the main providers of healthcare, paying directly for the construction of Cottage Hospitals throughout the coalfield. This was also seen as integral to the revolutionary struggle, which has its roots deeply set in nineteenth-century ideas of social transformation and care that was brought about by the hands of working men. As captured in Emile Zola's classical

French novel *Germinal*, which although depicting the brutal realism of mining communities during periods of hardship and oppression, marked by tales of personal tragedy, ends with a healthy and reproductive image of worker liberation as the planted seed brings forth a new political horizon of hope:

> Beneath the blazing of the sun, in that morning of new growth, the countryside rang with song, as its belly swelled with a black and avenging army of men, germinating slowly in its furrows, growing upwards in readiness for harvests to come, until one day soon their ripening would burst open the earth itself.

Sadly for the valleys, its days of plenty and warmth never arrived. The darkness simply took different forms. As a metaphor for describing bleak times, we often fall back upon the Victorian period as a base level standard for measuring the lived realities of social neglect. Such conditions were most evidenced in the valleys of South Wales, as places such as Merthyr have already testified. This has given rise to a number of historical comparisons, notably to the image of the world so evocatively captured by Charles Dickens. I am reminded here by the fact Dickens partly wrote his classic tale *A Christmas Carol* in direct response to *The Employment and Conditions of Children in Mines and Manufactories* report published a year before the book came out in 1842. The Ghost of his Christmas Present would take the novel's main protagonist to a "bleak and desert moor where monstrous masses of rude stone were cast about as though it were a burial place of giants". The horrors of the present leading directly to "a place where miners live, who labour in the bowels of the earth". From food banks, fuel poverty and widespread social deprivation that notably affects children, there are ample reasons to describe the valleys of today as being Dickensian. But we also need to be mindful of such terminology, for in seeking to making comparisons, too often the reality becomes purely allegorical and stripped of its contemporary realism and the very kinds of humanistic response Dickens wanted to inspire. This is not in any way to downplay the importance of the literary field. Like poverty, the lived effects of a society marked by chronic sickness cannot be captured by statistical measures alone. We need the literary imagination to bring to life the darkness and death that surrounds. Nobody understood this better than Dickens, who gave to us a visual language for reliving the blighted past. Victorian squalor means nothing without his ability to paint with words the landscapes of its impoverished despair. Yet, in order to speak of sickness as a condition of life in the valleys today, we need to move away from Dickensian images of broken-backed men, prostituting women and street-worn children whose dirty faces also bear the hallmarks of an Empire in its prime. The aesthetics of poverty has changed, which some often mistake for being a measure of material progress and the realisation of more prosperous and healthy times. Today's sickness is marked by cheapened obesity, sedated bodies and hidden away anxious children who no longer can be seen in the gutters looking at the stars, but longing into their broken screens — the Empire of their times, which offers back only the delusions of hope to accelerate further mental states of anguish and disillusionment. Yet to make full sense of these changes, we also need to let the memory of a lived history be our guide. There is a need to look more intently at the past and consider what's changed in the physical and psychological conditions of the valleys' people.

Pupils that arrived at the comprehensive school in Treorchy in the mid-1980s were immediately drawn into a cultured setting, which was also bound to the social economy of health. As founded rumours of random assaults and submersion often meant you stayed away from toilet facilities, the site of notable transgressions was ironically hidden behind the sports hall, or what was termed "the Dutch barn". Undoubtedly as ill-reputed as areas of Amsterdam, some of the more promiscuous would often be seen venturing behind there, two by two. The thin mud track was policed by the more unsavoury characters in the school, who replaced the dust that once colonised the lungs of the miners with nicotine and other addictive substances. It was a thin concealed track, mostly identifiable by the watchout appearance of a worn down spotted face that had already lost all the shine of youthful exuberance and radiance. Theirs was a rite of notorious passage, which was sadly populated by already vanishing souls, whose appearance were as whitened as that ghosting child from *Salem's Lot*. Of course, there are no statistics except one's memory to rely upon, but it seemed a truism that many of its tribal gatherers would end up becoming alcoholics and drug addicts, while many of the lured girls the first in the school to leave due to teenage pregnancy. On the one occasion I plucked up the courage to venture into its forbidden pass following a bet with some school friends, I was bitterly disappointed to find my presence completely ignored by a pack of dishevelled smokers sat on the wet embankment, probably too low on life to care, while a row of three couples leaned against the wall ferociously eating one another in an act of kissing that looked more like a collective robbery of breath. Dante, it seemed, could have learned a thing or two about the tortured reality of a purgatory intent on reproducing itself until the Gods lost all interest. A second cultured happening was experienced by every child sometime during the first week of term; that is, for those who followed the timetable. The biology laboratory's cabinet of curiosities was as bizarre as rumoured. While the encased exhibits of a taxidermized blackbird and rat have no doubt been embedded deep into my subconscious, it was the liquified presence of a premature child, or the "baby in the bottle", which was the most surreal and the focus of morbid fascination. I have no idea what purpose it was meant to serve, except perhaps to remind us we were all largely part of a gigantic biological experiment, though who exactly were the exhibits was difficult to tell. Accompanying the child was also a piglet, which was preserved in a similar way and perhaps taken together suggested a novel adaptation of William Golding's classic. A tale that would have no doubt resonated with the stranded behind the barn, should they have had the inclination to prize their bloodshot eyes onto unfamiliar pages. Still, despite these hiding dwellers' willingness to participate in their own demise as they filled their toxified mouths with smoke and saliva, they were still living at the threshold of an emerging social condition that would distinctly change the human look of the valleys.

The enduring image of death that darkened the human landscape of the industrial valley was the blackened lung. Once coal dust entered into the breathing chamber it couldn't be removed. It permanently resided and started to engulf the body with an inner shadow, which x-rays revealed as to being a veritable void. The blackness colonised from within and often led to large cavities being torn on the surface of the organs. Once the blackness settled, the condition was incurable. While the image of this shadowing is deeply symbolic to the political and biological history of the South Wales valleys (what critical theorists have abbreviated and called "bio-politics"), it has been replaced by an equally symbolic ailment that's altogether more visible to the naked eye, even if its implications are often written away. One of the most prevalent of killers, the black lung has been replaced by the failing heart. Directly attributed to the decline of industry, the shift towards sedentary and unemployed lifestyles has resulted in a notable deterioration in physical health. Stood in between the earlier presented figures of the anabolic man and the emaciated addict, now stands a larger dejected body of a population that's literally growing. While there has been a history of people being overweight in the valleys as a result of bad diets based on limited food choice, this was largely kept in check by social conditions that often resulted in rationing and scarcity. Since the 1980s, however, there has been an explosion in recorded levels of obesity, which is part of a new sugar-coated economy that keeps the masses politically and socially suppressed as it feeds them on addictive diets of fast food, which literally speeds up the demise. Cheap food has become plentiful at a time when the energies of production declined. And bodily excess has ironically become one of the surest signs of economic want. This has been associated with an exponential increase in Type 2 diabetes, further adding to the problem of heart failure that is also exacerbated by anxiety disorders and syndromes linked to high blood pressure. While the well-established links between obesity and socio-economic deprivation are again most apparent and acutely felt in the valley towns, with areas such as Merthyr having more than 60% of its population being categorised as worryingly overweight, the same towns have become the heart failure capital of Europe. In Merthyr alone somebody dies every 48 hours from a heart condition, which in the end will be the primary cause of death for one out of every four in a town where the vast majority are inactive. But this is not just about the individual health of people. It's about the body of valleys life.

When he was redesigning the first modern city of Paris, Baron Haussmann looked upon its alleyways and boulevards like a surgeon looked down about a cadaver. Believing that Paris was a city plagued by infection, he drew upon the ideas of William Harvey, whose discovery of the movement of blood gave rise to an entire economy of thinking based on the idea of "circulation". Not only was circulation important to a healthy body, it was also important to a healthy social system, where everything from people to money and goods could flow and reveal back to us the character of a people. Whilst these principles could invariably be applied to all major cities, as they were from London to Mexico City and New York, they needed to be rethought in the valleys. Circularity in the valleys' urban design most often meant a spiral of destitution. While the direction of traffic was most often linear and determined, notably what was precarious entered and what was enriching tended to be extracted. Since the linearity of the valleys' streets opened onto a social body that was therefore more rooted and defined by Newtonian laws of a fall to the bottom — whether we are talking here about the way money fell down until it reached the castles below or of people simply falling without any safety nets to catch them — what becomes the picture of health is also more static in its impression. Indeed, while the valleys' roads are marked by their curvatures and their ups and notable downs, there is still a straight line of history cutting through. A simple time-spanned inventory of the life of the valleys' main town streets reveals back to us so much about how the aesthetic look of its poverty has changed. During the early 1980s, every main street would have featured an independent butcher, bread maker, fruiterers and grocers. There would have been takeaways that probably included one fish and chip shop and another which probably belonged to a Chinese family. Today, the look of the street makes the mining families' reliance on beef dripping on bread (basically the insertion of fat directly back into the body) seem positively healthy by comparison. Valley streets have been dominated by takeaways, which have become symbolic of towns whose excessiveness is a measure of decline, and whose abundance is the surest indication of lack. Much of this again can be traced to dynamics that really accelerated elsewhere during the Thatcher/Reagan years, whose special relationship produced more desperate offspring. It was during this time that the older vision of aristocratic gluttony was firmly displaced by the seductive lure of MTV culture and its vision of glamour which equated the wealthy with being healthy. Conversely, those who watched on, tasked to simply exercise their minds, would increasingly be drawn into lifestyles that numbed ambition. Outsiders always seem struck by the appearance in the morning of mothers who drop their kids off at school while still wearing their pyjamas, slippers and dressing gowns. Why bother dressing if the day is simply a dressed rehearsal for a yesterday that's already past and which showed back in the mirror nothing was going to ever change?

Each time I go back to the valleys it's hard not to be overwhelmed by a sense of loss for people and things which are no longer there. Mourning is woven into every memory of return. But some losses are more meaningful than others, even if we do always need to be mindful of not falling back into nostalgia or romanticising a vision of life that never really was there to begin with. There was, however, a romance to the valleys, but that could only be properly explained by posing today two very direct questions: What does it mean to call a place a heartland? And what happens when the failing heart of a people, which was once beating so strongly that it was a vessel for the world, becomes the symbol of their shared sickness? The beating heart of a community is defined by its productive energies. The very idea of a heartland speaks to such forces that bring forth a theory of natal power that is able to regenerate across time. We also know a healthy heart is essential to the circulation of blood, which at the start of modernity was just as powerful a metaphor as any image of mechanised machines for progress. There is no coincidence the flag of socialism which first flew in Merthyr was red, for there is no heart without that colouration. It was the spirit of our belonging. Besides, there is no passion without the blood. The passionate heart of the valley was its unmediated truth. It bestowed life and gave meaning to a people who married with layers of history the red with the black. The heart of the valley was also the symbol of its courage. Courage is a poignant word to explain the lived condition of those who have needed to continually fight, and which is derived from the Latin "*cor*", simply meaning "heart". The people of the valleys once spoke from the heart. They were in modern times amongst the first with the courage to speak truth to power. A phrase today which has become moribund in equal measure, such as the terms "radical" or "critical" have become redundant. Maybe part of the issue now is that the heart has been displaced by the mind in terms of the value society places on its organs of social importance. Post-industrial bodies feed into an emotional economy of a less physical kind with an emotional mind-gamed politics to match. Theirs belongs to a bloodless world. Indeed, narratives of blood are also seen as cause for concern. This shift from a cardiological to a craniological sense of being is no doubt compelling. Yet the problem for the valleys is both of these are seen to be failing, for the mind also is a dereliction subjected to its own internal blackening born of isolation from the heart of life. People of the valleys used to often recite the importance of "speaking to the heart". Wearing one's "heart on the sleeve" was also a measure of honesty and pride, which challenges so many of the false assumptions that uneducated peoples don't speak of emotion. But that heartland has gone. Its beat can no longer be heard as the sickness has fully taken hold. Indeed, if there is a sickness it needs to also be measured in these political terms. For beneath the green surface, the black valley today simply looks like an ailing heart, which calling out for love, needs to connect the mind with the body in more liberating ways.

When we were young, the idea that you would want to stay indoors was beyond all comprehension. There was always excitement to be had, which often meant simply taking a football into the street, walking a few blocks and before you knew it, there was a game to be had on the local pitch. You didn't need to ask; the intuition of a game was enough for fellows to join the parade. While some pitches were closed off, many were unguarded and could be used without concern. As the 1980s progressed, however, not only were by-laws enacted that prevented groups of children from playing in the streets, but the football fields were also increasingly fenced off to apparently preserve their integrity and damages caused from being overplayed! That didn't stop us improvising, including making use of a field that was once officially used by miners who played football there at the turn of the last century. Access though wasn't so straightforward as it involved crossing a railway track, which thankfully as we were concerned was running less and less frequently, and scaling barbed-wire fencing that often made a spectacle of a dangling child once the train eventually passed. Given the field was surrounded on two sides by the River Taff, there was also a good chance you'd spend part of the afternoon chasing a wayward ball that flew off target and was now intent on reaching the stadium lights in Cardiff. Even inanimate objects here had their own dreams of escape. It's hard not to see these simple shifts that made the rudimentary activity of children more difficult and restricted, as the start of a process that would slowly lead them to play less in the fields and either simply hang out in spaces of dereliction or retreat into an online world that's a false approximation for any meaningful notion of connection. The children of Generation Z have been subject to enough studies to emphasise how the world of social media has led to the hyper-acceleration of all worrying symptoms concerning insecurity, isolationism and self-deprecation. Such symptoms become all the more apparent when the child is already full of self-doubt, having been born into a situation where they are marked by their deficits. While some may talk of the educational benefits of the digital revolution, what we see in these towns is how it has more pressingly brought greater anxiety, which further feeds into the normalisation of sedentary forms of living and the associated mental and physical ailments already set in train.

A year before I was born, my parents were married in St Albans church, which was at the far end of the valley in Tynewydd near the Fernhill colliery. This was almost as far as religion would go. Once a place that could seat around 350 members, it shut at the turn of the Millennium. Childhood sweethearts, they were 18 years old when this ceremony took place in which they spoke of their commitment to each other "In sickness and in health". A phrase that has since become more synonymous with a drab and lazy racist television show, which was always a poor approximation of comedy. From the perspective of my parents, the former at least would be relevant and the surest test of their vows. Without a home at the time, my newlywed parents spent their honeymoon in the spare room of a family member in a rented maisonette on the Penrhys estate. It was not far from where we would eventually live. Maybe they wanted to be closer to the stars for a night and forget all the troubles that surrounded their world? Then just as the film *Rocky* was being released in 1976, which told of a physical fight against all the odds, my father suffered severe internal haemorrhaging and pains that resulted in months of surgery and hospitalisation. They were just two years into their marriage with a two-year-old child in arms. He was also diagnosed with diabetes, further hindering his recovery and instigating a deterioration in his other vital organs. At twenty he had to face the reality of permanent disability, even though this physical diagnosis would be continually assessed by benefits agencies. The mental effects were barely considered for at least the two decades after the surgery, whose brutal scars were more than just physical. In the year after his surgery, my father's weight plummeted to around 30 kilos. That weight didn't however simply vanish. It was placed deep into the centre of his troubled mind. It took him years to simply get back to a recognisable weight, though as always, the road to mental recovery was never so easy. There were times, as I recalled, when his optimism returned. But I now see how that was masked as he sought to hide away all his conditions and fight hard to suppress the lingering pain deep within. He had created a deeply cut valley within himself, which was coursing with a different kind of blackness. He once told me he went to sleep every single evening believing he wouldn't awake the next day. Perhaps that's why he kept a knife under the bed? To ward off a different kind of intruder who would arrive like a thief in the dead calling of the night?

For many years my father lived an isolated existence. The home became his only real security. When he did venture out, he became dependent on my company. I am not exactly sure who was doing the shadowing. Fear of dying stopped him living for so many years. It was another kind of debilitation. However, as I have also learned, the more things appear stationary, the more invisible forces can be moving at lightning speeds. I now see my father was always running; it was just a different kind of race. Throughout life he's been running from death, who's never once left his side. And that's burdened him with an exhaustion I couldn't possibly understand. While I often feel guilty for raging against him and blaming my sense of impoverishment on his inability to work, the greatest guilt I carry is knowing I was running from that same condition too. I would be lying if I said I felt no sense of relief having made my escape from the valley. Being able to breathe was also not having to live each day within a lived condition that is known to only get worse with the passage of time. That condition was personal. But it was also seeping out of every crevasse in the valley's floor. I deluded myself into thinking it could be defeated by only returning home when I had the strength. Maybe I was already mourning a father who wasn't defined by such a debilitating illness? Maybe some of us do come close to death a few times in our lives, while others dance with her every day? And that kind of waltz is paid in a psychological spin that only pauses to foxtrot between anguish and despair. My father, however, was a prize-fighter who belonged in an alternative ring. I would slowly recognise the fight he was continuing to wage to live another round despite the hardship and pain of it all. He never possessed a white towel. Even if Apollo, Lang and Drago were merely bit-part players who could never dance the way this foe could. My father suffered more than most. But he is not alone in the valleys. There are many others for whom sickness has become inseparable to their identity.

The Valleys are Twin Towns. They are twinned with death and mourning. And they are twinned with economic and health inequality. Nevertheless, despite these chronic conditions affecting so many of its inhabitants, the political tides of radicalism that were birthed here have been subject to a double movement of localised flight and external appropriation. Indeed, while hopelessness is also part of a sickness inseparable from the palpable sense of loneliness blanketing the hills, a new social media vanguard would have us believe the valleys embody the worst of our concerns as its people fall back into nativism and the reassertion of identities lost. Yet while the white middle classes were rejoicing at the throwing of the statute of Edward Colston into the harbour in the City of Bristol in 2020, cheer-led by an army of social media academic activists who were asking all white people regardless of lived economic realities to check their own privileges, the selective outrages of this new (apparently more emotionally and historically attuned) intelligentsia were brought into sharp relief. This was after all during the height of the pandemic, when the very same activists were openly condemning those who were calling for an easing of the lockdown so they could return to work. Colston was a monster who should have never been put on a plinth. That doesn't however mean to say we should place the blame onto the shoulders of the poor whose desperate lives are part of the same systemic production of human misery across generations. As the debates concerning Colston continued to rage as the focus rightly turned to consider structural violence (though often in ways that relegated economy), official government figures released showed that five out of the top ten areas in the entire country having the highest per capita Covid deaths were in the South Wales coalfield. The top two being the Rhondda Cynon Taff and Merthyr Tydfil districts. Such disproportionate mortality rates could not simply be accounted for in terms of the indiscriminate nature of the new variant of the disease. It was as discriminate as police violence in the United States, whose victims are also overwhelmingly defined by the appearance of poverty. In terms of Covid, as replicated elsewhere, a wider and more historically considered microscope was required, which in its analysis was inseparable from the underlying causes of social deprivation and the related ill-health of impoverished populations. We have since recognised that the lockdown was a monumental overreaction, which in the long run enriched and empowered beyond all measure the technological, energy and pharmaceutical corporations. Yet should societies have properly conducted an assay of vulnerability and coordinated security measures to protect those in need based on the prevalence of pre-existing conditions (which prior to the pandemic was the World Health Organisation's standard guiding containment strategy) instead of basing its policies on models that worked to hypothetical worst-case scenarios, the valleys of South Wales would have still been largely sealed off. But even that would have had limited impact on the prevalence of death as a result of this latest affliction. People of the valleys simply didn't have the luxury to take time off from their already limited work, nor did many of them qualify for furlough due to their precariously contracted working arrangements. Moreover, a vast majority couldn't avoid public transport which was the only means of collecting their weekly food supplies. So, while the prevalence of death meant everybody knew of somebody who died (my family shared this grief), so the blackness returned — albeit without the dignity of a funeral gathering, which was a further unnecessary encroachment by a government whose own flouting of the rules is one of the most egregious episodes in recent history. Covid killed those without the economic right to live with the secure conditions good health provides. That is the real measure of privilege. And the terror it brought upon a population occurred in the very moment those populations were being denied their own voice to call upon historical injustice, which so many close intimately felt. I didn't detect a single profiteering Twitter-theory of emotional affect dealing with this reality.

Covid was just one of many epidemics to have swept over the life of peoples in the valleys in the past century. Of course, while the variant of a familiar virus was marked out as being exceptional — hence demanding of a state of emergency being declared — when epidemics can be neatly contained, they have no associated response. Poverty is an epidemic. Obesity is an epidemic. Heart failure is an epidemic. Isolation is an epidemic. Diabetes is an epidemic. Addiction is an epidemic. Hopelessness is an epidemic. Depression is an epidemic. Male suicide is an epidemic. Dereliction is an epidemic. And denial is an epidemic. None of these lead to the shutting down of entire nations until resolved. There would be no state of emergency if epidemics only concerned contained communities like those who are living with such chronic pressures in the valleys of South Wales. If one of the positive outcomes of a catastrophe is to show what was already broken within a system, what Covid really showed was how so many were already living so close to the immediacy of death. The virus was merely an accelerant that showed how truly precarious the conditions of existence were for those who lived on the forgotten edges of the world. Indeed, in many ways it was death's little finger that simply needed to give the slightest of touches, knowing full well so many bodies were already feeling exhausted and that a chronically underfunded health service, whose proud impetus was first imagined in these towns, didn't even have enough ventilators to keep them from suffocating. None of this, however, is new. For over 100 years the people of the valleys have had to fight to breathe. All that changes are the forces that continue to pass over the baton for a race with death whose end result is never in doubt.

When communities are caught in a dance of death, it often results in some of their members throwing themselves into the absence. Or we might say, when a future is denied and people feel that all they can do is live in the moment, yet learn that moment offers nothing, what is sought is something, anything, that makes them feel alive and numbs them all the same. They become searchers for a pacifying high, which throws them into an abyss, for at least in there their troubles melt as sure as the walls that are being looked up through a barely visible light. Deindustrialisation had a marked impact on substance abuse and levels of addiction across the United Kingdom. Much of this has been well documented. In the 1980s, it was on estates like Penrhys where valley concerns with heroin and later crack were most concentrated. Increasingly sensitised to the issue, locals started to refer to the "druggies" in their midst as if they were referring to an entirely new species or creature. The reference was initially said to simply explain the notable deterioration in appearance, which was painfully emaciated even by valley standards. But as the problem slowly crept down onto the valleys' floor, as known rancid dens of iniquity started appearing in every town, so the concern became more widely felt, especially as addiction was being directly linked to local theft and burglary. Frequent violent attacks on pensioners in their homes soon turned into vigilante hunts, while any discussion on the conditions that gave rise to addiction were cast aside. Most of us were after all living with some kind of desperation, so was there really any excuse? Since that time there has been an ongoing battle in terms of whether addiction should be seen as either a criminal or health issue, which has profound implications for policy responses. While stories about the activities of the addicted were increasingly visualised through the parading of photographs of both the users and their victims, for the most part you barely came across them. They preferred to stay in the dark. That said, the drug dens were easy to identity and common knowledge to most in every town. Curtains were permanently closed, signalling perhaps an even more fatalistic kind of mourning that truly wished the outside world away. Very soon, signs of their infested squalor started appearing outside, notably the littering of syringes and broken bottles, which were as wilfully abandoned as the lives that were also being disregarded. In the early days at least, most of the addicts kept to themselves and would only really be seen scurrying in the dark alleys or doing their best to avoid eye contact in the bright lights of the local Spar store. As children you know there's something going on, though for us they were just another form of entertainment as we used to creep up to the windows and try to goad them into giving chase, knowing full well there was something preventing them from even acknowledging our existence. It was only later when the reality of the valleys' ailments became clearer.

I vividly recall an incident in the summer of 1987 when the emerging realities of the valleys' new economy of addiction, ill-health and violence made an initial calling into my life. I know it was August because the sun was blazing, and as we entered into the playground of the nearby Bronllwyn School in the neighbouring village of Gelli, the sound of Tiffany's "I Think We're Alone Now" was ringing out from the loudspeakers. The cover was played to death that summer. Fittingly, the song was originally written as a warning against teenage pregnancy, though the line that stuck with me was more about running just as fast as we could. The yard was open for a free fete that was organised by the local youth club situated on the same premises.

A number of us entered and swiftly had our faces painted in white and black in badly drawn homage to the US rock band Kiss. The running paint from the sweat already made us look more like a crossover between a Francis Bacon painting and the Joker from *The Dark Knight*. Then across the yard the appearance of trouble came into sight. We spent most of that vacation on the lookout for this particular boy from the nearby streets, who by his own admission was a "bit bonkers". His father was notably tough, and he was one of those children that trouble seemed to shadow. For some reason he had taken a liking to our company, even though his presence always ended in some kind of disaster. Our previous encounter involved a box of matches and a rather large fire on the side of a mountain. He arrived as calm and delightful as any model child and even offered to buy us all a round of ice-creams out of a large wad of cash he had in his torn jeans. Solemnity in such souls is however always but a brief distraction. As the band of face-painted brothers were sat on the wall adding to the composition a new vanilla layering, in the distance a feared gang of kids a few years our elder from Tonypandy could be seen running towards us. They were split in two. While a sprightly rabble of bicycle chain-carrying skinheads fronted the charge of this red-cheeked light brigade, their oversized leader whose nickname was synonymous with a rounded biscuit, yelled out knowing his voice could travel far faster than his legs. Somewhat startled, we looked to the side and witnessed trouble leg it across the yard and swiftly scale the drainpipe that took him two stories up onto the roof of the school. As he clambered over its steep slated sides, the disorganised gang ran around the building trying to ensure he didn't get away, while reminding him "You're dead" at every possible opportunity. How they imagined this rooftop acrobat escaping was beyond me. And yet, as our troubled acquaintance shifted gear and defied the laws of gravity by running directly over the top of the roof, so one disbelieving chaser cried out, "I've lost him, I tell you, I've lost him!" Just like that, he vanished and with us having promised to let them know if we ever knew of his whereabouts again, we carried on with our day sure of our own theoretical explanations for the remarkable Houdini act. I never saw him again. I heard he spent some time in the Borstal system, which was known for educating tough kids on the futility of violence by brutalising them in all kinds of abusive ways. A number of years later I read of his death from a heroin overdose, which was not long after I became aware of the passing of the biscuit boy from more natural causes. Neither of them lived to see in their eighteenth birthday, as sadly is too often the case in towns where newspaper obituaries are dedicated to the premature.

Since those early epidemic years, the valleys' recorded levels of addiction, overdose and drug-related deaths have continued to rise on a year by year basis. In 2020, it was reported that alongside Neath and Swansea, the Rhondda valleys had the highest prevalence of drug deaths in Wales, with misuse having risen over 80% in the past decade. Local charities noted how the lockdown only exacerbated the problem, along with alcoholism and the furthering of a sense of alienation from local communities. It also added to the anxiety at a time when support services were being significantly curtailed. A simple audit of newspapers in the Rhondda, Merthyr or Neath valleys shows that not a week goes by without a story of another local youngster dying from an overdose or associated drug complications. All the while the troubling spectre of male suicide remains. But even the solutions here have become part of the problem. Research has shown that in some towns in the valleys, one in three people are on proscribed anti-depressants. This is creating another layer of dependency and addiction, which simply sedates the symptoms, until it awakens a more vitally oblivious state of anxiety induced consciousness that is caught in a vertigo of mediating suppressants, which does little to address the underlying causes that would require reversing a century of depression.

Sickness is a condition. It is a condition that is deeply personal as it affects our most intimately felt senses of being.

But it is also a condition that is profoundly social. It creates surrogate conditions of dependency and also reaches into the future as it cultures a furtherance of despair. Understanding the social implications of sickness is crucial, especially if we are to have any serious conversation about the divisions and perversions marking the political landscapes of today. Social sickness deepens the exhaustion felt by too many who have long carried the invisible weight of history. And within that history is where another theory of injustice resides. Why them? Why all of them? When you live in close proximity to people whose sickness has become an integral part of who they are and what they believe they stand for in the world, so you also become an intimate witness to processes that have a profound bearing on contemporary claims of social belonging. Processes today which are overwhelmingly defined by narratives of vulnerability and competing claims over victimhood. Those who feel defined by a tragedy of a physical and/or psychological kind appear to be inescapably torn between the desire to fight against its consumption and a self-absorbing tendency to present themselves as victims of some monstrous injustice. While the latter is invoked to often compel empathy and pity, it becomes more problematic once it becomes the defining element in relations of power. It is one thing to say that for individuals and societies, we need to recognise and try to deal with the reality of an injustice. It's a completely different thing to say that should become the basis for a new kind of politics, whether we are talking about the politics of households or the politics of society at large. Mobilised victimology brings everybody into the orbit of anxiety and insecurity in order to steer everyday behaviours in a particular direction. It can in fact become all-consuming. There is a treachery of victimisation, which reveals a more uncompromising authoritarian tendency that is fully inseparable from the embrace of vulnerability, along with a manipulative politics of lament that denies a people the tools to properly resist what are intolerable conditions. At their brilliant and wonderful best, those whose lives feel marked by the tragic reach directly into the darkness and find a different kind of courage, which laughs at that thought they are possibly even more ill than the dead. At their all-consuming and performative worst, those who embrace the figure of the victim compel allegiance, denying others their say for fear of hurting a fragile sensibility, which by its own admission is vulnerably cast. Our problem as a society today is that such a condition of vulnerability has become the default setting for a particular vision of radical politics that is therapeutically wrapped in a bourgeois dream. There was a time when people refused to see themselves as victims of history. That was problematic insomuch as it denied us asking more searching questions about the lived effects of violence. We have however today gone to the other extreme, where the sickness is openly welcomed, while serious narratives on the meaning of death are all but denied. I don't really know if I have an answer to this, except to say that a politics of victimisation is the worst kind of individualism. Perhaps it is no coincidence that the culture wars taking place in popular entertainment, and increasingly in educational settings such as universities, correspond to the dominance of American influence and its vapid individualisation of both places. Cancel culture is a product of Americanisation and a self-centred belief in the inherent sickness of the self, which parading as some kind of emancipatory politics places us all into boxes marked "Fragile". The irony being those who are collectively classified as medically sick are the ones being stripped of their agency on account of some non-existent benefits. We don't resolve this crisis by falling deeper into a well of vulnerability, which born of a surface-level performative ethos only proves how it has no depth at all. What we can do is insist upon a better relationship with the tragedy of existence, so that we can recover a more affirmative conception of life that's freed from the tyranny of victimisation. Jean-Jacques Rousseau once claimed that, "Man is born free but everywhere is in chains". A German by the name of Marx would adapt this and tie it directly to the alienating nature of capitalist production. That gave rise to a century of battle in which people fought for their rights. Little did they know that at the moment one chain was being destroyed a more powerful and more invisible one was being set. Indeed, the more they fought, the more they were exhausted, until they finally lay on a giant rock, too tired to notice the world was still upside down, and whose falling corrosive energies that weighed upon the soul sickened the body and numbed the mind.

The train is leaving the small town. This is the last time I will make this journey on these tracks as the valleys lines are to close and will be replaced by a more automated electric system that is yet another signal that the engine of industrialisation is truly over here. Sat on the carriage I also read of the closure of the fairground in Porthcawl, which makes me realise what I am writing already belongs to a past. Will its words resonate beyond my generation? Or will they fall silent and become as obscure as Richard Llewelyn, whose book millennials would surely have never come across? Looking out of the window, I see the mountainside towering over the village on fire and the smoke rising into the grey skies. Maybe the local youths really are trying to communicate something to somebody beyond these hills? Or maybe they are still trying to kill a sickness by returning to traditions which turn the mountains black so that they can be reminded of what lies beneath? If the blackness belongs to the past, it is the fire that becomes us. But what inferno awaits? On this journey, I have recovered what I believe to be something of the idea of the valley. Undoubtedly tragic and full of suffering, there is nevertheless a poetry to this place, which promises tales as epic any that have been written in the deepest of black inks. This is not however the poetry of Dante and his journey into a world of redemption. We began with the salvation, only to witness the most intolerable suffering that has left us in the wilderness of doubt. Such doubt however is also revealing, for the reversals we have lived through return us back to an image of a world that breaks apart the false assumptions that others write about the story of the valleys. Having travelled back along these broken tracks of life, so I have been forced to reassess my own shameful compromises and failures. I used to think the valleys was a simple place and that beyond its perimeters the complexity of existence was to be found. What I have since learned is places like the valleys have far greater depth than any bourgeois gathering, which is far easier to navigate than the straight lines connecting these towns. It is theirs which is simplistic, predictable, repetitive and vacuous.

So what is my role in the drama of this history? Do I even have a position to speak of? I know that in the past I have learned to move away from debating the big ideas and instead followed a path that collapses the personal into the political as I sought to over-theorise the world by being attuned to a more intimate sensibility. This was not unfounded. Like many people of the valleys, I know that politics is a matter of life and death. But I have witnessed first-hand the corrupting tendencies of the emotional appeal, which is part of the sickness today. We don't suffer from a lack of feeling; we are suffocated by them. What we lack is the capacity to think in ways that free us from dogmatic and morally certain chains. None of this is inseparable from what some identify to be the crisis of the left today, which is a crisis of the political imagination. While there are good enough reasons to argue that familiar demarcations between the left and right have lost all meaning, I am troubled by the alternative. What chance is there for a people, when knowing socialists of old failed them, the political parties that claimed to represent merely took them for granted and ultimately abandoned them, while those who claim some radical lineage from those past revolutionary struggles now look upon them as if they are the sickness and part of the source of society's ills? Reluctant to use the words "Third Way", to lift the sickness of the valleys requires a different kind of politics. Whilst this politics must resist the fall back into nostalgia and lament, while being ever mindful of the forces of populism and revivalist fascist tendencies, it must also be wary of emotional vanguards, who claiming to speak with a radical voice continually swipe over the complexities of history and through their embrace of identity politics look to censor, shame and judge every indiscretion that doesn't live up to their privileged standards. One of the greatest betrayals of radicalism has been the disavowal of the radical spirit of outrageousness, which is inseparable from the poetry of the tragic and the black-hearted humour of the poor. Having said this, it is not my place to deny a people like those in the valleys the right to find value and meaning in identity, even if I am aware of the violence fixed identities have permitted in the past, especially the nationalistic. Though it does help that we have the best god-damn flag on the planet. We all need to accept that freedom means the freedom to see, feel and believe the world differently, and if our politics is to mean anything, it's to be able to speak across those differences and be open to the disagreement. This means recognising our own contradictions and admitting we are not always on the right side of history. Indeed, if radicalism is to mean anything today, then it cannot be about running head-on into a world of technologically-enabled liberation, which evidently biased towards those who benefit from the digital world, is based on endlessly repetitive proclamations that lead further in the secluded righteousness of truth. To be radical today means seeing the world from the perspective of those who are Other, not in terms of the simple and essentialised othering of identity, but about taking the time to listen and engage with those who possess different and challenging ideas about the world. Only then might we begin to appreciate how there is more uniting than dividing poor people, despite those who profit from such divisions, including those who now insist with a moral certitude to be the progressive. Those who are continually washed by the dust of history know the future isn't always rightful.

The valleys are dying. They have been doing so since the day I was born. Can that sickness be lifted? I don't know. Maybe there is too much history to be undone, too much future already loaded against its possible recovery. Then again, maybe we are looking at the problem the wrong way around and need to enact another reversal. What if it's not the people who are sick but the system that's producing them? A sickness that has been reasoned, rationalised and set on such communities that are utterly disposable to its plans. And a sickness today that's attuned to the therapeutic language of vulnerability that obscures a logic of power manifest through a technological fanaticism, which if left to its own devices will ensure that alienation will become more pronounced, the unemployment everlasting, the tensions more fraught and the frustrations more violent in their hate-filled expressions. Faced with such conditions, the desperate social and psychological problems will only get worse and it's difficult not to be fatalistic. Still, it is precisely when all hope seems lost, when the nothing seems to prevail, that is when we have to hold onto the glimmer within the darkness, for maybe it's within the silent shadows of the black valley where the poetic fire will be rekindled, and its flames burn anew. Backdropped by the fern-covered horizon of a fading but not forgotten dream, as Dylan Thomas imagined as he walked the invisible line connecting the memory of an unrecoverable past to a future held in the grip of a near certain death, "Time held me green and dying, though I sang in my chains like the sea".

DYING OF THE LIGHT

It's winter in the valleys. The Breconshire Beacons are set in the twilight of their long-shadowed dawn, blanketed by a cerulean blue light that pictures an eternal presence which bounces back to the heavens a calm defiance. I feel myself lifted by the spirit of the Rhondda as I glide over the top of its unmistakable rugged beauty. The mighty waterfall is frozen in this landscape of its own seasonal time, naturally creating a cathedral in the crag as sharp and clear as any crystalised memory to ever have been formed upon its commanding watch. I have found my way back home, still a stranger who has recovered something worth recovering from the black dust of history. Yet among the serenity of my world that is finally at peace with itself, I still remain haunted by the ghost of a question: "Who am I?" A child of the valleys? An outsider destined to be always looking back? A writer digging into the blackness to excavate a written fragment from an immortal language, knowing full well they will soon be forgotten as sure as our words crumble into the earth below? An invisible witness to an unfinished symphony on the most unworldly of stages, which is as tragic as anything the ancients of Greece foretold? Or merely a traveller, whose life and fate were destined to remain, until this planet upon which we occupy finally burns out to reveal a giant black rock that will eventually float, shatter and break in a tremendous universe of absence, only for it all to be recomposed again and a new concert of energy formed?

Here I am the ghost. I was always destined to be passing through. Writers are always ghost-writers of a kind. We are always playing with stories that have died but whose apparitions still fill the mind with fascination and terror, clarity and madness, intrigue and despair. We are always dealing with glimmers of a fading light, interpretations of truth, whose very meaning changes as the memories of forgotten time are refracted by the material realities of the equally unforgiving and neglectful world we now inhabit in this moment. These pages are full of hauntings. They are populated by people who no longer exist. Yet still they wander. How I wish the words before you could have been printed in coal, read once then wiped away just to remind us that when things are erased, there is always a trace of something that remains and still holds onto the promise of being understood anew. My recollections have taken me deep into the unknown depths of a wounded place, mirroring a fractured time which for some will be unrecognisable today as it may even have been back then. It is chilled by the sentencing of unwritten stories, unspoken words, unachieved ambitions, unannounced feelings and unrequited losses, which creates a sense of foreboding that is just as important as anything officially stated and pronounced as the truth. And it is deluded by the spectre of unimagined futures that are yet still part of the story of the valleys' tomorrows.

I travel along the now familiar break the frozen river is settled upon. Everything is still, except the children who are at play in the fields of ancestral spirits. The spirit of my thoughts has drifted. I stand at the irrepressible summit of the Pen-Pych mountain some 1,400ft above the valley floor. I look down upon the round, snow-covered estate of Tan-y-Pych that sits below. My body is warm as I am once again in the company of my grandparents. They lived on those streets, soaked by the forgotten memory of the ancient blood of the bulls, which penetrated deep into these lands of past refusal. I feel the heat from the black-coaled fire surrounding my being, as I lay in front of the hearth and look into the burning embers, which once again captivate my imagination. Such fires were always volcanoes in my childhood mind, full of energy, passion, homeliness and loving care. A frozen tear marks my presence and falls to the floor like a momentary snowdrop that has always been waiting to arrive. I lay for a moment on the snow and feel the weight of history lifted. As I recover my sense of flight, I now see this mountain for what it truly is. I occupy the most privileged vantage point in the entire valley, which affords uninhibited views for miles down its corridor. An image flashes before me, which pictures the most famous of all political illustrations. The mountain is the Leviathan of the Valleys. Regal and majestic, powerful and demanding of our respect, it is the guardian and watcher over this land. As I turn my head and look upon the perfectly rounded stone that has a crack in its centre, I can't help feeling that was where Excalibur was pulled from. But what if the legend was wrong? Maybe it wasn't the sword that had the power, but the wise old stone. I have never felt more humbled, knowing this Leviathan will be here until time itself crumbles and falls. The sacrifice of the bulls wasn't incidental. Nor was it merely a warning. It was an offering to a power whose mysticism will only be revealed once the dragon sleeping within is finally released.

I keep thinking about the loss. Hauntings can be haunted too. We come from the death of our past memories and dreams to try and say something about this life, often knowing our words will fail us. That is why we always need a better language. Everywhere I look, I can only see the young. A valley of children playing in the sunlit snow, careering down the mountains in the only race that matters. Towns without children are towns without promise, the people of South Wales know this reality better than anyone. And these children still have the dreams of tomorrow there, even if today is all that matters. The houses too are so full of merriment, regally coloured in the festive trimmings of yuletide. Cold and warmth can happily coexist together, just as the blackness can exist with the white. I watch a child carefully sculpt the perfect snowball in their hands. If only the world could be that simple. At least it won't melt away for them today. Yet as I approach the familiar town of my childhood, I notice one home where no small footprints have been left. The curtains are half-drawn as a solitary candle flickers inside. As I peer through the frosted window, I see the young girl Myfanwy sat alone yet perfectly content. She has no desire to play on the mountains, for the adventure she seeks begins in the mind. Myfanwy reaches beside where the candle is stationed and pulls out a black book written in time. *A Christmas Carol for the Valleys* is inscribed on its cover, its old leather-bound pages bring comfort and delight. As she opens the book its pages are lifted, floating images accompany the tales of our lives. It is a story that reads quite familiar and telling. It speaks of the girl child visited by three spirits, in a reflected world of optimism and suffering where past, present and future collide.

As Myfanwy starts to read, she soon realises that she is the story, and the pages were being written in a dance that follows the movement of her eyes. Is she an author or merely a witness? Does that ink appear from deep within the pages carved away by the labours of a now forgotten tribe? She doesn't seem too bothered, for she trusts her imagination. She has learned how to let wandering thoughts and poetry be her guide. Her *Carol* begins by explaining its setting, it's a wintery place of hardship yet where so many loving families reside. There is however no Scrooge in her adapted fable, his benevolent transformation couldn't happen in these times. So the spirit of the past appears before her as written, it is a majestic white horse that transports her to a dusty black mountain where a single boy dwells. Myfanwy knows this journey and the path it has taken. But those mountains seem different, like they belong to another distant world. The spirit steps aside to let these travellers be together, it is after all just a follower who reveals the past through the pages of new eyes. The children are children, so have no problem in making a connection. They smile and laugh and dance around in circles, his blackened face contrasted by her pale complexion that so delicately smiles. They continue to share their dreams of children, ignoring the smouldering fires situated behind. But the faster they dance the more the boy becomes uncomfortable, the time passing over leaving him short of breath. But still they dance in a union of exuberant defiance, finding trust in the hands of a simple child's touch. As Myfanwy looks away for the briefest of seconds, she returns to find herself all alone on the smoking pile. She cannot tell if it's burning within or being damped by mist raining from falling skies. Then the snow starts to fall, and the boy reappears, they are now on top of the hillside where the Virgin keeps watch. A song rings out which speaks of her namesake. She knows of its tune yet has forgotten the words. The boy stands in the snow and sings like a deep choir of Welsh angels. A chorus rings out, carried through the enchanting trees in the forest beside. Still — something isn't right, and a rumbling swiftly brings an unholy silence. The boy looks anxious and pulls Myfanwy closer in his arms. He continues to sing as the black earth begins to open. Why so much anger, filling those dark eyes? As they stand on the edge, she holds his hands tightly, until he lets go and she is returned to her chair.

The second spirit arrives and carries Myfanwy above the roof-topped streets of the warm pastured present. It is a powerful black dragon that makes her tremble with pride. As it pulls away from the earth and into the atmosphere above them, Myfanwy looks down upon the valleys and sees it complete. A transformation begins as the black mountains are covered, the greening of the hillside no sceptical doubter can deny. She gazes upon a landscape so full of promise, but she turns to the dragon and asks, "Why do all the people still hide?" The dragon stands still, and no answer is given, then it swiftly flies down and brings her back to home. Myfanwy now looks at her mother stood crying. Her father is comforting even though there's little food to eat. Together they have warmth, he tells her in silence, they have learned how to communicate in suffering without the children able to hear. The winter returns and the child is unsettled. Everything is perspective, the dragon will advise. The snow all around now feels more unwelcoming. A blizzard returns and bites at her feet. No shadows can be seen on the

ground before her. She turns to the dragon and implores him
to breathe. I cannot intervene in this world, the black beast
reminds her. What happens to you and your kind only humans
can change. Myfanwy asks why the elements can't be kinder.
They are ambivalent dear child, make of them what you will.
Myfanwy takes leave and walks past the grown-ups. Why are
all the children so locked away? She reaches into her pocket
and pulls out an instrument. Today I will be the pied piper of
the valleys and call the children out to play. One by one she
sees an alternative reality appear; it was one that was always
there if only others cared to look. The poor children empty
their pockets full of sorrows and run to the snowy mountains
as their watching parents happily cry. The others that queue
for the charitable hand of forgiveness return to their homes
and paint dignity on their doors. The present stands still as
the heart of the valleys slowly starts beating. And as its drums
ring out, it is the sense of worldlessness that declines. The
black dragon vanishes, leaving Myfanwy to contemplate the
meaning of this day.

A week and a day have passed, and nothing further has been
written. Myfanwy has been waiting, patiently confused by it
all. How do these people still manage to smile at each other?
Why has our history been so denied? The young child is back on
the chair, her legs swinging with wilful abandon, the candle is
still alight as it has been for all this narrated time. As she turns
the next page, an inscription appears, "roll for the future" as
a dice gently falls into her hand. If you roll 1–3 the first story
will happen, if you roll 4–6 then another fate will inevitably
preside. Just as Myfanwy is about to question, the third spirit
enters, which intrigues her the most. The spirit stood before
her appears as Myfanwy's reflection, yet there is one notable
difference which sets them apart. The resembling spirit is
happy and calming, though the colour of its appearance brings
a curious doubt to Myfanwy's mind. "Why are you painted all
red?", the young child enquires. "I am also the colour of this
land", the spirit replies. Myfanwy then councils this red spirit

for guidance, "How can my future be so open to chance?" The spirit responds by saying that is how the game is written, leading Myfanwy to refuse to take further part. She closes the book, unable to conceal her displeasure. I will not let my future be determined this way, she gestures. The red-spirited child takes the book in its possession, advising Myfanwy the story must go on. Still Myfanwy will not partake in such an elaborate deception, so the spirit agrees it will read the scenarios to come. In the first it tells of a valley that is continually fading. It speaks of a dereliction too unimaginable to explain. It is a land that is falling deeper into its suffering, where hatred becomes rampant, and anger fills every vein. The greening still continues, but now is purely envy. Matched only by a blackness that's totally isolating and inescapable. Such a world was once sold over to a new technological promise, yet all it returned were permanent armies of redundant minds. So the decline continued until everything imploded. And all that remained were lost shadows invisible at birth. The second was painted in a language of recovery, where a people were so proud all were welcomed to see. The fruits of their labours brought harmony to their surroundings and the local streets bustled with local delicacy and pride. This was a valley where the children felt valued, where meaning was restored, and no future denied. It was a valley that reignited the ancestral fires of resistance, and where children were less concerned with the black screens that colonised minds. It was not then a place where the future was fatal. But a valley, the red spirit told her, where a culture was brought back in time. A valley resplendent with the poetry and wisdom of the ages, and where the people of its towns were at long last set free.

Myfanwy awakes on the black leather chair and wonders if the story of the *Carol* in the valleys was just a frightening yet fantastical dream. She wouldn't put it past herself, the young girl reasons. She rubs her cheeks and pulls up the bright red blanket that's been partially covering her as the evening sets in. Her mother lovingly calls from the kitchen to tell her supper is ready. She doesn't answer but raises a gracious smirk. As the night-time descends, she moves her face closer to the worn-down white church candle that's perched on the reading table. How long has it been burning, she wonders. Beside it she sees a black dice that wasn't there before. Myfanwy closes her eyes and starts to whistle a familiar melody. She keeps them shut tight as she softly chuckles while shaking her head from side to side. Once again, I become aware of my own small presence in this part of the world. As I look upon Myfanwy still refusing to roll the dice, an almighty gust of wind blows me from behind. It bursts open the frosty window and carries over to where she is unrepentantly sat. It sweeps over her face, blowing the square, numbered object violently across the room. The winds of change wash over my body with a tremendous warmth and unbearable coldness, which combine to strike lightning in the street where I am stood. As old weathered time slows down while the dice continues falling, I see the flicking light of the candle start dying as the young child Myfanwy looks at me straight in the eyes. And into that shared darkness one world is surely surrendered. So just as it started, everything returns to black.

INDEX OF ARTWORK

Cover: Chantal Meza, "My Black Valley". Charcoal, ink & pastel on sanded paper. 2023. 210mm x 150mm

Chapter 1: Chantal Meza, "Land(e)scape". Charcoal, watercolour, pastel & graphite on sanded paper. 2023. 140mm x 170mm

Chapter 2: Chantal Meza, "Black Ecology". Charcoal, watercolour, pastel & graphite on sanded paper. 2023. 140mm x 170mm

Chapter 3: Chantal Meza, "A Colony Within". Charcoal, watercolour, pastel & graphite on sanded paper. 2023. 140mm x 170mm

Chapter 4: Chantal Meza, "One Hundred Years of Depression". Charcoal, watercolour, pastel & graphite on sanded paper. 2023. 140mm x 170mm

Chapter 5: Chantal Meza, "The War at Home". Charcoal, watercolour, pastel & graphite on sanded paper. 2023. 140mm x 170mm

Chapter 6: Chantal Meza, "Aberfan". Charcoal, watercolour, pastel & graphite on sanded paper. 2023. 14cm x 17cm

Chapter 7: Chantal Meza, "Derelict Gods". Charcoal, watercolour, pastel & graphite on sanded paper. 2023. 140mm x 170mm

Chapter 8: Chantal Meza, "A Boy from Nowhere". Charcoal, watercolour, pastel & graphite on sanded paper. 2023. 140mm x 170mm

Chapter 9: Chantal Meza, "Pride & Prejudice". Charcoal, watercolour, pastel & graphite on sanded paper. 2023. 140mm x 170mm

Chapter 10: Chantal Meza, "In Sickness & In Death". Charcoal, watercolour, pastel & graphite on sanded paper. 2023. 140mm x 170mm

Chapter 11: Chantal Meza, "Dying of the Light". Charcoal, watercolour, pastel & graphite on sanded paper. 2023. 140mm x 170mm

ACKNOWLEDGEMENTS

How does an author begin to give any sense of recognition to those who have contributed to a monologue, which has literally been a lifetime in the making? There were moments when writing this book that I felt the prose had somehow already been written and I was simply scribing through words something that was already in the world and just needed to be revealed. That perhaps is a defining part of stories from people like those from the valleys of South Wales, who have so many tales to tell, yet due to the forces of history, seldom see their truths and fables presented as part of the historical record. But even history itself can be part of the problem. Whose history do we recount? What happenings do we elevate as important in our own memories, which invariably take on new meaning and importance with the passage of time? How could I know that a group of dishevelled children sat in a graveyard on a bitterly cold evening, just wasting the time, would come to have so much relevance to me today? What I can say is that the story of my life, which I believe is so similar to many in the valleys in which I was born, is a ghost story of a very peculiar kind. It was written as I spoke with memories of people long since forgotten by others. It is haunted by the sense of injustice so many have felt. It has taken inspiration from ancestors who I have never met. And it has been challenged by phantoms from the past, including the ghost of myself — that boy from nowhere.

While the book may now appear like a determined ambition I have always possessed, in truth I doubted whether it would ever be written. Why the valleys? Why me? It was only when I spent some time back in the Rhondda during 2018 as I was going through a profound transformation in my personal life that the necessity and belief in the book was truly realised. For that I owe everything to my wife, Chantal Meza, who visiting the United Kingdom for the first time during those spring months, forced me to properly confront the blackness that was locked deep inside. Having her presence visibly felt throughout these pages with the inclusion of her artwork doesn't however do enough justice to the way in which every sentence speaks to how she allowed me to confront the shame I was feeling of growing up in poverty. She saw the valleys for what it was as beautifully captured in her artwork "My Black Valley", featuring on the cover. Yes, it is a place. But it is also a contradiction. It is a black ecology of the mind raising so many complex and deeply felt emotions. Or, as the artwork on the cover questions: What exactly is my black valley? Is it a doorway or a place we look down upon? Is it an opening in the earth or is it something that is closing in upon us? Does it live in the distance, or does it exist within us? Is it a cut into the land or is it a tear in the fabric of time itself? Is it an empty abyss into which all existence is eventually thrown? Or is it a beckoning void of possibility? Is it a deep psychological wounding? Or is it something that just might reveal in the incommensurable darkness traces of the ancestral or poetic spirit?

Once I was committed to this project, I knew I wanted to write a people's history of the South Wales valleys. But I didn't want it to be a typical history book, following roteformats that so often take away both the passion and the lived trauma of a place. That is why for me the inclusion of art instead of photographs and maps was an important intellectual choice. I wanted to evoke a human history of the valleys, which stirred that untameable vortex within. And it is within that vortex that I have encountered so many from my past to whom I remain indebted. This book belongs to the people of the valleys of South

Wales. It owes everything to those who were part of my life growing up there, friends and foes, those who frequented my house on weekends during those now legendary house parties of youthful inebriation, kind neighbours and utterly miserable family members, who have each made a mark on the world I once inhabited. You are too many to mention, but I thank all of you just the same. Some people do, however, require a special mention, for their love and support also made this book possible. My parents Wendy and Steven are equally woven into the fabric of each and every page of this story. Their strength and humility are what properly bind the words together. I know reading these pages have been difficult. Whatever positive tales I have to tell belong to you, the bleakness and the desperation was never your fault. And to my grandparents Sidney and Morfydd, to whom this book is dedicated. My valley begins with you, and in many ways, it ends as the light of your generation finally fades into the darkness. I will also mention my siblings Gavin, Christian, Rebecca and Leonnie, who I have learned so much from and continue to admire what you have become. Christmases in your shared company is enough to reveal how the bonds of family can survive most things, including football, politics and religion! My daughter Amelie remains a source of inspiration and great pride. A final family mention should also be extended to my father's sister, Helen Pick, you showed my father kindness and support when others simply turned away. I am very grateful for this.

It's a bit of a cliché to say that writing a book of this kind is therapeutic. That's not fully true. The past can be dealt with in a cathartic way, but along the way you feel the arrival of a different kind of weight. When I realised writing was actually something I could pursue as a career, I would be lying if I didn't say I wanted to have my thoughts read and discussed by the chattering middle classes. But this project weighed differently. For I know the real measure of its success will be if it connects with the people of the valleys and others like them whose lives and fates have been left to the mercies of a disregarding post-industrial world. Along the way, I have taken council in many trusted colleagues and friends, who have all provided insightful commentary and criticism in the proper spirit of collegiality. Again you are too many to mention. Henry Giroux, Ray Bush and Mark Duffield must, however, be acknowledged here, not just in terms of this project, but the friendship, mentorship, encouragement and guidance you have always afforded me throughout my career. A notable mention must further go to a former school friend Richard Wilde, who read many of the early drafts and whose generous words gave me the confidence that I was touching something close to the truth of valleys. I must also thank the staff and fellows at the Käte Hamburger Centre for Apocalyptic and Post-Apocalyptic Studies at the University of Heidelberg, with whom I spent a number of months at the start of 2023, courtesy of a grant from the German Ministry of Education and Research. The support afforded the greatest luxury of all, the time to complete the manuscript and the chapter that weighed the heaviest upon me: "Aberfan". To the people of that town, I sincerely hope that what I have written does justice to the memory.

I have enough experience now to know the production of any book is dependent upon the editorial team and wider publishing support. I also know from experience the difference between good and bad editors. Tariq Goddard at Repeater was a real pleasure to work with. His lucid comments and edits improved the prose considerably, and his overall approach that respects the integrity of the author is a testament to the best in the editorial profession. Josh Turner's copyediting and general support throughout have been most appreciated, while I would also thank Johnny Bull for putting up with my constant demands for aesthetic perfection on the cover design, which invariably you ended up producing far better than I ever could!

Ultimately, the weight of this book, however, is mine alone to carry and take responsibility for. I just hope in a small and humble way that I can bring the voices of the peoples of the valleys more into the neglectful arena of political and social concern. Whatever limitations this book has belong solely to the author. Whatever strengths it may have belong to an indescribable collective fire, which is at the heart of any viable sense of community whose stories we must fight to continually tell.

REPEATER BOOKS

is dedicated to the creation of a new reality. The landscape of twenty-first-century arts and letters is faded and inert, riven by fashionable cynicism, egotistical self-reference and a nostalgia for the recent past. Repeater intends to add its voice to those movements that wish to enter history and assert control over its currents, gathering together scattered and isolated voices with those who have already called for an escape from Capitalist Realism. Our desire is to publish in every sphere and genre, combining vigorous dissent and a pragmatic willingness to succeed where messianic abstraction and quiescent co-option have stalled: abstention is not an option: we are alive and we don't agree.